Inkscape for Metal Clay and Etching

Free Vector Drawing in Black and White

Inkscape for Metal Clay and Etching

Free Vector Drawing in Black and White

P. L. Hartman

Inkscape for Metal Clay and Etching

Table of Contents

Acknowledgments

Special thanks to Ellen, my rock, without whom I would get nothing done.

Thanks also to Wendell Wiggins, my computer guru and explainer of mathematical concepts I should have learned in high school. As DrWiggly, he is responsible for rescuing my favorite extension, the Guilloche extension, after Inkscape's migration to version 1.x. He has also been my cheerleader through the whole process of writing and publication. More than any of that, I count myself lucky to have had his friendship for almost more years than I can count.

Thanks to photographer-extraordinaire Kevin Olds for his patience and good conversation.

To the Metal Clay and Jewelry Arts Guild of Northern Ohio, thanks for inspiration, opportunities, and friendship.

My gratitude and admiration for the programmers and staff of Inkscape, who have dedicated countless hours to creating this fine application, and to all the other people who keep the concept and reality of Open Source programming alive.

And finally, thanks to Tavmjong Bah, whose book, *Inkscape: Guide to a Vector Drawing Program*, opened the door to vector drawing for this neophyte user.

Cover Photos

Photography by Kevin Olds Imaging   https://kevinolds.com/

Front Cover: Counter-clockwise from top

Tsymbaly   bracelet panel links 30.5 x 18.5 and 12 x 18 mm
Function plotter extension, machine etched

Burst   40 x 27 mm
Guilloche Pattern on oval, stencil

Mesa   42 x 29 mm
Traced photograph with pattern on path for frame, photopolymer plate

Astra   29.5 mm diameter
Layered Guilloche Patterns on a circle, machine etched. Colors are liver of sulfur.

Moonweave   (Reverse of Sunweave lentil, back cover)   44 x 35.5 mm
Drawn with spiro lines, framed, photopolymer plate

Back Cover: Counter-clockwise from top

Supernova   29 mm diameter
Guilloche Pattern on star, machine etched

Apollonia   46 x37 mm
Apollonian external extension, machine etched

Capulin   30.5 x 22.5 mm
Traced photograph, machine etched

In it together / Love   Two-sided half-lentil   47.5 x 39 mm
Hand traced map, text, photopolymer plate
Text on spiral path, machine etched

Bandannas   31 x 27; 60 mm including wires
Whirl extension on framed grid, photopolymer plate

Seascape   35 x 30 mm
Logarithmic spiral via function plotter extension with Guilloche Pattern waves, machine etched

Sunweave   (Reverse of Moonweave lentil, front cover) 44 x 35.5 mm
L-system basket weave, photopolymer plate

Gallicia   25 x 22.5 mm
L-Sytem Van Koch Snowflake variation, machine etched

Introduction

What is Inkscape?

Inkscape is a free, open source computer program that can do many of the same things as expensive drawing programs like Adobe Illustrator and Corel Draw. It produces vector images, that is, images you can enlarge or shrink without losing clarity. In Inkscape, each element you draw can be altered, skewed, moved, copied, deleted, or grouped with other elements in an infinite variety of ways, all while preserving the individuality and scalability of the original element until you purposely combine the parts. It is used by professional illustrators and hobby artists alike.

Inkscape can be used on Windows and on Mac computers, though it may run a little more slowly on Macs. An Inkscape document is saved as an .SVG file (a vector file), but a file can be exported as a .PNG or .JPG image for upload to the Internet or for further use in other graphics programs that use raster (such as most photo editing programs). An Inkscape document can, of course, be printed.

Why would jewelry artists want to use Inkscape?

This book is directed mainly at two kinds of jewelry artists: those who etch metal, such as copper, brass, or bronze; and those who work with metal clay. Both etching and metal clay can greatly benefit from high quality, original designs in stark black and white. Inkscape can certainly make gorgeous full-color illustrations, but what will concern us here for etching and metal clay purposes are crisp black-white images that will translate into raised or incised surfaces in your metal.

Enamelists, too, will find Inkscape useful for designing and laying out the various color cells of a piece. Even more than some other jewelry artists, enamelists are dependent on clean designs and the ability to tweak lines that will be holding enamel. While almost no attention is paid to color in this book, rudimentary use of colors such as enamelists may need for planning will be obvious enough.

What does this book cover?

Designs in black and white are the goal here, so we will be looking at getting from the idea in your head to the design sheet that you will either iron onto your metal for etching, burn into your photopolymer plate for texturing metal clay, or import into a cutting machine such as Silhouette.

idea ─▶ black & white graphic ─▶ page of graphics ─▶ transparency or printout ─▶ etching, cutting, or mc process

In that graphic, we don't want colors or shading or gray-scale. We just want white or transparent where the material will be etched and black where it won't be (or vice versa). Thus this book will not cover many of the usual techniques of the illustrator such as shading and gradients. This will not be a book about design, nor is it a comprehensive guide to Inkscape. It is a guide to many of Inkscape's useful functions for the purposes of jewelry artists.

This book actually began as notes for myself so that I would not forget how to do a task in Inkscape once I had figured it out. As someone who is neither a programmer nor an illustrator, I am aiming at simple and clear directions for using a complex program for a specific goal. However, I assume that you know basic computer functions, including the following:

- opening and closing a program,
- opening, closing, and saving files,
- resizing a window,
- using the left and right buttons of a mouse, as well as the wheel,
- cutting, copying, and pasting,
- scrolling,
- using a keyboard with **Shift**, **Ctrl**, **Alt**, and **Backspace** keys.

Inkscape was developed for Linux and Windows users. It will work on a Mac, but requires extra installation steps and may run more slowly. I am a Windows user and have written this book from that perspective; though most of the same information should apply to Inkscape on a Mac once you are past the installation, I cannot guarantee all details.

How is this book arranged?

This is not a project book, but rather a guide to using the Inkscape program for black and white drawings. One short chapter is meant to help you through installing Inkscape and familiarizing yourself with the Inkscape window. Following this orientation is a sort of floating reference chapter about saving files, setting up documents, and printing. You can skip this until you need it. From there, you will progress from basic and indispensable features like shapes, patterns, and lines to more complex processes like path effects and bitmap tracing that will allow you to trace existing pictures. Topics have been arranged in what is hoped to be a logical sequence like a long, multi-part tutorial. If you are a quick study, though, and you just need help on certain topics, you will find the table of contents and index useful.

Once the common functions of Inkscape have been covered, an additional chapter will help you turn your Inkscape drawings into printed sheets for etching or into photopolymer plates for use with metal clay. These sections don't require much knowledge of Inkscape, so as you are playing with Inkscape early on and you produce a drawing you'd like to immediately turn onto a photopolymer plate or etching-ready sheet, by all means skip to Chapter 21 to learn how to do that. That chapter will also include some basics about getting your Inkscape drawings into a form compatible with cutting machine software.

Some Important Limitations of Inkscape, Vector Drawings, and this Book

Inkscape is a very powerful and extensive program that will serve you well, especially if you are realistic about what to expect. Here are some points to remember.

1. Vector programs treat each item you draw—a line, a circle, a spiral, for instance—as a separate thing, unless you take certain steps to combine it with other things. Most objects will remain accessible as individual objects that can be edited, even if they have been grouped or combined.

2. If you are familiar with raster graphics programs like Photoshop, GIMP, or Corel Paintshop Pro, getting rid of parts of your drawing in Inkscape will take some getting used to. Erasing does not work in vector programs the way it does in raster. You can delete, resize, or reshape whole objects and lines with no problem at all, but selecting and deleting a <u>piece</u> of an object requires some thought. We'll devote a chapter to the subject. Really, this is a minor issue. Mostly, you will love the freedom of being able to resize and manipulate your drawings infinitely.

3. .SVG files, the native format for Inkscape, will not currently show up as thumbnail images in the Windows filing system. You'll see only the Inkscape logo of each file. Add-on apps are available and will be covered under **Saving and Organizing** in **Chapter 2**.

4. Inkscape is a free, open source program dependent on donations and produced by dedicated, brilliant professional and volunteer programmers. That is a tremendous plus. The downside is that development can be a little uneven, and you may occasionally find a bug that may not get fixed promptly. Check for program updates and reinstall when they occur.

5. There is no indexed help feature in the program, but tutorials and FAQs are available under the **Help** option on the top line of commands. In addition, an Internet search will find good explanations and even videos for most functions. There is an active community of users online. YouTube is also a good source for how to do things. *Inkscape: Guide to a Vector Drawing Program,* by Tavmjong Bah, is available in book form and online from Inkscape's Help function for those who want to pursue the fine details of Inkscape, especially as it applies to illustration—and color. That manual, however, has not been revised for Inkscape 1.x.

6. The program is complex and flexible enough for use by professionals, but this means there may be numerous ways of doing the same thing. A myriad of techniques will *not* be covered in the coming pages. Even the seemingly simple step of selecting objects to manipulate can be done in at least a dozen ways, only a few of which will be mentioned in this book.

Time invested in learning to use Inkscape will be time well spent. The many cool things you can do in Inkscape may prompt your creativity in ways you haven't considered before. The idea is to expand your creative choices.

Chapter **1**

Getting Started

Installing Inkscape

To download Inkscape, go to https://inkscape.org, where you will find a download button that will take you to the download page. There you will see buttons for the different operating systems. You will most likely choose either Windows or Mac, but there is also a button for Linux if you happen to use it.

If you have installed Inkscape before and you want to reinstall it or install a new version, be sure to **uninstall the previous version first**. This is very important.

This book will assume that you are using Windows, but most of the directions provided will also pertain to Inkscape on a Mac.

If you click on the Windows version, you must choose 32-bit or 64-bit, depending on your computer. Follow the download instructions on the page. On the next page, you will choose the installation format. Choose **.exe** unless you know differently. You'll be asked if you want to save the file. Say **yes**.

Find the Inkscape download on your Windows computer wherever you usually find downloads. If you are not familiar with how to do this, you can use **File Explorer** and then **Downloads** to locate the file. Double-click on the Inkscape.exe file. There will be a version number on the file. The version at the time this book was written was 1.1.1. Your double-click will start the installation process.

Say **yes** when asked if you want to install.

Choose the language for installation, probably **English**. Click **next** and agree to the license agreement. Unless you know better, let the program choose the components and installation location for you and click **install**.

Once installation is complete, open the program and have a look around.

Finding Your Way Around the Inkscape Window

When you open Inkscape for the first time after installation, you will see a window with several lines of tools and commands. At first these may seem overwhelming, but you will soon learn where things are by using them. You will find a brief key here, but Inkscape gives you a definition of each icon if you simply point at it without clicking. You can even skip this section entirely and plunge into Chapter 3, where you will find step by step directions that aim to familiarize you with some of the important functions and commands.

Like all window-based programs, the Inkscape window can be resized to your liking. As you probably know, the three buttons at the top of a typical Microsoft window are, from left to right, the minimize button (–), the maximum/medium buttons (☐   ☐), and the close-program button (X).

If you want the Inkscape window to occupy your whole screen, make sure the double box symbol shows at the top right. If you want the Inkscape window smaller, click on the double box symbol so that it becomes a single box. Then point at an edge or corner, pressing and holding the left mouse button and pulling or pushing in the direction you would like the window edge to go.

Getting to the Default Screen Arrangement

The tool and control lines of Inkscape can be arranged in various ways. This book will assume you are using the default arrangement described in the next pages. If, however, your installation happened not to put the control lines in the default arrangement, please do that now, so you can follow along with my instructions more easily. To check that you are in the default arrangement, go to **View** in the top line of commands. At the bottom of the list, you will see circular buttons next to **Default**, **Custom**, and **Wide**. Make sure **Default** is selected.

The Controls

1. Top line: the **Drop-Down Menus**. Clicking on an item in this row will open a drop down menu. All of Inkscape's most important commands will be found here.

File   Edit   View   Layer   Object   Path   Text   Filters   Extensions   Help

When a command from these **Drop-Down Menus** is discussed in this book, it will be shown in bold with a caret like one of these:

Edit > Copy
Object > Pattern > Objects to Pattern
Path > Object to Path

To activate such a command, for instance **Edit > Copy**, left click on **Edit**, then left click on **Copy** in the drop-down list. Occasionally there will be still another drop-down list, as in the second example above.

2. Second line: **Iconized Commands**. The most frequently used commands from the drop down menus have been turned into icons for convenience. Point at each to get an idea of what is here.

3. Third line: **Tool controls** for whatever tool is selected in 4. At the moment, these are the controls for the **Select Arrow**.

In this book, the first three lines of the screen beneath the Inkscape title line will be referred to as Line 1, Line 2, and Line 3.

4. Left column: **Drawing Tools**. These are the basic tools for production of any graphic. Point at each one to see its description. A few of these will not be covered in this book because they have to do with color or charting, of little use for the black and white drawings we want. The 3-D box tool will also be ignored.

Left clicking on one of these tools will turn the cursor into a specialized cursor for that tool: making a square, drawing a line, writing some text, etc.

5. Far right column: **Snapping Controls**. These determine how elements like objects and lines are attracted to one another or to a grid you can set up. Until you get used to drawing in Inkscape, you might want to click the top button to turn snapping off. Make it white/light gray. Medium gray means it's turned on.

6. Colorful bottom line: **Palette**. Here you can quickly choose the colors of the **stroke** (a line or a border) and the **fill** of objects you draw. Mostly, you will want black or white or nothing, but occasionally you will temporarily want a bright color to make an element easier to distinguish from other elements while drawing. Notice that there is a scroll bar just under the palette strip. That is

because most computer screens are not wide enough to show the entire palette. For our black and white images, we will not need the rest of the palette.

7. Bottom line: **Notifications**.

| Fill: N/A | | | | | | | | | | | |

- Moving from left to right, the first box tells you what **Fill** and **Stroke** are currently being used, if any. None is selected here, nor have you drawn anything, so you see N/A for Fill and Stroke and 0 or perhaps 100 in the Opacity box, which is grayed out.
- Next comes information about what **Layer** is active. It is possible to have several layers to your drawing stacked one on top of the other. If you aren't familiar with layers, don't worry about this right now.
- The longest section tells you what is currently selected. A **Selection** is what will be operated on. The same area also provides information and hints about the active selection.
- The **X** and **Y** tell you the current position of your cursor/pointer to help you with precision placement. See section 8 below for more about **X** and **Y**.
- The **Z** box allows you to zoom in and out precisely. Easier ways of zooming will probably mean you'll use this function rarely, if at all. Don't confuse this with **Z-order**, explained in the next section, 8.
- Finally, the **R** box shows you the rotation of your page box. You will seldom want to change this from its usual orientation.

8. Middle: the **Canvas**, within which a Page appears.

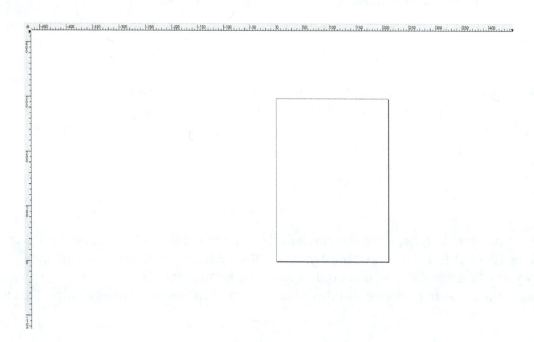

The page dimensions can be set for printing. You can draw anywhere on the canvas, not just on the defined page. If you find the page constricting or annoying as you draw, you can pretend it's not there by turning off **Show page border** in the **Document Properties** dialogue under **File**. You can turn the page back on when you need to set up for printing. Or you can just ignore it till you need it.

The canvas itself is bordered to the left and across the top with a **Ruler**. The ruler corresponds with the **X** and **Y** positions at the lower right of the Inkscape window. As you move your cursor around the screen, the **X** and **Y** numbers on the lower right will change.

Note that 0 for both **X** and **Y** is located at the top left corner of the **Page** outline. As you move farther right, the **X** number rises. As you move farther down, the **Y** number rises. If you move to the left of that lower left page corner, the **X** number moves into minus numbers. If you move up from that corner, the **Y** number goes into minus numbers.

There is also an invisible third dimension, called **Z-order**. This is the order in which you draw objects. If you move these objects on top of each other, they are automatically stacked in the order drawn. The first one drawn is at the bottom of the **Z-order**, the next drawn is next in the **Z-order**, and so on. Objects remain in this order unless their **Z-order** is deliberately changed.

9. Another portion of the screen will not show up until you click on a triggering command or icon, such as the colors (or N/A) to the right of **Fill** and **Stroke** in the bottom left-hand corner. Try that.

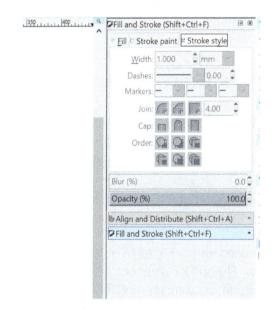

A **Dialogue Box** pops up on the right side of the window and will remain there until you close all of the dialogues. Several dialogues for different commands can appear in this box, one on top of another, accessible by selecting the appropriate tab at the top of the space.

This box can be undocked and moved around your screen if you wish. (I myself prefer to leave it where it is because I have a large screen with plenty of drawing room.) When you are done with a particular set of controls, you can close its section using the little x to the right of the dialogue title. As mentioned, additional controls will also pop up in the same area as you use other features. They will stack one above the other with the most recent at the top. You can reach them via their tabs.

This dialogue area is sometimes referred to as **Dockable Dialogues** because they can be moved around.

If the Dialogue Box is too wide or too narrow, you can point your cursor at the left margin of the box and drag the double arrows to change the width. Some dialogues are particularly wide. Once you've finished with such a dialogue and closed it, you may want to narrow the width of the area to regain your drawing space.

Keyboard Commands

If you like using keyboard commands instead of the mouse, you will find the corresponding keyboard commands defined as you point at a tool or command on the various menus. Some of them are common to many Windows-based programs, such as **Ctl + c** to copy, **Ctl + x** to cut, and **Ctl + v** to paste, as well as the essential **Ctl + z** to undo. As you become more adept at the program, you may find learning a few of these will speed up your process. You can find a complete list of keyboard commands under **Help** at the end of the top line. The Help document is called "Keys and mouse reference."

Right Mouse Button Commands

You will find that clicking the right mouse button will also provide you with common commands in Inkscape, such as **Undo**, **Copy**, **Cut**, **Paste**, and **Duplicate**. Aside from keyboard commands, this is the fastest way to access the most-used commands.

Customizing the Screen

It is possible to customize the Inkscape screen in many different ways, moving the various menus around and prioritizing items you use most. For this introductory book we will leave things where they are.

Using a Drawing Tablet or Touchscreen

Drawing Tablets: A graphics tablet is by no means a requirement for effective use of Inkscape. Its chief advantage appears when you will be doing a good deal of freehand sketching. If that is the case, you may want to investigate a tablet that can be plugged in to the USB port of your computer.

We are not talking about a free-standing tablet like an Ipad or Android—one commonly used for surfing the Internet, reading books, playing games, and, yes, drawing cool doodles and sketches in some much more limited program than Inkscape. We're talking about a dedicated drawing tablet that can be used with a stylus to imitate the feel of a pencil or brush. The best known brands are probably Wacom, Huion, XP-Pen, Gaomon, and Ugee. Entry level tablets of this kind can be purchased for well under $100, but fancier models can range up to to nearly $1000.

You will need to weigh the added cost of a tablet against the advantages. Unless you are planning to use Inkscape on a regular basis and unless you will be doing calligraphy or sketching, you may be better off sticking to the mouse. Most Inkscape functions will involve the mouse anyway, even if you have a tablet. If you do decide to add a tablet, the information provided in **Help > Tutorials > Inkscape: Calligraphy** is essential. You will also find good information online about setting up a tablet and testing it. Those topics will not be covered in this book.

Touchscreens: Computers frequently come with touchscreens now. Like the drawing tablet, a touchscreen can be used to good advantage for drawing with the three Inkscape line tools, though pressure sensitivity will not be available. You will want a good stylus to use with it. You certainly don't have to have a touchscreen to use Inkscape, but you may find it especially helpful for drawing lines freehand.

Backup

You surely know that sinking feeling when a program or computer crashes in the middle of a document you've been working on for an hour. While Inkscape is fairly stable, it is going to crash on you occasionally. Don't be left weeping: enable backups now.

Setting Backups

1. Click on **Edit > Preferences** (at the bottom). Click the arrowhead next to **Input/Output**. Click **Autosave**.
2. Check **Enable autosave**.
3. If you are computer savvy and want to change the **Autosave directory**, do so. Otherwise leave it.
4. Decide on the **Interval** and **Maximum number of autosaves**. The defaults are reasonable.

You're done. Close **Preferences** and restart Inkscape.

Finding Backups

Backups are in the **User Cache**. The easiest way to find them is the following:

1. Click on **Edit > Preferences** (at the bottom). Click on **System**.
2. Find **User Cache** in the list. Next to it is a computer address in a box. Highlight and **Copy** the address. You'll need to right-click to copy.
3. Click on the **Windows** symbol to the left of your **Start Bar**.
4. Click on **Documents** (the page symbol). The address bar will probably say **This PC > Documents**.
5. Click in the white space of this address bar and then right-click to paste the address you copied. That address should begin with **C:\Users**....
6. Click and find **Inkscape** in the list that comes up. Open it.
7. In the list, find the file you want, probably the last file. Open it. Feel relief (we hope)!
8. Don't forget to **Save**.

Chapter 2
"Utility" Reference:
Documents, Files, Saving, Printing, and Organizing

What is in this chapter is a bit like your utilities—your gas, electric, and water. You definitely need them but probably would rather spend your time thinking about other things until you have to pay attention to turning on your lights, cooking your dinner, or taking a shower. In other words, this chapter is for reference. Skip or skim it until you need it. Really! Do some fun stuff first.

So why is the chapter here, instead of hidden in the back of the book somewhere? Simply because you should know it's here waiting for you the minute you...

- Have enough drawings to start organizing them into folders...
- Need to create a page of drawings...
- Want to set up a **Grid** or **Guidelines** to help position the lines you are drawing...
- Want to understand **Snapping**, the force that can sometimes pull your lines where you don't want them or can be harnessed to help with precision drawing...
- Need to print a page of drawings...
- Want to understand more about file formats and exporting....

Saving and Organizing Your Drawings

Saving Files: Unless you choose a different file type, you will be saving in .SVG, the native vector format for Inkscape. When you save an .SVG file, you are saving everything that is on the Inkscape screen, even items that are outside of the page boundaries. You may be familiar with file types like .JPG, .TIFF, or .PNG. but you will not find them here on the **Save As** list, although you can easily export to these formats, as you'll learn below. The many other file types listed under **Save As** are for specialized computer graphics purposes and will not concern us. The only familiar file type on the list is .PDF, and you will not need that either, until you print, and maybe not even then. In the meantime, just save as .SVG. That will retain the flexibility of the vector format.

> **Tip!** Be sure to save everything you draw as .SVG files unless you are absolutely sure you will not want the vector drawing or its components again. Saving a vector image is the only way you can be assured you will be able to resize something you've created. Other formats will not be as resizable.

Where to put a file: Where you save your Inkscape files is up to you. I have a dedicated folder for these, but you may prefer to file your Inkscape drawings along with other graphics types in folders by subject, such as trees or portraits or geometric flowers.

How to find it again: In both Windows and Mac, once your files are in these folders, the file name is going to be the only thing that will distinguish one file from another because there will be no handy thumbnail image, just the Inkscape logo in a black rectangle, like the one on the right.

You'll either have to name your files descriptively or get an add-on application. I recommend the latter if you are going to use Inkscape for more than a few drawings. Some of these add-ons can be found on the Web along with instructions about how to install. You can search for something like "SVG thumbnail." The most popular result seems to be the SVG Explorer Extension, although I have not used this particular one. When you download, be sure you have the right version for your computer, whether 32 bit or 64 bit. Another option for Windows is PowerToys, which offers a constellation of utilities beyond just an SVG thumbnail viewer.

If you do install a thumbnail viewer, to make it work you must make sure that the image you want to show up on the thumbnail is actually on the page in Inkscape's canvas, and large enough to see. The viewer only shows the page, not the whole Inkscape canvas.

Setting Up a Page

The Inkscape canvas is made up of lots of free space with a page outline in the middle. You can draw anywhere, whether on the page or on the canvas outside of it. The only magic about the page is that in order to print, your image or images must be on it. The default page for Inkscape is for the international standard A4 paper, which is slightly different from the USA standard 8 1/2" x 11" page. If you live where A4 is the standard, you are good to go: no need to change the display units or paper size. If you live in the USA, you will learn here how to set up the USA standard paper size:

1. Click on **File > Document Properties**. A large dialogue box will appear.
2. Click the **Page** tab.
3. Under **General**, set the **Display units** to **mm** (I find inches too big for the general display, which controls line width, among other things).
4. Choose **US Letter 8.5×11.0 in**.
5. Keep the default **Portrait Orientation** for now. That means the page is taller than it is wide. Change it if you need a landscape orientation for some reason.

That's all there is to it. There is no "Set" or "Apply" button to click. You are ready to print once you have filled up a page—or sooner if some blank page space is okay with you.

The default is A4, so each time you open a new Inkscape document, the page will be an A4 page. You really don't need to worry about this, because it doesn't usually affect your drawing. Just be sure to set up a proper page before you print.

If you want to change the default permanently, there's an easy way.

1. Open a blank Inkscape document.
2. Open the **Document Properties** dialogue.

3. Change the **Display units** and **Page Size** as directed above.
4. Click on **File > Save Template**.
5. In the box that comes up, give the template a name, such as "Default Page."
6. Check **Set as Default Template**.
7. Click **Save**.

The next time you open a document, the page will be **US Letter 8.5×11.0 in**. and the display units will be in millimeters if that's what you've chosen.

If at some later date you need to get rid of this default template you've created, go to **Edit > Preferences**. In the list on the left, click **System**. In the main panel, find **User templates** under **System info**. Click **Open** to the right in that line. A new page will open. In the list of files you will find the template you have named. Delete it.

Grids, Guidelines, and Snapping

Grids and **Guidelines** are ghost lines that can be set to show up on the canvas but that will not print or copy. Sometimes when you are drawing, you will need a grid or guidelines to help place your lines and objects where you want them. In conjunction with **Snapping**, grids and guides can even help you by "snapping" a line or object into place like a magnet, with only a nudge from you. Even if you don't regularly use grids or guides, they can be especially helpful when you are setting up a page for printing. A grid can help you see where to put your margins and can block out regular measured spaces for the various graphics you are putting on the page.

Grids. Let's suppose we want to print a number of 2" x 2" images. Return to the **Document Properties** dialogue to set up a **Page Grid**. Half inch spaces should make an adequate grid for our purposes. Click on the **Grids** tab. Make sure **Rectangular Grid** appears. Click **New**. Check **Enabled**, **Visible**, and **Snap to visible grid lines only** if they are not already checked. In the **Spacing X** and **Spacing Y** boxes, type **.5**. You can adjust the grid line colors by clicking on the color if you wish—perhaps a pink major grid line. In the slot, **Major grid line every,** choose 4. Now you have a grid line every half inch with a major grid line every two inches. You can turn the grid off or on under **View** depending on your preference.

When you actually set up to print, don't forget to leave a margin, because the page won't print all the way to the edge. How big a margin you need will depend on the printer. The grid lines can help you position images within the margin.

It is also possible to set up an **Axonometric Grid**. That's a grid with diagonal and vertical lines. You will find this option if you return to the **Grid** tab of the **Document Properties** dialogue. Under **Creation**, where **Rectangular Grid** normally appears, the other option is **Axonometric Grid**. You can choose the angles of the diagonal lines as well as the size of the spaces.

You can have both an **Axonometric Grid** and a **Rectangular Grid** turned on at once.

Obviously, you can reset any of these grid numbers at any time to whatever works best for you.

Guides, or guidelines, are long, single lines that run from one end of the canvas to the other horizontally, vertically, or diagonally. They can be dragged out of the ruler lines at the top or left of the canvas to help you position your lines or objects. As you point at the edge of the top ruler, a little black triangle will appear. If you left-click on that and drag downward, a line will appear. You can position it as you wish. Or point at the left hand ruler and pull a line to the right. If you point at one of the top corners of the canvas, you can drag down diagonal lines.

You may notice that each **Guide** has a tiny red circle on it. That is a rotation circle or anchor. To change this center of rotation, you can move it along the line by using the left mouse button to drag it with the little hand that appears. To rotate the line, hold the **Shift** key down while pointing at the line. Once a double arrow in a circle appears, you can drag the line around the center of rotation.

If you double-click on a **Guide** while the little hand is visible, a dialogue box will come up. There you can choose the position and angle of the line numerically. The X and Y boxes at the bottom of the screen give you the position of the rotation circle.

You can add as many lines as you wish. You can then turn these on and off under **View > Guides** from **Line 1**, or drag an unwanted line back to the ruler to delete it. If you need lots of lines, you might be better served by turning on a **Grid**, also under **View**.

Snapping forces the lines you are drawing to coincide with other objects, grids, or guides. It feels almost like a magnetic field force. While **Snapping** can speed up precision drawing, it can be frustrating if you're not used to it.

Snapping is controlled in three locations in Inkscape:

- A Snapping menu on the far right of the Inkscape screen contains a number of icon buttons that you can click on or off, depending on what you want to snap to what. The top button can turn Snapping off altogether. Snapping is great for rapid placement of lines if you know just what you want to do, but for casual drawing you probably won't want it. Truthfully, I keep it turned off most of the time.
- More controls for Snapping can be found in the **Document Properties** dialogue once again: **File > Document Properties**. Here you can choose how you want snapping to behave and with what force. Until you need it to be stronger, you may want to set all snapping to be weak. Click on <u>Snap only when closer than</u> under each of the categories. On the slider, move <u>Snap to objects</u> all the way to the left. Move <u>Snap to grids</u> to 4. Move <u>Snap to guides</u> to 4.
- A third set of controls can be found at **Edit > Preferences**. Until you are adept with Inkscape, you'll probably want to leave these as they are.

Printing, Exporting, and File Formats

The minute you send a file to a printer, no matter whether it is a laser or an ink jet printer, *your vector image becomes a raster image.* So, you might wonder, just what is the point of doing a vector image in the first place? For metal artists, it all boils down to being able to reuse and recombine elements of a drawing in infinite ways, and to resize repeatedly without losing clarity. When you lay out your images on the document page, be sure you have the sizes you want for your jewelry—perhaps several sizes. It would be counterproductive to ask a copy shop technician to blow up or shrink a paper copy you have printed. You probably wouldn't lose a lot of clarity, but even a little bit might make a difference.

How to print from your home computer on paper or transparency. Just click **File > Print**, and choose your printer and the number of copies. Then click **Print**. Whatever is on the actual page on your Inkscape screen will print.

How to print from a copy shop computer. Copy shop printers are usually very good, so if you want to put your work on a USB thumb drive, your local technicians can give you some excellent results. However, printing choices can be a little more complicated. You will have some decisions to make about what material you want to print on and how you want to present your file to the technician. We'll look at all this in more detail in the chapter about photopolymer and etching (see pp. 356 ff.).

If you are already versed on those subjects, here's what you need to know to take that file to the shop.

1. Copy shops are usually <u>unable</u> to print .SVG files. Most simply don't have Inkscape or another .SVG program on their computers. That means you'll need a different file format: .PNG, .JPG, or .TIFF.

2. Exporting files. The .PNG format is now very common in Web work, and that's why it has been adopted in Inkscape as the default export. It is a raster format like .JPG or .TIFF, but is more efficient in ways that matter on the Web. If you'd rather save a .JPG or .TIFF file, most copy shops will print those, too. What is said about .PNG files below pertains to the other formats as well.

    a) For all intents and purposes, exporting is like saving. It just means that you can't reopen the exported file in Inkscape again and treat it like an .SVG because it no longer is one. You can, of course, save the original .SVG file as well.

    b) You can export a single Inkscape image as a .PNG, .JPG, or .TIFF, or you can export a whole page in one of these formats. You might export a single image if you ever want to open it in your favorite raster program like Photoshop or Paintshop Pro in order to do something to it that can only be done in a raster program. You will want to export a whole page as a .PNG or .JPG in order to to take it to a copy shop.

    c) In either case, click **File > Export PNG Image**. Shortly you'll be able to choose a different format if you prefer.

d) A floating dialogue box will appear. The top tabs allow you to choose what area will be exported.

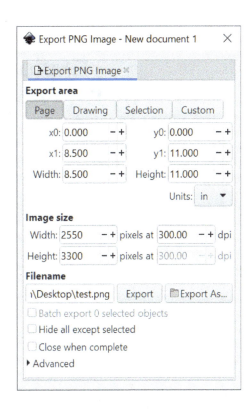

e) **Page** gives you the whole page with margins. **Drawing** gives you only the part of the page with actual drawing(s) on it. **Selection** gives you only what you have selected with the **Selection Arrow**. The numbers will be set automatically unless you have reason to change them. Under **Image size**, you can choose more **dpi** (dots per inch of line) for a finer-grained image. Choose 600 or 1200 dpi to avoid jagged edges.

f) When ready, click **Export As** and give the file a name that you and the technician can find. Find the location you want to save to, such as a USB drive. If you want to save as something other than .PNG, you'll find others listed under **Save as type** toward the bottom of the save box.

g) Click **Save** and the export is done.

3. Saving as a .PDF file. This is another option for your copy shop excursion or home printing, though the previous formats are easier and more straightforward.

Click **Save As**. Give your file location and name and choose **Portable Document Format (*.PDF)** from the drop-down menu. Then click **Save**. An additional box will pop up. For most of the choices, the defaults will be fine. However, if you have put any text in your drawing, you will probably want to check **Convert text to paths,** not **Embed fonts.** That's because if you used a font that is not in the PDF library, the PDF format may change the font to something you don't like. Converting the text to paths should take care of this issue.

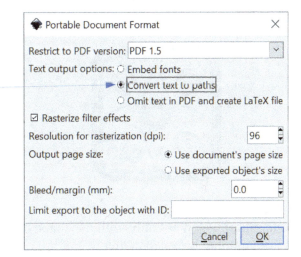

Chapter 3
Exploring the Shape Tools
by Drawing and Combining Shapes

Inkscape provides five different **Shape tools** on the left-hand tool bar: rectangle/square, 3-D box, ellipse/circle, star/polygon, and spiral. Point at each with your mouse to become familiar with their locations. Notice that the definition of each tool comes up as you point at it.

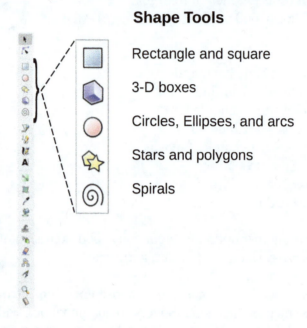

Shape Tools

Rectangle and square

3-D boxes

Circles, Ellipses, and arcs

Stars and polygons

Spirals

Since the 3-D box is of minimal use for our purposes (interested as we are in stark black and white 2-D), we will ignore it. We'll try out the remaining four.

An Example to Build

Drawing the graphic above will familiarize you not only with the shape tools, but with some of the basic functions of the program. The graphic is less than lovely, but it covers some commands you'll want.

Choosing Colors

Before drawing the outer rectangle, we will need to choose colors so that we can see what we're doing. Otherwise, we'll be drawing invisible shapes! All drawings in Inkscape are made up of **Strokes** (outlines) and **Fill**. Most of the time we will want only black and white or nothing/transparent.

On the color strip near the bottom of the window, you will see a range of colors in little boxes.

Here we can select a color for **Stroke** (the outline) and a color for **Fill** (the interior). For our current drawing, we want black for the stroke and white or nothing/transparent for the fill. "Nothing" shows up as white in a vector program, unlike the checkerboard background you may see in a raster program.

On the color strip, the leftmost group of little boxes is black, shades of gray, and white. Directly to the left of the black box is an X. Clicking on that selects <u>no color</u> (invisible, transparent or "nothing"). That is what we have now: no color, which shows up as white on the screen.

Now point at the little black square right next to the X. Pointing without clicking will bring up instructions on the bottom line of the window:

>   Color, **Black**; **Click** to set fill, **Shift + click** to set stroke.

We want the stroke to be black, so hold down the **Shift** key and click on the little black box. No need to set the fill. The fill will print as white if no fill is selected. The only time you actually need to select white as a fill or stroke is when you are putting objects on top of each other and you don't want one or more of the objects to show through.

Drawing Rectangles

With the colors selected, we can start drawing. You can draw anywhere on the canvas, not just on the page. Remember that any figure can be easily resized, so feel free to draw large figures that make it easier for you to see what you are doing.

Click on the **Rectangle tool**. Hover your mouse pointer over the canvas.   Each shape has a different cursor. Here the cursor is a tiny plus sign with an adjoining tiny rectangle icon.

A little icon will always show up next to the + to remind you which shape or other tool you are using. The crossing point of the + is where a corner of the rectangle will begin.

Hold the left mouse button down and drag the mouse in the direction you want. Release the button and you will see a rectangle with a tiny empty square in the upper left corner, another in the lower right corner, and a tiny empty circle in the upper right.

Those are handles which we will use momentarily. The X in the center of the rectangle marks the rotation center of the shape. Sometimes the rotation center looks like this instead: ✛ .You will also notice a broken line over the rectangle stroke. This is the **Bounding Box**, which is always rectangular, no matter what shape it surrounds. It indicates an active figure and will go away if you click on a blank part of the canvas. Try that.

Now let's get rid of the rectangle, just for practice. Activate the rectangle again by <u>selecting</u> it with the **Select Arrow** in the upper left of the tool box. First click on the arrow. Then click on the boundary (stroke) of the rectangle you have drawn. The **Bounding Box** will show up again. To delete the rectangle, either **Backspace, Delete** or click on **EDIT > Delete**.

It's also possible to draw a shape from the center out. Just hold down the **Shift** key as you drag. Try that and then delete the figure again.

Coming up, we'll draw the base square of our graphic for real. But first we'll need a few other commands.

Setting up the page

If you have already set up a page as described in Chapter 2, you can skip this section. If you took my advice and plunged right into Chapter 3 and drawing shapes, you'll need to set up a page now so that you can print once you're done with this exercise. Here's a quick recap of those directions.

Click on **File > Document Properties**. A large dialogue box will appear. Click the <u>Page</u> tab. Under **General**, set the **Display units** to **in** for inches. Choose **US Letter 8.5×11.0 in**. Keep the default **Portrait Orientation** for now, making the page is taller than it is wide.

Stay in the **Document Properties** dialogue for a moment. We will also set up a **Page Grid** to help size the graphic so it will print in your chosen size. For this first example graphic, we will aim for a size of

2" x 2." Half inch spaces should make an adequate grid for our purposes. Click on the **Grids** tab. **Rectangular Grid** should appear. Click **New**. Check **Enabled, Visible**, and **Snap to visible grid lines only**. In the **Spacing X** and **Spacing Y** boxes, type **.5**. Adjust the grid line colors by clicking on the color you want. For **Major grid line every** choose 4. Choose a color. Now you have a grid line every half inch with a major grid line every two inches.

Set the snap properties as well. Click on the **Snap** tab. Snapping forces the lines you are drawing to coincide with other objects, grids, or guides. While snapping can speed up precision drawing, it can be frustrating if you are not used to it. We will make the snapping very weak so it won't force you to draw what you don't want. Click on **Snap only when closer than** under each of the categories. On the slider, move **Snap to objects** all the way to the left. Move **Snap to grids** to 4. Move **Snap to guides** to 4.

You can now close the **Document Properties** dialogue.

There is an iconized **Snap** menu at the far right of the Inkscape window. There you can turn off snapping altogether with the top button or choose from a number of other options. I usually work with snapping off.

If the grid lines become distracting, you can easily turn the grid on and off. Go to **View > Page Grid** for that.

Tip! Actually, most of the time you can ignore the page except when you prepare to print. All printing is done from your page, so at that time arranging your items on the page will become crucial. Otherwise it's quite possible to work anywhere on the canvas, or even to turn the **Page Border** off (**File > Document Properties** > uncheck **Show Page Border**). If you turn the border off, however, most thumbnail extensions won't work.

Zooming

Zoom so that you have a large enough area of the page to work in. By far the easiest way to zoom is to hold down the Control key (**Ctrl**)— while scrolling with the mouse wheel. If you have no mouse wheel, you can click **View > Zoom > Zoom in** or click the magnifying icon on the tool bar. That will give you several choices, the simplest of which is the + icon. Once the magnifying glass is active, you can left click to zoom in and right click to zoom out.

Drawing the square with rounded corners in our model

Click on the **Rectangle tool**. To draw a square rather than a rectangle, hold down **Ctrl** while dragging the rectangle. The control key will force one of two types of rectangle, either a square or a rectangle with the "Golden Ratio." Aim for a square as you draw, and the program will snap to an exact square.

Aim for a rectangle, and you'll get one with the "Golden Ratio." Don't worry about the size at this point. Stop when you have a square of any size with the three corner handles.

As you can see, the base of the graphic we want to imitate is a rounded square, not one with corners. To round the corners of your square, click on the **Node Tool** (or **Node Arrow**) directly below the **Arrow Tool** on the left-hand tool menu. Point the **Node Arrow** at the tiny circle in the upper right of the rectangle until the circle turns red. Then depress and hold the left mouse button and drag the arrow downward. The corners of the rectangle will all become round.

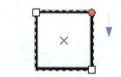

Drag circular handle downwards

Tip! Get in the habit of paying attention to Line 3 of the screen. This shows the controls for whichever tool is active. The controls allow you to precisely choose the characteristics of the object you are drawing.

Click on the rectangle tool to select it, and note what has happened in Line 3, the tool's control line. For the rectangle, you can choose the dimensions numerically by whatever measurement unit you want —pixels, millimeters, inches, and so on. You can also adjust the curve of the rounded corners with the **Rx** and **Ry** boxes. If you want to imitate the model exactly, you can make it 2 inches square and type .336 into the Rx and Ry boxes.

Change: W: 2.000   − + H: 2.000   − + Rx: 0.336   − + Ry: 0.336   − + in ▼   ⌐

If you make a mistake, you can always **Undo** previous commands. Click **Edit > Undo** or use the yellow **Undo** arrow icon in Line 2 of the commands. **Ctrl-Z** is the keyboard command.

The next time you draw a rectangle and want sharp corners, you may need to select the angle icon in Line 3 of the commands.

Since we are aiming to use Inkscape to produce jewelry designs, consider what the graphics we draw will look like on a piece of metal. For this particular graphic, we want a nice thick line to provide a raised frame around the edge of our metal. Thus, we need to make the stroke of our rounded square thicker. We'll need further command options.

By this time, a new section of the screen should have appeared between the canvas and the rightmost snap commands. This large section, the **Dockable Dialogues**, is where many further commands can be set. These dialogues are called up by certain commands and stay in their portion of the Inkscape window until closed. They can also be dragged away from their normal position and placed where the user wants them. We will just leave them in place or close them.

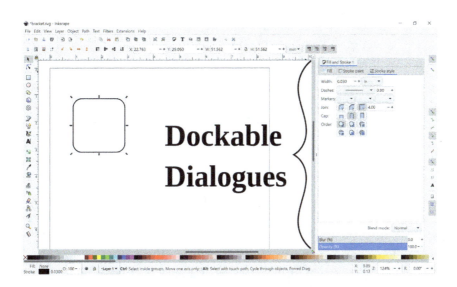

Some of these dialogues can be called up with the icon commands on Inkscape's Row 2.

In this case, we are looking for a dialogue called **Fill and Stroke**.

Click on this button or use the keyboard command, **Shift + Control + F**). The **Fill and Stroke** box comes up in the Dockable Dialogues.

Click the **Stroke Style** tab near the top of the box.

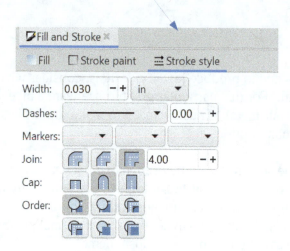

 This is where you change the width of the stroke and choose whether the line is solid, dashed, or dotted.   You will also see selection boxes to choose what the corners should look like, whether a line is rounded at the end, and how lines stack.

 If you like to measure in pixels, choose px first. Or you can choose millimeters or inches, etc. Now set the width of the stroke to a border you like. I have used 16 px.

Never freak out if an object seems to disappear while you are setting colors or stroke width. Just keep going. When you have everything set, the object will reappear. If worse comes to worse, you can **Undo (Ctrl + z)** repeatedly.

Tip! There's a neat shortcut to changing the stroke width on the fly. In the lower left of your Inkscape screen, just to the right of the boxes that tell you what Fill and Stroke colors are currently chosen, you'll see a number. If you right click on that number, a vertical box appears. At the top are measurement types--inches, pixels, and so on. Beneath them are numbers you can use to set the stroke width. This method allows you to try out different widths easily and quickly.

Further adjustments to the square are made by clicking on the black **Select Arrow** at the top of the tools column. Do that now. Note that the handles of the square have been converted to double arrows.

To adjust the <u>size</u> of the rectangle on the page, hold down **Ctrl** to maintain the square proportions, grab one of the corner double arrows, and drag outward or inward. Alternatively, you can type in the dimensions if you have not done so already. To do that, select the rectangle and then go back to the **Rectangle Tool** by clicking on it. **Tool Controls,** line 3 of the menu, will now read **Change**, followed by dimension boxes. We want 2.0 in the W and H slots and **in** (meaning <u>inches</u>) in the slot where you can choose units of measurement. This will give us a 2" square, appropriate for a pendant. Obviously, you can always resize your work to any dimensions you wish. Illustrations in this book are often not full size.

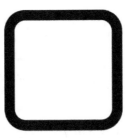

If you want to move the square around on the page, click once again on the **Select Arrow**. Double arrows appear again around the square. Point at the black border and you will get a little four-way arrow next to the regular select arrow:

This is the **Move** symbol. Click, hold, and drag the rounded square where you want it on the page, using the grid lines as a guide if you wish. The dotted lines of the bounding box will help you see the grid below.

Moving objects onto the page as you work will be useful when you go to print your page.

Drawing a four-pointed star

The star/polygon tool is capable of producing a remarkable number of figures. Take a few minutes to try it out on a blank area to the left of your page. Keep an eye on the **Tool Controls** (now reading **Change**) in Line 3. Choose the five-cornered polygon icon. Draw a figure. Note that you can change the number of corners and choose whether they are rounded or pointed. Try out some variations. Then try **Randomized** and see what chaos follows!

When you're finished playing, the little gray and white x icon at the far right will reset the tool to the default polygon.

The star can produce even more amazing figures. Experiment with corners, spoke ratio, and rounding. You will soon be drawing mandalas.

Another feature of the star/polygon tool is manipulation handles. If you look carefully at a star you have drawn, you will see two tiny diamonds. One will be at an outside corner near the bottom. The other will be at an internal corner. The outer diamond controls size and rotation and can be found on both stars and polygons. The inner diamond works only for stars and allows you to change the spoke ratio and also skew the shape by rotating. Try these out to see how you can alter a star on the fly.

For our four-pointed star, work in the space to the left of the page. We will combine our star with the square frame momentarily.

To begin, draw a star and make sure it is selected with the **Select Arrow**. In the **Tool Control**, or **Command line,** put the following numbers in the boxes: **Corners** 4, **Spoke ratio** .4, **Rounded** 0, **Randomized** 0. Now select the star with the **Select** arrow, point directly at the star's border, and drag it to fit inside the rounded rectangle. To maintain the same shape as you resize it to fit, be sure to hold the **Ctrl** key down before you drag.

Set the stroke width of the star to 1 or 2. This will vary as you resize. Once in place, mine is 3.5. Again, use the dotted lines of the bounding box to help you center the star inside the rectangle. Don't worry about exact centering at this point. Shortly, you'll learn a good way to do this precisely.

Tip! Because you're making an approximate copy of a graphic prescribed here, you are using numbers in the **Tool Controls,** line 3. When you are inventing on your own, you will probably be winging it most of the time and may not need to pay attention to the numbers. It's good to know how to use them though, in case you need to be exact.

Drawing ellipses and spirals

Just as you draw a perfect square by holding down the **Ctrl** key as you drag, so too you can draw a perfect circle using the **Ctrl** key. We don't want a circle this time, though. Instead, just draw an oval ellipse. Try drawing several in the space to the left of the page. Your oval doesn't have to be the same dimensions as in the example figure, but if you want them to be the same, enter 7.0 mm in the Rx slot and 10.0 mm in the Ry slot in the **Tool Control** line, Line 3.

Next, try a spiral, using the **Spiral Tool**. In the **Tool Control** in Line 3, give the spiral 3.00 turns with a divergence of 1.000 and an inner radius of 0.000. Move and resize the spiral until it fits inside the ellipse. (By the way, each end of the spiral has little sizing diamonds similar to the handles on the star tool. This time they adjust the number of turns of the spiral. You can try them out or ignore them, as you wish.)

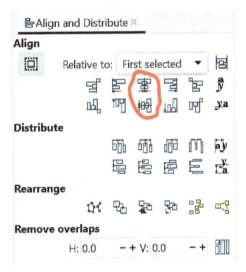

You can exactly center objects with the **Align and Distribute** dialogue, which we will call up in the **Dockable Dialogues** area to the right.. Click on the correct icon (third from the right) on Line 2 or find the same command under **Object > Align and Distribute** or (**Shift Ctrl A**). A dialogue will pop up over the **Fill and Stroke** dialogue. I actually keep both of these dialogues open most of the time because I use them frequently. You can toggle back and forth using the tabs at the top of the dialogue.

With the **Shift** key depressed, click on both the ellipse and the spiral. **Shift** allows you to select more than one object at a time. You should now see <u>two</u> bounding boxes, one around each shape. In the **Align** controls at the right, click on **Center on vertical axis**. Then click on **Center on horizontal axis**. The figure should now be centered.

Center on vertical and then horizontal axes

While you still have both the ellipse and spiral selected, join them together to make the next steps easier. Click on the icon in Line 2 to **Group** selected objects,

or find the same command under **Object > Group** (**Ctrl G**). Now you will see only one bounding box. The two objects will move and enlarge together until you **Ungroup** them (**Object > Ungroup**).

Next, we need to rotate this spiral-ellipse. Click in a white space with the selection arrow to make sure everything is cleared. Click on the spiral-ellipse. Click again in the same spot. This time, instead of straight double arrows that indicate simple selection, you should see double arrows that parallel the perimeter and wrap around the corners of the bounding box. If you drag one of the corners, you can rotate the figure. Turn the figure to about a 45 degree angle.

We need four of these figures, each one lying in a different direction. Copy the rotated figure and paste another figure. Space the two so they look like the top two in the first set below. Align these horizontally with the **Align and Distribute** dialogue. **Group** these two spiral-ovals by selecting both and using **Ctrl + G**. You now have a group with two levels.

Tip! To copy and paste, it works well to use the right mouse button—especially for pasting. That way you can position the copy where you want it to go. If, instead, you use the paste command on the command lines, you will have less control over where the copy will end up. Better yet, try **Duplicate** instead (**Ctrl + D**). This puts duplicates right on top of the original. Then you can move them wherever you want. <u>This is a keyboard command worth learning</u>.

Next, copy or duplicate the twin figures and arrange the two sets of twins in two rows of pairs, as in the first set of four below. You can now align the two pairs vertically using the appropriate symbol in the **Align and Distribute** dialogue.

Now **Ungroup** the objects <u>once only</u>. That should make the spiral-oval combinations independent. Next, **Shift-select** both of the two bottom figures and click on **Object > Flip Vertical** or simply **V** on the keyboard. Click elsewhere to clear. Now **Shift-select** both of the two right-hand figures and click on **Object > Flip Horizontal** or simply **H** on the keyboard. You should have four symmetrically designed figures ready to move into place on the graphic. Select all of these and **Group** (**Ctrl + G**) them. Now you can resize them or change their stroke to fit the graphic, all at once. Move the grouping into place in the square.

Note: Don't try to use the **Clone** command to make the copies for this figure. Cloning produces copies that make it possible to change all of the copies in the same way at once. That would not work here because of the different orientations of the spirals/ellipses.

Drawing another star

The central figure for our graphic is a 24-cornered star with a spoke ratio of .400, 0 rounding, 0 randomized. Draw, adjust the stroke and move the new star roughly to the center of the 4-cornered star.

You can use **Align and Distribute** if you want accuracy.

Adding to the Border Square

Assessing the graphic, we might decide that the border is too heavy for the rest of the figure, and yet we may still want a strong frame. We can try out some alternatives for breaking up the border while keeping the width. A thinner white line on top of the border might be just the thing. First, copy the black frame by clicking on it to select and then using **Edit > Copy** or the copy icon in Line 2. Paste the frame to the side. Readjust the stroke of this square to a thin line (see p. 19-20). Depress **Ctrl** while dragging the border slightly smaller. Drag it on top of the original border. Since it is black, only the boundary box will be visible. Depress **Shift** while clicking on the white color box in the palette at the bottom of the screen. Adjust the stroke width and position to your liking. You can, by the way, experiment with dashes under the stroke style to see if you prefer some sort of broken line.

Adjusting the Alignment

Once all the elements of the graphic are the sizes you want and the strokes are as you like them, do a final alignment of the concentric elements. Select all four concentric figures, holding down the **Shift** key. In the **Align and Distribute** dialogue, click first on **Center on vertical axis** and then on **Center on horizontal axis** as you did before.

Now tweak the positions of the spiral/oval figures, using the grid. If you want to be exacting, you can put one where you like it and then select its opposite horizontal or vertical figure. Use **Align Vertical** or **Align Horizontal** on these figures to line them up exactly.

Remember that you can zoom in and out (**Ctrl** + mouse wheel) to make the figure easier to work on. As you do that, the grid size will change proportionally.

Tweaking the Stroke Width

It's possible that all the resizing has changed the stroke width in ways you don't like. Before unifying the figure, you may want to make some adjustments. To make components have the same stroke width, select all those components you want to share the same width by holding down **Shift** while clicking on them. Then make your changes in the **Stroke style** tab of the **Fill and Stroke** dialogue. The stroke will now be uniform in all those components.

Important Tip! When the **Select Arrow** is active, there are some symbols at the end of the control line you need to know about.

These control how strokes, corners, gradients (not relevant for us), and patterns behave when you scale an object—that is, make it smaller or larger. Most of the time you want these all to be selected (gray). That will make the stroke and corners, for instance, grow or shrink proportionally with the size.

Unifying the Figure

If you are finished with the figure and you want to make sure you can move the whole thing around without missing some of the elements, you will want to **Group** all of the elements. There are two alternatives for selecting a number of objects to group.

Method 1, which you already know:

Select each element, using **Shift + click**. You may find it easier if you zoom in to make all of the elements easier to click. On this figure you will probably find that the spirals and ovals are still joined from a previous grouping.

Method 2, rubber-banding:

Instead of clicking, hold the left mouse key down while dragging from one corner of a group of objects to the opposite diagonal corner. You surround or "rubber-band" a group of objects with a rectangular bounding box and thus select all at once. All of the items now have bounding boxes.

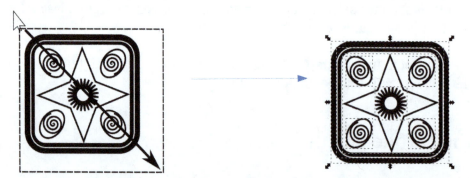

Rubber-banding: select all objects by dragging from one corner to another.
All now have bounding boxes.

Once each element has a bounding box, click on the icon in Line 2 for **Group selected objects**, or find the same command under **Object > Group**. Now the figure is a unified whole and can be moved around. Note that this grouping can be reversed. If you decide you want to change something you can **Ungroup** the elements, the next command in the row.

Saving Your Work

As with any file, save your work often! Inkscape projects are saved as SVG files. If you don't have a folder for vector images, I recommend you make one now.

It is also possible to export an image as a PNG, JPG, or TIFF file, which can be used in other graphics programs or on the Web. Exporting as one of these files will convert the image to a raster image, so if you do that, be sure the image is exactly the size you want it to be so you don't have to enlarge or shrink the raster file. You will no longer be able to manipulate its elements in Inkscape.

Warning! When you save in Inkscape, you are saving everything on the canvas. If you want to save only a particular image, you will have to delete everything else on the canvas. A workaround is to copy the image you want, open a new Inkscape file, paste the desired image on the new page or canvas, and save that. I like saving the various pieces and experiments along with the main image I'm keeping. I never know when I might want a scrap. See p. 8-9 for more ideas about saving and filing your work.

A Suggestion

Before jumping into the next chapter, practice the skills you've learned by creating images of your own using the various shapes and combinations. As with any new skill, using the shapes will begin to seem natural only when you've used them for a while. Simple though they may be, the shapes will soon have you creating a myriad of beautiful images appropriate for your jewelry.

Definitions and Anatomy of Shapes and Drawings: Review and More

A **Shape** is produced by the **Shape** tools: **Rectangle**, **Ellipse**, **Star/polygon**, and **Spiral**.

The **Shapes** all have handles (tiny squares or circles along the perimeter or inside) that can be dragged to change the shape. These handles function differently for each shape.

Rectangle: square handles resize the rectangle; the circular handle rounds all corners simultaneously.

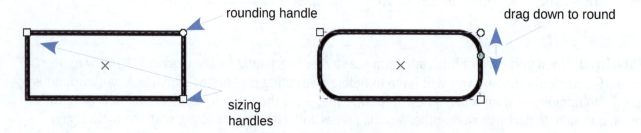

Ellipse: square handles resize the ellipse or circle; dragging the circular handle turns the ellipse into an arc. The top resizing handle drags vertically only; the left resizing handle drags horizontally only. Dragging either square handle while depressing **Ctrl** turns the ellipse into a circle.

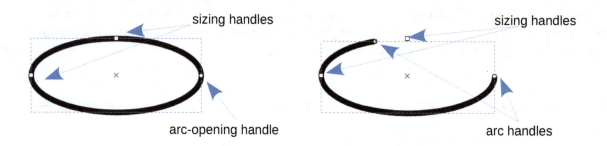

Star/polygon: a star has a diamond-shaped outer handle that rotates and resizes the arms and an inner handle that skews; a polygon has a diamond-shaped outer handle that rotates or resizes the arms.

handle to skew

handle to rotate or resize arms

handle to skew

handle to rotate or resize arms

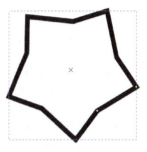

other positioning via the handles

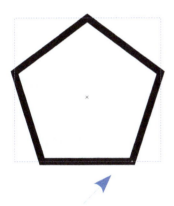

handle to rotate or resize

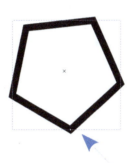

handle has rotated and resized

Spiral: handles at both ends of the spiral line allow for more winding or unwinding of the spiral.

handles to unwind spiral

spiral unwound from inside

spiral unwound from outside

As long as a **Shape** has not been converted to a **Path** (see pp. 46, 73), you can always click on it with the appropriate **Shape** tool and alter it as a **Shape**, using all the **Shape** controls, even if it has been **Grouped** with other objects.

- In this book, an "object" or "drawing" is anything produced by Inkscape, including **Shapes**, but also including complex figures with several components of varying kinds. "Object" is the general word most used by Inkscape for these things.

- All **Shapes** and any objects/drawings that have been **Grouped** or **Combined** have a rectangular dotted **Bounding Box** when clicked with the **Select Arrow**.

Bounding Box Arrows

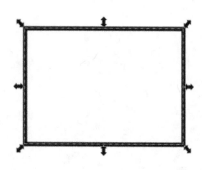

- The first click produces arrows perpendicular to the lines of the **Bounding Box**. These can be dragged to <u>resize</u> the figure in vertical and horizontal directions.

- 45° arrows will also appear at the corners. Dragging one of these <u>enlarges</u> the image. To keep the proportions, hold down **Ctrl** at the same time.

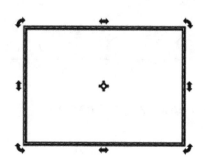

- A second click produces double curved arrows at the corners. Dragging these will <u>rotate</u> the figure.

- There will also be arrows parallel to each side. Dragging these <u>skews</u> the figure.

- The second click also reveals a **Center of Rotation** marker: ✛ . If rotated, the drawing uses this point to <u>rotate</u> around.

- The **Center of Rotation** marker can be dragged, so that the object/drawing rotates around a point other than its own center. This feature is used especially for automated processes like cloning (see pp. 97 ff.).

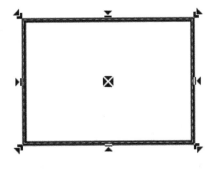

- Actually, there is a new **Bounding Box** click that is available optionally as a third click.

- This feature is for "on-canvas alignment." It can be turned on or off with the little blue box in the upper left corner of the **Align and Distribute** dialogue. It is supposed to provide a more intuitive way of aligning objects. I myself feel that it interferes with my use of the other **Bounding Box** features, but details of the feature will be covered later (see pp. 203 ff.). You can decide whether you like it.

Some Commands to Remember and Practice

- Undo a command: **Ctrl + z** or yellow undo arrow or **Edit > Undo** or **Right-click Undo**.
- Set fill: Click on color on the palette or on X for no color/invisible/transparent.
- Set stroke: Shift-click on the palette or on X for no color/invisible/transparent.
- Draw a shape: select shape tool and drag a shape diagonally. Refine with control bar.
- Activate a figure: click with the **Select Arrow**. This is known as **Select**.
- Delete a figure: **Select** + **Backspace** or **Delete**.
- Zoom in or out: **Ctrl** + mouse wheel
- Scroll left or right: **Shift** + mouse wheel
- Round corners of rectangle: use **Rectangle Cursor** to drag red circle or set in control bar.
- Resharpen corners: click corner icon on the rectangle tool control bar.
- Change stroke width: set by number in the **Stroke Style** tab of the **Stroke and Fill** dialogue or right click on the stroke number in the bottom left corner of the screen.
- Align objects: various iconized commands in the **Align and Distribute** dialogue.
- Resize an object: click with the **Select Arrow** and drag the little arrows. Click-hold **Ctrl** while dragging to main the same proportions.
- Rotate an object: click twice with the **Select Arrow** and drag the little corner arrows.
- Move an object on the canvas: point at the object to get the 4-arrow icon, then click, hold, and drag.
- Draw a perfect circle or square: select the tool and hold **Ctrl** while dragging. Allow to snap to the circle or square.
- Select more than one object: hold **Shift** while selecting, or "rubber-band" by dragging the **Select Arrow**. Alternatively, **Alt-drag** draws a red line through objects to select them.
- Copy: **Select** and then **Ctrl + C** or right-click copy with the mouse or use menu commands.
- Paste: **Select** and then **Ctrl + V** or right-click copy with the mouse or use menu commands.
- Duplicate: **Ctrl + D** and then drag copies off the original.
- Flip an object vertically: **V**.
- Flip an object horizontally: **H**.
- Group objects together: Select all the objects and click the **Group** icon in Line 2 or click **Object > Group** or keyboard command **Ctrl + G**.
- Ungroup: Select the group and click the **Ungroup** icon in Line 2 or click **Object > Ungroup** or keyboard command **Shift + Ctrl + G**.

<h1 style="text-align:center">Chapter **4**</h1>
<h1 style="text-align:center">**Learning some variations: Arcs and Patterns**</h1>

Metal clay and etching artists are always on the lookout for new patterns for texture. Why not create your own? In this chapter, we'll begin with arcs, just so you have those elements in your tool chest. Then we'll play with making patterns for textures using just copying and pasting. We'll move on to the ready-made Patterns in Inkscape and how to manipulate them. Finally, we'll apply a newly created Pattern to objects.

Drawing Arcs

In Chapter 5, you'll learn how to draw lines, which can certainly include arcs. But starting from a circle or oval is usually the easiest way to produce an arc, whether open or closed:

Open or closed arcs are easily drawn with the **Ellipse** tool.

First, make sure the fill is set to nothing/transparent: click on the X at the left end of the palette line (Line 6). Set the stroke to black: **Shift + click** on the little black box directly to the right of the X.

Now click on the **Circle/Ellipse** tool on the left hand menu. Draw a circle by holding down **Ctrl**, pointing at a blank area of the canvas, and dragging the ellipse icon until you have formed a circle. The figure will hesitate back and forth between oval and circle. Encourage a circle and you will get a perfect one. You will get the feel for this.

At this point, <u>don't</u> switch to the **Selection Arrow**. Stay with the circle tool with the circle selected. Take a moment to look at the **Tool Controls,** line 3, where you'll see slots for the horizontal and vertical radii and the start and end positions of the circle.

To the right of these slots you will see four little icons in faint grays. If you squint, you may see that the first shows a closed arc—almost like a pie with a piece missing. The second shows an open arc—no line to show the missing piece. The third shows a closed line across a portion of the circle. The fourth restores the complete circle. As you go through the next steps to create arcs, you can make some changes and corrections by clicking on these little icons.

Next, look at the circle you have drawn. You will see two tiny white squares, one on the left side and one on top. With the little squares, you can pull the circle into an oval one direction or the other. If you want to try this, remember you can use the **Undo** command (**Ctrl-z**) or, alternatively, **Ctrl-click** on one of the tiny squares on the circle's perimeter to get the oval back to a circle.

On the circle's right side is a tiny white circle. It is actually two circles, one on top of the other. These circle handles can be used to produce an arc. Put your cursor over the little circle and it turns red.

Drag the red circle handle down and most of the circle disappears so that you find yourself redrawing the circle's circumference. On the other hand, if you drag the red circle handle up, the circle will open up into an arc. Depending on which of the little icons at the end of the control line happens to be checked, the wedge may be closed or open. Notice that the minute you open the circle, the grayed-out icons turn blue and are much easier to see.

If you click on the first of those four little blue icons in the **Tool Controls,** line 3, the line(s) between the outside of the circle and the center will be drawn in black. Click on the second of the little icons in the **Tool Controls**, and the black radii will disappear, leaving you with an open arc. Click on the third icon and you'll get a straight line joining the ends of the arc. Finally, the fourth brings you back to the original circle.

Depending on whether you start with a circle or an oval, you can produce many different arcs, and you can, of course, use the handles to pull the arc into still other arcs. If you then click in a blank area, click on the **Selection Arrow**, and click again on the arc, you can pull the arc this way and that, producing more variations. Clicking twice on the arc with the **Selection Arrow** will allow you to rotate the arc with the corner double arrows or skew the arc with the side double arrows.

Unless you are fond of the arc you've created, get rid of it by selecting it and backspacing.

Draw a circle again to try out one other command. The **Tool Controls** we've just looked at also allow you to precisely choose the rotation of an arc—how close or far it is from being a complete circle. A circle is 360°. An arc is less than that. An arc you have drawn in Inkscape starts at 0.00, the position of the tiny red dot at the beginning of the process. You will see 0.00 in the **Start** slot. The **End** slot tells you how far around the arc goes toward being a complete circle. Change this **End** number and see what happens to your drawing. A perfect half-circle arc is half of 360° degrees, which is 180°. If needed, you can draw very precise arcs by entering your chosen numbers in the **Start** and **End** slots.

"Hand Building" a Pattern from Arcs

What we'll try next is a pattern based on arcs. I'm calling this "hand building" because there are more automated ways to create a pattern that we'll cover in later chapters.

A pattern is simply a repetition of lines or objects or other patterns, so you could create patterns using any of the shapes we've tried so far. We'll just use an arc for practice in this chapter. If you already have a perfect half-circle arc, you can use that. Otherwise, start fresh with these directions.

Click on the **Ellipse** tool.

In a blank space, draw a circle by holding down **Ctrl** and dragging. If one of the arc icons is still active, you may end up with an arc. Just so we're starting from the same place, change it back to a circle by clicking on the circle icon at the end of line 3, the **Tool Control** line. Find the tiny white circle on the right side of the main circle's perimeter. Drag up or down to open up the circle. Make a half-circle arc of about an inch—large enough to work with easily. If there is a line closing the arc, click on the second icon at the end of the **Tool Controls**, line 3. That will give you an open arc. Also be sure the slot labeled **Start** is at 0.00 (degrees) and the slot labeled **End** shows 180.00 (degrees) so that you end up with a perfect half-circle.

In the **Fill and Stroke** dialogue box to the right, change the **Stroke Style** to a width that produces a pleasing bold line. While you're at it, round the ends of the arcs so the figures will look less ragged. To do this, on the **Stroke Style** menu, find the various choices for the **Cap**. Choose the rounded middle option.

Click the arc with the **Select Arrow** to activate the arrows of the bounding box. Copy or duplicate the arc. Paste it onto the canvas and move the new arc into the cup of the old arc. Turning on the **Page Grid** under **View** may help with positioning.

Shift + click to select both arcs. Copy again. Paste the two new arcs to nest above the old. Under **Edit**, click on **Select All**. Again, paste the new group to nest above the old. You now have 8 nested arcs.

Reminder: Another way to select multiple objects is to hold down the left mouse button outside the cluster of objects and drag a bounding box across all the objects. When you let up on the button, you will see that all of the objects in the cluster are selected. You will actually find this "rubber-banding" technique more useful than **Select All**, because the latter will pick up all objects currently in the workspace, and you often won't want that.

Select all your nested arcs. Now make sure all the arcs are centered vertically. Click on the **Align and Distribute** icon third from the right in **Line 2**. That brings up the **Align Dialogue Box** to the right. Click the **Align Vertical** icon (third from left). You'll also want to be sure that the arcs are nested evenly one within the other. Under **Distribute**, click the button for **Make vertical gaps between objects equal** (fourth from left on the second line of **Distribute**).

It's time to make all these arcs function as one object. With all selected, click **Group Selected Objects** icon on **Line 2** or click **Group** under **Object** in **Line 1**. Using **Group** is reversible. You can **Ungroup** the objects again if need be.

Now copy or duplicatethe whole figure again. Paste or position it. Then click **Flip Vertical** under **Object** in **Line 1**, or hit **V** on the keyboard.

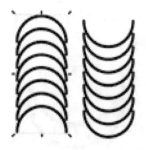

Move the new figure so that it overlaps the first figure in a way you like.

Group and copy the whole thing and make a couple of additional rows.

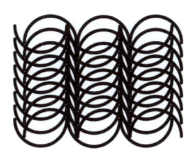

Select the entire figure and **Group** it all together into one. You will notice that you can now grab a double arrow and pull the image this way and that to distort it in various ways. If you want to maintain the same stroke width, be sure to check **when scaling objects scale the stroke width by the same proportion**, in the group of symbols at the right of **Line 3.**

Distortion and rotation in still other ways is available if you click twice on the image with the **Select Arrow** to get the rotate handles. Try the various handles to see what happens. Then **Undo** everything to get back to the undistorted image.

At this point you have an image that could be used for texturing metal, using one of the processes in Chapter 20. If you are bothered by the "tails" on either side of the image, you will see how to deal with these shortly.

Save your pattern before continuing, giving it a name you can find again. We will be using it again soon.

Exploring Inkscape's Ready-Made Patterns

Inkscape provides several common Patterns that can be used as fill for the objects you draw. To try these out, first draw an ellipse.

Go to the **Fill and Stroke** dialogue on the right. You may need to click on the tab if it is covered up with another dialogue. If it has been closed altogether, you can reopen it with the **Paint brush** icon directly to the left of the **T** icon on **Line 2**. Or from the keyboard, use **Shift + Ctl + f**.

Under **Fill and Stroke**, click the **Fill** tab to open it. You will see a line of icons with an **X** and several boxes. Click the fourth box, the one with the small checkerboard Pattern.

The label **Pattern Fill** will appear, along with a drop-down box with various Pattern names. Take a look at what's there and try out a few. If the ellipse you have just drawn is selected, it will fill with the various Patterns as you select them. The black and white Patterns would, of course, be appropriate for metal designs, while the shaded Patterns would not.

Once you have applied a Pattern to an object, you can further manipulate the Pattern, as you are about to see. You can make it larger or smaller within the boundaries of your object. You can rotate the Pattern. You can move it up and down.

Tip! Until you are used to this process, for the next steps it will help to have an uncluttered canvas so that you can see what you are doing. Keep your object, the ellipse, well away from the top left corner of the page outline. You will see why shortly.

To make these Pattern adjustments, first apply the Pattern you want. The smalls checks provide a good practice example.

Next, select the ellipse with the **Select Arrow**. Then click on the **Node Tool** just under the **Select Arrow**. In the upper left corner of the page outline, you should now see a faint **X**, a tiny circle, and a tiny square. Don't mistake the sizing handles on the ellipse for these handles. The former are two squares and a circle right at the edge of the object, and the object may also have an **X** to mark the center. Confusingly these are the same size as what you're looking for. The handles you want are

<u>outside</u> of the object. The x, o, and square form the points of an invisible right triangle. The handles for ready-made Patterns will usually be found neatly stowed at the top left corner of the page, but they are only visible with the **Node Arrow** turned on.

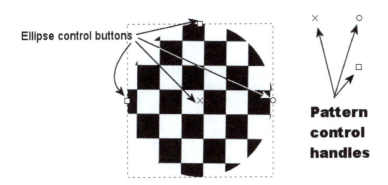

The three **Pattern control handles** do the following jobs:

x : Moves the center of the Pattern. This will be most useful in a non-concentric Pattern. You can see the checks need to be centered here.

o: Rotates the Pattern around the center (the x of the ellipse).

□: Resizes the Pattern in relation to the object. Resizing can happen in width and/or height. If you want to maintain the original shape of the Pattern and just make it smaller or larger, hold the **Ctrl** key down as you drag.

Once you are satisfied with the size and position of the Pattern in relation to the object, you will need to stabilize it so it doesn't continue to move around inside the object if you move or resize or rotate the object. Click the **Select Arrow**. At the right of the **Tool Control** line, Line 3, are four icons. Point at each to see what they do. Make sure the fourth one is selected (highlighted by a medium gray box) to stabilize the Pattern within the object.

Reminder: The **Undo** command is your friend!

39

Using Patterns for the Stroke

If you use a **Pattern**, most of the time it will be to <u>fill</u> an object—that is, put it in the space bounded by the lines of your object. It's also possible, however, to use a **Pattern** for the <u>stroke</u> of an object. Obviously that's not going to work well if the stroke of an object is thin, but if it's thick, it can be an effective design element.

To use this feature, go to the **Stroke Paint** tab of the **Fill and Stroke** dialogue. Select an object that has a thick stroke, choose the Pattern you want, and adjust the size and orientation with the handles, just as you did with patterned fill.

An oval with a thick stroke with a Pattern applied.

Warning! You may be dreaming up possibilities for drawing an object with one Pattern for the stroke and a different Pattern for the fill. This might not work out as you expect. You will discover that the fill and stroke Patterns will overlap when the background is transparent, as it is in most of the ready-made Patterns. This may create an unacceptable mess, or it may produce a fortunate new pattern at the overlap. If a result like the star on the left is not what you had in mind, you will need to stack one star within another. The outer one would have Stroke Paint with no fill; the inner would have a Pattern fill with or without a stroke. To get an outer stroke on the third figure, you would need to stack another star with a black stroke below the other two.

Single star: overlap of fill and stroke Patterns

Two stars: outer with stroke Pattern, inner with fill Pattern

Two stars: black stroke added to inner

40

Patterns Via an Alternate Fill and Stroke Option: Paint Servers

The **Paint Servers** function is a different means of using patterns. Like the **Pattern** sections of **Fill and Stroke** that we've just been looking at, **Paint Servers** offers a number of ready-made Patterns, some of which are the same as those you have already seen. To access these, click on **Object > Paint Servers**. A new menu will pop up in the dialogue area.

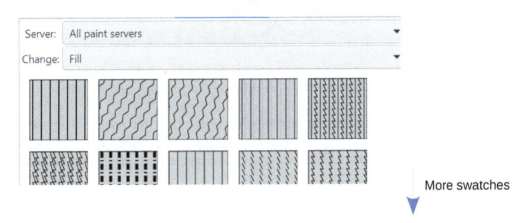

More swatches

To view what's available, it's best for beginners to select **All paint servers** next to **Servers.** You will see swatches, many with a gray background. The gray here represents a transparent background. Remember that if you try these Patterns on both fill and stroke on the same object, you will get overlap anywhere you see gray in the Patterns.

With an unfilled object selected on your page, click a few of the Patterns to try them out. Some of these can be manipulated with the **Node Arrow** in exactly the same way as you did with the **Pattern** function. The hatches, however, currently come one size only (they will be resizable in a future Inkscape version). Right now, you can get around the resizing problem by making the object you are filling very large or very small and then resizing the whole object.

Applying Your Own Custom-made Patterns

You can design your own Patterns and turn them into **Pattern** fills or **Paint Server** fills to use with the objects you draw in Inkscape. Thus you could have several objects with different custom or ready-made fills in the same drawing.

The word *pattern* is used in this book in two senses. Lower case *pattern* is used here to refer to any repeated elements arranged in a design intended to please the eye. Upper case *Pattern* is used of the objects that Inkscape converts and calls a Pattern, which can then fill another object. Such a Pattern is its own peculiar type of object in Inkscape.

> **Warning!** Custom fills you devise will disappear when you close Inkscape. Always save your Pattern as an .SVG document so you can use it at a later time. Later in the book we'll look at a way to use Paint Servers to save Patterns to Inkscape more or less permanently.

To practice using a custom **Pattern** fill, we'll use the arc graphic that you built and saved.

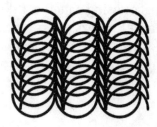

Open your arc graphic. It should come up in a new Inkscape document to start fresh.

If you are planning to use this Pattern as a transparent Pattern, just leave it as is. However, understand that if you then put an object decorated with this Pattern <u>on top</u> of another object, the other object will show through this Pattern. If you want to prevent that from happening, you will need to make the background opaque. You can do that by putting this line-graphic on top of a white rectangle of the same size. Such a rectangle would need to have no stroke and a white fill. Just move your line-graphic onto the white rectangle. In order to see the background rectangle, you may want a temporary stroke, which you would then turn off once the line-graphic is in place.

What if the white rectangle covers up the line graphic? That happens if the rectangle was drawn last and is therefore on the top of the **Z-order** (see p. 5). To correct this, select the rectangle and click **Object > Lower**, or **Object > Lower to Bottom**. Remember to turn off the stroke of the white rectangle.

Once the Pattern graphic is as you want it, click the **Select Arrow** and rubber-band the entire graphic to select it.

In **Line 1**, go to **Object > Pattern > Objects to Pattern**.

To try out the Pattern, draw a new shape of your choice somewhere on the screen, and select it.

In the **Fill and Stroke dialogue** to the right, chose the **Fill** tab if it is not already up. Then choose the little blue and white checkered Pattern box. Your custom Pattern will probably immediately fill the shape, because that Pattern will be first on the list. It has been given a number for a name. If you have created more than one Pattern during your Inkscape session, you will have to try out the numbered Patterns to figure out which is which, because unfortunately there is no preview and you can't easily name the Patterns. Do remember that when you shut down Inkscape altogether, <u>the custom Patterns will disappear</u>. Remember to save a copy of the Pattern graphic so you can use it again.

Now that your shape is filled with the custom Pattern, you will want to adjust it. It is probably too large or small for the shape and the orientation may not be pleasing. To get the adjustment handles, first select the shape and then click the **Node Tool** just under the **Select Arrow** in the Tool menu on the left.

Locate the Pattern control handles. You'll remember that when you were using the Patterns included with Inkscape, the control handles showed up in the upper left of the page. Unfortunately, they are not so well-behaved with custom Patterns you have made. Most often they will be floating outside the shape below and to the right. Sometimes they will overlay the shape, making it a little tough to see them. You may have to zoom <u>way</u> out or move the shape around to find them. Once you see the handles, you can grab the x and drag it toward your shape to get the handles close enough to the shape to work with them. The square handle can be moved closer to the x to help you see things better. Now you can play with the adjustments. Remember □ is the sizer and o is the rotator.

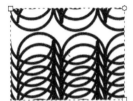 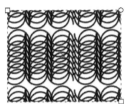 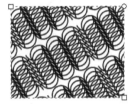  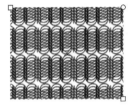

On the left is the unadjusted Pattern as it showed up for me. Shown next are four other possibilities after adjustment, all appearing in a rectangle shape. You could fill any shape of your choosing.

You might remember that when we first produced this arc pattern, we left open the question about the "tails." In all of these examples of adjusted Patterns, the tails have become part of the Pattern. If, however, you don't want them, you can work with the scaling and centering until the "tails" are out of the boundaries. The result is the first image below.

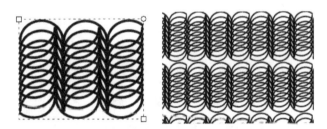

If you like this and want to make another Pattern from it, you can—or from any of the other adjustments you made. You will probably want to eliminate any stroke you have around your shape (**Shift + click** on the X on the color bar)—unless you want that outline to become part of the Pattern. To make a new Pattern, repeat the instructions you have already followed:

Click the **Select Arrow** and the graphic to select it. In **Line 1**, go to **Object** > **Pattern** > **Objects to Pattern**. The second image above shows one result from the new Pattern.

Why not just erase the tails? Erasing in Inkscape is not like erasing in a raster graphics program. That eraser tool on the **Drawing Tools** line is a fooler. It only erases objects or fill, not parts of strokes. Using Patterns is one way to edit edges. We will look at better ways to "erase" in Chapter 9.

Three Important Points about Patterns

1. A **Pattern** can be made from any object or objects from simple to complex. Even a single line or square can be converted to a **Pattern**.

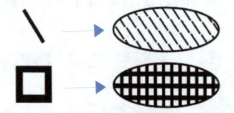

A line and a square converted
to Patterns to fill shapes.

2. When you convert a drawing to a **Pattern** it can't be edited as long as it is a **Pattern**. You can change it back to an editable drawing with **Object > Pattern > Pattern to Objects.**

3. Since custom **Patterns** disappear from the **Pattern** menu once you close your Inkscape document, you may want to start a page dedicated to Pattern swatches or even to particular kinds of Patterns so you will have a catalog of Patterns you can use in the future. Save the page. Then when you want to use one of these Patterns, you can copy and paste it into a new drawing page, make sure it's activated as a custom **Pattern**, and use it to fill new objects you're designing.

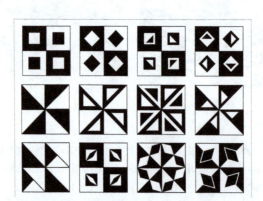

Save an Inkscape document with
Pattern swatches for future use.

Later in the book, we'll look at how to put custom **Patterns** in **Paint Servers** so that they don't disappear when Inkscape is closed.

Recap

To recap, we've practiced two skills in this chapter: first, the "hand-building" of patterns by simple repetition, and second, turning such hand-built patterns into **Patterns** in **Stroke and Fill** so that they can be used over and over to fill shapes you have drawn.

Looking ahead, we'll experiment with additional methods of creating patterns in upcoming chapters, especially using the **Clone** function to arrange copies of an object in an almost infinite variety of ways (Chapter 8). We'll also look at other pattern-making functions, especially for making seamless patterns. These assume more skills in Inkscape and will not be covered until much later in this book (Chapter 19). There you will also learn a method for saving your custom Patterns in Inkscape more permanently. If you want to skip ahead, feel free.

Before delving into other ways of making patterns, we'll cover a number of other basic skills in Inkscape, especially creating and using lines.

Chapter **5**
Exploring Lines and Paths

So far, everything we have drawn in Inkscape has been based on objects produced by four **Shape** tools: the **Rectangle**, the **Circle**, the **Star** or polygon, and the **Spiral**. We will permanently ignore the 3-D box tool. While designs based on the **Shapes** could occupy you for years, you may still be feeling a major limitation on your creativity without that most basic of drawing elements, the line, which will allow you to produce arbitrary shapes and details. It's time to add lines and paths to your Inkscape repertoire.

A few basic definitions

Lines and **Paths** are pretty much the same thing. "Line" is not a term used much in Inkscape, but it will be used in this book to refer mostly to the objects drawn by the three drawing (or line) tools: the Bezier pen, the freehand pencil, and the calligraphic pen. The term "Path," on the other hand, appears everywhere, because all Inkscape drawings are ultimately based on paths. In a vector program, a **Path** is the computer formula for each object you draw. It is made up of points and instructions about how to connect those points. Strokes and fills and shadings—the stuff we can actually see—are just additional attributes, like the clothing on a person. The person is still a person without clothing, and a path is still a path with or without the attributes of strokes and fills, though this path may be invisible to us without these attributes.

A **Shape** (**Rectangle, Ellipse, Star, Spiral**) is a particular kind of path. Whereas a **Path** is defined mostly by the positions of its points, **Shapes** are defined mostly by comparative dimensions. For example, a rectangle might be 5 × 3 with 90° angles. A circle might have a radius of 8. **Shapes** can be converted to **Paths** in Inkscape, meaning that the program will then define them by the positions and relationships of their points instead of their dimensions. But the opposite is not true: a **Path** cannot be converted to an Inkscape **Shape**, even though it may look just like a shape.

A **Path** can be very simple or very complex, but it must be continuous to be defined as a single path. If you hand-draw an object without lifting pencil from paper, you have the equivalent of a single path.

simple —————————————————————————▶ complex single paths

Most drawings are made up of a number of paths piled on top of one another. All of those below are made up of more than one path:

If you're comparing the last drawings in each of the lines of drawings above and wondering how they are different, take a close look at the wide V-shaped lines that join the various layered spirals in the first set. These lines have made the path continuous. In the second set, there are no lines joining the spirals. They simply sit on top of one another.

The number of paths in an object or drawing will become important when we start doing path operations in a Chapter 9.

Getting started with lines and paths

This chapter will first look at the **Line tools** and their characteristics. Once we've practiced a few basics, we'll move on to the essential topic of **Nodes** in Chapter 6 and how they can be used to edit the lines we draw. If you become frustrated with the line tools, hang in there until we get to nodes, where you will gain much more control.

A word about the mouse versus other input tools: if you are a casual user of Inkscape, you can get along just fine using only the mouse. However, a drawing tablet or touchscreen (see p. 6-7) would certainly make freehand or calligraphic lines easier and more intuitive if you plan to do a great deal of freehand work. This book will not treat drawing tablets in detail.

The Line Tools or Drawing Tools

In the toolbox at the left of the screen, Inkscape provides three tools for drawing lines:

 The Freehand "pencil"

- Draw unaided or with degrees of smoothing.
- Draw in one of three modes for different types of curve.
- Draw straight lines by clicking.
- Draw dots with Ctrl + left mouse; + Shift or + Alt adds sizes.
- Choose shapes to control how line-width varies.
- Alter using node control points.

 The Bezier "pen"

- Draw in one of three modes for different types of curve.
- Drawing is constrained by the rules of the mode through clicking and dragging.
- Draw straight line segments and dots with two additional modes.
- Choose shapes to control how line-width varies.
- Alter using node control points.

 The Calligraphic "pen"

- Draw single lines of varying widths and styles.
- Use most effectively with a drawing tablet, but capable of interesting effects even with a mouse.
- Uses both stroke and fill.
- Alter using node control points.

Tip! The default stroke width for the pencil and Bezier pen tools is one pixel, which you will find hard to see. If you would prefer a wider initial line, you must set it in the stroke style—say to a millimeter or two. The trouble is, once you have drawn a line, the stroke will go back to the default. If you want to keep it at a wider setting, go to **Edit > Preferences > Tools >Pen > Style of new objects > Last used style**. Now once you set the stroke, it will stay that way until you change it. If you want to go back to the default, do the process again and choose **This tool's own style**.

Try out each of the line tools in turn. If you haven't used graphic drawing tools before, these will take getting used to. As always, experimentation and practice are the answer.

If you would like some guided practice, try drawing the figures offered in this chapter. They will demonstrate what each tool is good for and will also show its limitations. Don't worry if your efforts seem far from perfect or if you think there are better ways to draw some of the elements—just think of them as scribbles. Be sure to keep your results handy, because once you have drawn the initial efforts, you can practice editing them using the node tool we will introduce in the next chapter.

The Freehand Drawing Tool, or Pencil Tool

We'll jump into drawing in a moment, but first, this section is placed here as a reference, since using the pencil tool effectively will eventually require some understanding of the pencil's control bar. The various parts of the control bar are numbered below to help with explanation. Come back to this for help once you start drawing.

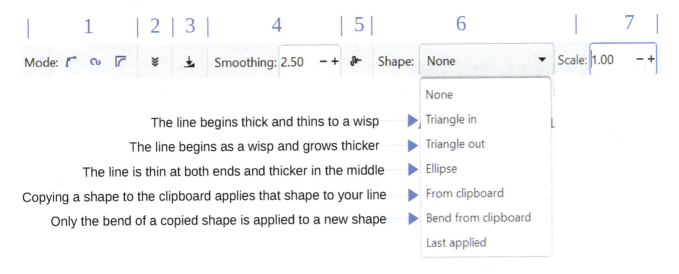

1. **Modes** control the kind of curve available when you draw. These will show up again with the Bezier pen tool. There are three modes: **Bezier**, **Spiro**, and **B-Spline**. The **Bezier** is the basic mode. In the Pencil tool, you won't be conscious of the Bezier curves. Instead, it's the most like drawing with an ordinary pencil; in the **Bezier Pen** tool, the curves will require a completely different approach.

2. Below are lines drawn in the three modes. Using a grid, I've attempted to make similar waves. You can see that the **Bezier** line is less curved and more subject to the irregularity that stems from a shaky human hand. The **Spiro** line produces rounded humps, while the **BSpline** humps are flatter and more forward leaning.

Bezier   Spiro   Bspline

The **Spiro** and **BSpline** lines can be altered after drawing in ways peculiar to these modes.

3. This button slightly alters Spiro and Bspline lines.

4. This button makes a drawing tablet sensitive to the pressure of the tablet's pen and is irrelevant if you are using a mouse or touch screen.

5. **Smoothing** allows you to get rid of shake in the lines you draw. You will almost always want some smoothing, probably around 20-30.

6. It is also possible to smooth a line after you have drawn it. Turning on this button calls up a dialogue for doing that.

7. Putting a **Shape** on a line makes it possible to draw tapered, elegant or oddball lines of variable widths. Using this option is quite different from choosing a stroke width in **Fill and Stroke**.

8. **Scale** is a way to control the width of a shaped line and only pertains to **Shape**. Note that there is also a tiny red diamond handle available at the end of the line if you click on the **Node Arrow** right under the **Select Arrow**. Dragging the red handle adjusts the width of the line.

A Doodle: Getting Ahead With the Pencil Tool

If you are using a mouse and not a drawing tablet, the **Pencil Tool** will probably be your go-to approach for drawing lines, especially once you are used to the **Smoothing** setting. Spend some time trying it out with the suggestions that follow.

Turn off **Enable snapping**, the top icon on the snapping bar on the far right of the screen. Snapping will be an annoyance in this freehand exercise because it may pull your lines to places you didn't intend.

Click to choose the **Pencil Tool** or use keyboard control **F6**. In the control bar, click the first **Mode**, the **Bezier** path. In the **Smoothing** box, write 1.00. Make sure the squiggle button next to **Smoothing** is selected (darkened).

Draw a doodle of a face. Don't worry about artistic merit and don't worry about other control settings yet. We'll get to those controls shortly.

| Doodle at 1 smoothing | Similar doodle at 30 smoothing | First doodle at 30 simplification with Path Effect |

Each element of your drawing—each line or path—is separate unless you intentionally join elements. If you hate a line, you can select it with the arrow tool and then backspace or delete to clear it. The last line you've drawn has the bounding box showing. To delete that line, just backspace or delete.

Your lines are probably pretty shaky, as mine are in the first doodle above, especially when drawing with a mouse. In fact, zoom way in and look at your lines to see just how shaky they are! Remember that vector lines are actually collections of points, or nodes, connected by curves. Every time your hand changes direction slightly, another node is laid in to change the curve.

Magnified left eye before and after smoothing or simplification.

There are remedies for the jaggedness. Don't erase this doodle. We'll come back to it.

Now look again at the **Control line** for the **Pencil Tool**, line 3.

You currently have the box for Smoothing set at 1.00. Set the number to 30. Now try drawing another doodle similar to the first face. You'll immediately notice that the lines are much less shaky, as they are in my second doodle face above. That's because the program is reducing the nodes as you go. Fewer nodes usually equal a less jagged line.

It's also possible to smooth your lines *after* you've drawn. Go back to your first doodle. If you have several lines in a drawing as you do here, you will have to group the elements of the drawing together for this method to work. Select the entire doodle. Then **Group (Ctrl + G)**. Keep the group selected. Next, open **Path Effects** under **Path** on the **Menu Bar** or **Shift + Ctrl + 7**. A **Path Effect** called **Simplify** will pop up in the dialogue box to the right. If it doesn't, click the blue + button to call up the **Path Effects** menu page. Click on **Simplify**.

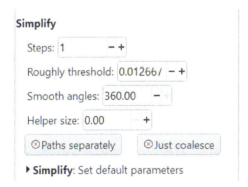

In the dialogue box, you'll see four variables with number selection boxes. **Steps** gives the number of times smoothing will be applied. This will be similar to what happened in the second doodle when **Smoothing** was at 30 in the control bar. In the **Path Effects** dialogue you can try 30 again and you should see a pretty similar result. Or play around with various numbers to compare effects. You can always undo.

The **Roughly threshold** has to do with the strength of the **Steps**, so upping that number will soon multiply the smoothing effect. It can be quite aggressive.

If you have angles you want to preserve or smooth, **Smooth angles** should help. The number can be set from 0.00 to 360 because the latter is the number of degrees in a circle and degrees are the measurement for angles. At 360, all angles will be targets for smoothing. At 90, any angle of more than 90° will be preserved, but sharper angles will be smoothed. If you want to preserve a 45° angle but smooth anything sharper, set the number at just under 45.

The remaining options are obscure and can be ignored for our purposes.

Applying a shape to the line width

In both the **Pencil** tool and the **Bezier Pen** tool, you can vary the width of the line from one end to the other. As you saw in the control bar comments above (see p. 49), this is called **Shape** and is set by a little drop-down menu. The four standard shapes are illustrated below at 30 smoothing.

You can also put a Shape or Path on the clipboard and incorporate it into the line you are drawing. For instance, a 4-pointed and a 3-pointed star drawn with the star tool and copied produce the figures on the left. The results depend on the smoothing, orientation, and curve of the line:

The figures on the right above originated from the same shape, unfilled and copied. This command is meant to allow you to create your own "brushes." Try with a square rotated to a diamond, for instance. Brushes can be all sorts of irregular shaped blobs or lines, and do not have to be closed figures. You can even construct a leaf or heart or bird, copy it, and then draw variations on the original with a stroke of the **Pencil** tool. If the brush is composed of more than one line, don't use **Group**, use **Path > Combine**, as in the leaves on the right, below.

All the shapes come with a tiny handle that will appear at the starting end of the line when you click on the **Node Arrow**. Drag it to alter width.

> **Tip!** If you're done with whatever you've drawn with your custom brush, you'll want to stabilize it by applying **Path > Object to Path**. Otherwise, if you reorient the object—rotating it, for instance—the object may morph into something you don't want.

Drawing with a built-in shape uses the **Path Effect** called **Power Stroke**. It will come up automatically if the **Path Effect** dialogue is open and if you select the **Node Arrow**. Among other things, **Power Stroke** allows you to choose how your line begins or ends. You'll learn more about **Power Stroke** later (see pp. 234-5). Similarly, drawing with a clipboard shape is linked to the **Path Effect** called **Pattern Along Path** which will also be discussed later (see pp. 231-3).

Bend from clipboard

This command was devised to allow you to copy just a curve from a path you have drawn. Applied to a new, straight line, the bend of the clipboard curve will transfer. This is meant to make it easy and intuitive to draw new lines with the same bend as previous ones.

Scale

For all of the **Shape** choices, you can decide the size of the effect with the **Scale** box. You can set this before or after you draw the shape. Setting it after drawing will allow you to see the different effects quite easily. If you draw with a copied shape, **Scale** will change the shape as well as the size.

Going dotty

The pencil can be used to draw precise **dots**. **Ctrl + left mouse button** produces a dot. Adding **Shift** doubles the dot size. Adding **Alt** to either **Ctrl** or **Ctrl +Shift** produces dots of varying sizes. The same dot feature is available in the right two modes of the **Bezier pen** tool (see below).

Pencil Pushing

With smoothing and shapes, the Pencil is capable of elegant, swooping lines or quick sketching. Try out all the various line choices, including shapes, to get a feel for what you can do with them. Here are a few more doodles.

The Pencil is truly a versatile and powerful tool and will even more useful once you learn to manipulate nodes in the next chapter.

> **Tip!** If, after using a shape to draw your lines, you go back to a plain line (**None**) and find strange results, it's probably because the **Fill** is turned on while you're trying to draw something that should just have a **Stroke**. Just turn the **Fill** to transparent and make sure the **Stroke** is black.

The Bezier pen tool: curving your enthusiasm

If you're new to Bezier curves, you may find that the Bezier pen tool takes some getting used to, but with a little practice you can master it.

Depending on what you are drawing, you may wish to turn on a grid (**View** > **Page Grid**) or use **Guidelines** to help you with line placement (see p.10-11).

Left click on the **Pen** tool and look at the **Tool Control** line, which has only two sets of choices. On the right, you'll see the same **Shape** and **Scale** choices that appeared with the **Pencil** tool. On the left are the **Mode** icons.

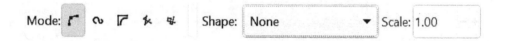

Mode also appeared with the **Pencil** tool, and we touched on them lightly there. With the **Pen** tool, the modes are essential to drawing. To use the **Pen** effectively, understanding the various characteristics of the modes is a must.

There are five modes, some with the same name as in the **Pencil**. We'll begin with the two new ones on the right, since those are the most easily controlled.

Allows you to draw **straight line segments** one after the other in any direction. Try drawing a zigzag line with several turns. To draw, left click on the canvas where you want the first segment to start. Click again where you want to make a turn. If you want to stop, double click or right click. If you want to continue, simply move to another point where you want to make a turn and left click. Continue as you wish, ending the series by double clicking or right clicking. You can also click **Enter** on the keyboard to end a series.

In addition, this mode and the next allow you to draw **dots**. To repeat the directions above from the **Pencil**, **Ctrl + left mouse button** produces a dot. Adding **Shift** doubles the dot size. Adding **Alt** to either **Ctrl** or **Ctrl +Shift** produces dots of varying sizes.

This works just like the previous mode except that it only allows you to draw segments at right angles. If you want these segments to be limited to either straight up and down or straight across, hold Ctrl after your first click. You'll be able to feel hesitations encouraging you to click in a vertical or horizontal direction, although you could choose to ignore that. Once you have made the second click, all your segments thereafter will be at right angles.

As mentioned, dot drawing is also available for this mode.

The B-Spline mode is the easiest of the remaining modes to control. It creates curves that approximate angles, but are rounded off. Each click of the mouse places the point of an angle, and between the two lines of the angle is your curved line, as can be seen here:

While you are drawing, the angles are in red and the resulting curves are in blue. Notice how the curves hug the angles. Once the line is finished, the red angles disappear and the line changes to the stroke color.

Tips!
- As long as there is a bounding box around the line, it can be deleted with **Backspace** or **Delete**.
- While you are drawing, the last segment can be deleted with **Backspace** or **Delete**.
- If you've ended a figure and then decide you want to continue it, click on the little box at the end of the line (the end-node) and keep going.

Another figure to try: a wavy frame

Let's suppose we want to put an evenly spaced wavy line around the edge of a square pendant—something like this:

55

We'll use the **B-Spline** mode of the **Pen** tool for this. As we've seen, the B-Spline is just a type of curve. To get the wave even, we need to set up a grid to guide us. Open **File** > **Document Properties**. Under the **Grids** tab, press **New**. Leave most of the defaults except for **Spacing X** and **Spacing Y**. Make those both 20.00000. Put 10 in the slot, **Major grid line every __**. Close the dialogue.

Enable snapping. That's the top symbol in the far right icon menu.

Make sure **Snap to grids** is also on, toward the bottom of those icons.

To make it easier to keep track of what we are drawing, we'll use the rectangle tool to draw a square around four of the squares formed by major grid lines.

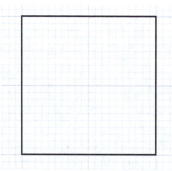

With the **Bezier Pen Tool** in **B-Spline** mode, begin drawing in the lower right corner of the first little grid square and move diagonally to the upper right corner of the next square and click. This point will coincide with the boundary of the larger square you have drawn. As you draw, your cursor will trail a red line to mark the angle and a blue line to show the curve.

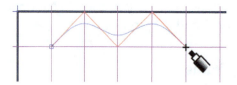

You don't have to be too exact about where you click, because the angle will snap to the grid. If you miss, backspace to the previous point.

Continue to weave back and forth between the boundary of the square and the grid line just below it. When you reach the last grid square, click on the lower corner and continue to the diagonal corner that coincides with the black outline, as shown below.

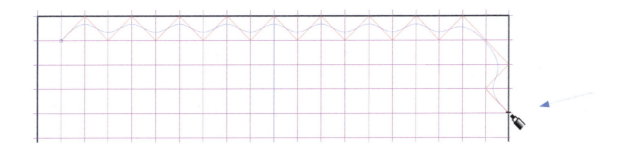

Continue all the way around the black square and click on the beginning point to close the line. If you have to interrupt the process, you can start again by clicking on the little square—the control point—at the end of the line. It may look as though the line is not continuing properly, but when you end it again, it will right itself.

Once you've made it around the perimeter, click on the black square and delete it. You will be left with the wavy square. You can now do any other of the usual operations to it, such as changing the stroke, adding fill, distorting it, copying it, and so on. Below, I have copied the figure twice and resized the copies, using the **Align and Distribute** dialogue to center all three wavy squares. Then I have widened the stroke a little.

Changing the weight of the B-Spline curve

Using the accompanying dialogue box (**Shift + Ctrl +7**), it's possible to change the "weight" of the curves you draw—that is, how closely the curves hug the angles of the lines you are clicking. The default weight is 33.3333. The higher you set the weight, the smoother and flatter the curves. The lower the weight, the more closely the curve matches the angle.

At 33.3333% weight (default)

At 10% weight

At 25% weight

At 45% weight

Tip! If you wish you'd placed the previous click of the B-Spline differently, pressing ALT will allow you to go back to the last angle and move your mouse around to get the curve you want.

The Spiro Mode: A circular argument

The Spiro line yearns to be circular, and it will fight you to get its way. As you might have guessed, the Spiro mode was named after the popular Spirograph toy that's been around for more than 50 years. Clicking sets the control points, each one allowing you either to continue in the same spiral direction or to reverse course to produce a graceful S.

As long as you click fairly often, you will have well-behaved lines. Try to force the line too far and you may suddenly find your screen full of a tangled mess of line that looks like your fishing reel after a really bad day on the lake:

Even if you accidentally like the swirly mass you end up with, you will find it very unstable and not easily resized or amenable to other operations. Best to get rid of it.

Try out some swirls, clicking often and changing course several times to get a feel for the process.

Spiro lines are particularly attractive when drawn with one of the line shapes. Note that the shape cannot be changed after drawing the line, but the scale can be. You can experiment with how much thickness looks good.

If you would like to try the same sort of wavy frame that we did with the B-Spline curve, set up your grid and square again. Make sure **Enable snapping** and **Snap to grids** are turned on. Be forewarned that as you weave from square to square, the line will protest by moving all over the place. If, however, you stick to your guns and click at each diagonal corner as you did with the B-Spline, the line should right itself. The very first curve you place will look much more circular than the others, but if you go all the way around and close the line, that curve will snap into place and match the others. You'll end up with a frame that looks a little like a ravioli.

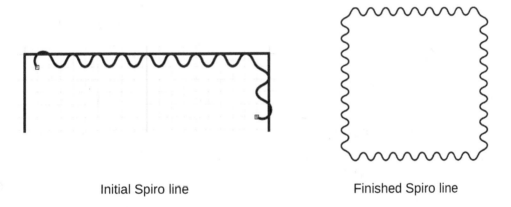

Initial Spiro line   Finished Spiro line

By the way, **Spiro** lines and **B-Spline** lines, unlike other lines, must be converted to a **Path** (**Path > Object to Path**) if you are going to add to or alter its nodes. Don't worry about this yet. We'll be looking at nodes shortly.

Tip! As in the **B-Spline** line, if you wish you'd placed the previous click of the **Spiro** path differently, pressing ALT will allow you to go back to the last angle and move your mouse around to get the curve you want.

The Bezier mode of the Bezier pen: getting a handle on your curves

Bezier (pronounced *bay-zhay*) curves are the most common type of curve found in drawing programs. Inkscape's **Bezier** curves show underline handles as you are drawing. You don't draw a **Bezier** curve by clicking on one point after another. If you do, you'll get a series of straight line segments. Sometimes these can be useful to alternate with curves, but if it's the curve you're after, click down and don't let up; then drag. As you drag to another point, a blue handle with a little circle on the end will appear, lying along the direction of your drag.

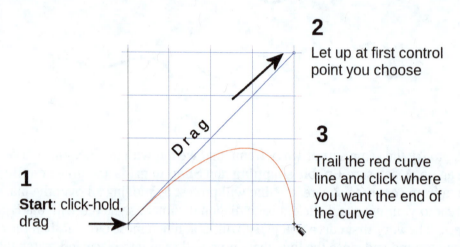

2 Let up at first control point you choose

3 Trail the red curve line and click where you want the end of the curve

1 **Start**: click-hold, drag

Drag

Let up on the mouse button. You will have a curved red line "stuck" to your pen point. Try trailing it this way and that to see what curves you can produce. When you reach the point where you want the curve to end, click again, and the line will turn green. Now you can either continue with another curve or right click to end the line altogether, turning the line black. If, instead, you click-hold at point 3 above, and drag again, you will continue trailing the red line into another curve. You can continue this way indefinitely, but you will notice that as you continue, each opposing curve will pull the former one into a shape you may not have predicted unless you are a mathematician. It may take a bit of practice to get used to how to produce the curves you want. Using a grid can help with this.

The Bezier mode seems best for drawing long, gentle, graceful curves. It will not easily produce the kind of arc found on a circle or ellipse, and is not the best choice for a single curve that is completely symmetrical. For that, try an arc made with the **Ellipse** tool instead.

The wavy frame conundrum

We can once again try the wavy frame experiment that we've done twice before, just to see how the **Bezier** curve differs from the others, but be forewarned: it will be very difficult, if not impossible, to draw even curves all the way around the perimeter of the square because the corners will be unruly. I have had to settle for a single line of arcs with odd tails at beginning and end to anchor the curves. I have then duplicated the line, rotated it appropriately, and overlapped the corner ends. This is the best I could do without using node-editing, which we will get to soon.

Set up your black square as previously and be sure snapping is on. Because of the difference in the way the **Bezier** curve is drawn, we can't just click on alternate diagonal corners as we did before. This time, we must proceed by the click-hold, drag, let-up, click-hold, drag, let-up action described above.

Start a row down from the top of the black square, the better to see the work as you go along. Here is a map of the points you will be clicking, following the directions below. **Please realize that you will not see the numbers or dots representing click points. They are merely a map here.**

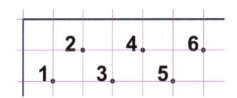

- With the **Bezier** mode selected, click on 1 and let up to anchor the line.
- Click on 2, hold, and drag to 3.

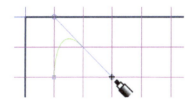

- Let up on 3.
- Trail the red line to 4.

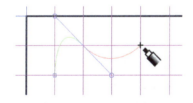

- Click on 4, hold, and drag to 5.

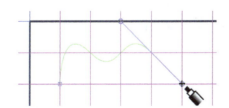

- Let up on 5.
- Trail the red line to 6.
- Click on 6, hold, and drag, etc.

Once you have reached a point two squares before the end of the line, drag down to the next point, as usual.

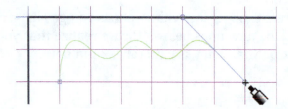

Click, hold, and trail the red line all the way up to the top edge of the black box and double-click to end the line. The extra tail is necessary to pull the last curve into place.

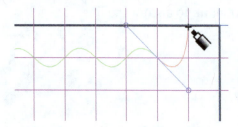

Here's the completed **Bezier** line:

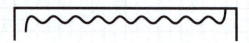

As mentioned above, to complete the wavy frame, it will be easiest to make three copies of the line, turning two vertical, and arranging them around the square. To tweak the positions, you may want to turn off snapping. Here are two possibilities for corner treatments. The second uses additional straight line segments in the corners to make flaps.

As you can see, the **Bezier** mode is not the best choice for this particular exercise, but at least you now have a sense for the difference in the curves produced by each mode.

Other options in the Bezier mode

Once again, you can use the various **Shape** choices to achieve different looks on your curves. The last two are made with copied shapes (see pp. 49, 52 ff.).

The Calligraphic Pen: fancying up your lines

You will have more natural control over your calligraphic lines with a specialized drawing tablet that attaches to your computer (see p. 6), but for the purposes of a metal artist, the investment may not be necessary. Much can still be done with a mouse, and this book will only cover what can be done without a tablet. A touch screen and a good stylus would be an alternative, though it would lack pressure sensitivity.

Unlike the **Pencil** and the **Bezier Pen**, the **Calligraphic Pen** uses **fill**, bounded on either side by two usually invisible sub-paths. This makes it possible to have a calligraphic line of highly variable widths, rather as if you were drawing by hand. A different color stroke can be added, so that the **fill** is one color and the **stroke** on either side is another. While that option will rarely be useful for metal artists, there may be a time or two when you will want such a double line. Below are examples with the Stroke increased to 10 and set for black, with the fill set for white.

Other Options for the Calligraphic Pen

Here's the control bar:

Some of these options only work with a pen and drawing tablet.

Since the basic width of a calligraphic line is fill, not stroke, it is controlled by an option on the control bar called—surprise, surprise—**Width**. It's the second slot on the bar. Width can also be varied on the fly by clicking on the left and right arrows of your keyboard. Left decreases width, while Right increases it. You can thus change the width of your line even while you are drawing it.

The other options, except for the leftmost set, are well explained when you point your cursor at the slot, though few will do much with a mouse.

> **Tip!** Raising the Mass number slows down the drawing of the line and has the effect of smoothing the line somewhat, even with a mouse.

On the left, where you will initially see **No preset**, there are six preset line types in the drop-down menu: **dip pen**, **marker, brush, wiggly**, **splotchy**, **tracing**. Try these out at different widths. Below are the six presets at a width of (initially) 20 px.

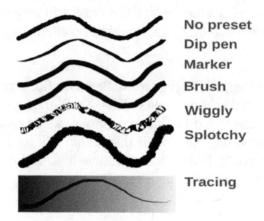

You may notice that, as you change from one preset to another, some of the other options will also change. Most of these presets—the first five—need no explanation. What you see is what you get.

If you devise a line that you especially like by fiddling with the other settings, like thinning, fixation, mass, etc., you can create your own custom preset for it so you can use it again. You add a preset by creating your line and then clicking on the tiny wrench symbol to the right of the preset slot.

Give your preset a name, and it will then appear in the preset list.

Tracing and hatching

The last of the standard presets, the **tracing** option, requires considerably more explanation.

https://commons.wikimedia.org/wiki/File:Hirs
chvogel_Self_Portrait.jpg

Before we actually look at **tracing**, we'll need to start with the concept of **hatching**. You've no doubt seen black and white engravings with the tiny parallel lines that give the sense of contour. To the left is an example from a self portrait by 16th century artist Augustin Hirschvogel. In this detail you can see both parallel and cross-hatched lines, the latter used for deeper shadow under the subject's cheekbone.

As metal artists working with stark black and white for our etching or photopolymer plates, we may sense opportunity in the fact that Inkscape provides a way to draw curvy parallel lines fairly easily.

The first step in hatching is to draw a line that will serve as your guide path, the path your additional lines will follow. Once drawn, the line must be selected:

Next, hold down the **Ctrl** key (and keep holding), choose the calligraphy pen, and start to draw. As you point at your guideline, a circle will appear, bounded in black with a cross in the center. As you move closer to or farther from the guideline, the circle will expand or contract. The center cross marks where the new line will go.

Once you click to begin drawing the new line, the circle will turn green and the diameter—or distance from the guideline—will lock.

If you stray from the correct distance, the circle will turn red. If you aren't happy with the line, you can undo it and try again. Take it slowly, drawing as many parallel lines as you wish. Because each new line is modeled on the previous one, some variation will accumulate, lending a more hand-drawn look.

If you prefer to model every line on the first one, you can change the preferences for the Calligraphy tool: **Edit** > **Preferences** > **Tools** > **Calligraphy**. Uncheck **Select new path**. Now when you position the circle for the next line, you will see that the diameter of the circle has grown so that the edge of the circle can still follow the original line.

This automated hatching can use any path as the guide path.

You may see possibilities here for making Zentangle-like drawings.

Now let's get back to the **Tracing** option under the calligraphy pen's presets in that first drop-down menu in the tool's controls. Tracing allows you to draw a line that varies in width according to the lightness or darkness of what's behind it. A white background produces a very thin line; a darker background produces a wider line. The idea seems to have been to further automate the drawing of hatched lines on top of a shaded background, so that the background could be removed, leaving just the hatched lines to indicate the contour. Unfortunately, this option frankly doesn't seem to work very well, and there are currently much better ways of achieving hatching (see, for example, pp. 135-6, 223-4, 244-7). Here is my rather poor attempt to demonstrate this option.

| The shaded background object | The lines drawn | The background removed |

Calligraphy and a Tablet

If you are using the **Calligraphy Pen** with a drawing tablet you will want to click the little downward arrow on the control bar to activate the pressure sensitive feature of the pen.
The more pressure you use, the wider the line.

Practice and Create with the Line Tools

Now that you've learned some of the characteristics of the various lines available in Inkscape, spend some time playing with them. Drawing with these lines takes a little getting used to, but before long you will find yourself creating some original drawings that will eventually be suitable for your metal jewelry. If you are a little frustrated by mistakes and uneven or misplaced lines, hold on! Major help is on the way in the next chapter!

Chapter 6
Editing Lines and Paths Using Nodes

The steering wheel

Drawing lines without using nodes to make adjustments is a little like driving without a steering wheel: it can be done but the results are not likely to be satisfactory for long! You may have found line drawing so far a bit frustrating. Never fear. You are about to gain much more control.

Any path you draw can be precisely altered using nodes. You can straighten curves, add curves, move parts of lines, join lines, split lines, change curves to sharp angles or straight segments and vice versa.

Draw a double Bezier curve something like this. It doesn't have to be precise.

Make several copies of your curve so we can use it again for other experiments.

Now select the **Node tool**, just below the **Select Arrow** in the left-hand toolbox.

You will see a different kind of cursor-arrow, a thin triangle pointer. Use it to click on the curve you have drawn. The nodes will become visible as tiny hollow squares, and the line will be surrounded by a node selection box. For this curve, there are three nodes: the beginning, the middle control point showing where the curve reverses, and the end.

You can drag on these nodes directly. Try doing that and see how the curve changes. Alternatively, you can drag anywhere on the line and alter the curve in various ways—the program is then using the nearby nodes to reshape the line. The exact way the curves are altered by dragging is governed by the properties of each of the three drawing tools or, in the case of the Bezier and Pencil pens, by the mode you are in. For instance, dragging the line itself for a Spiro curve will do nothing. You can only drag from nodes, or less successfully, from a blue handle. In the B-Spline mode you can only drag from the nodes or from a control line. The reshaping of the line as you drag on a node will also differ among the three modes since each mode draws a different type of curve. If you need to do more with the nodes of a B-Spline or Spiro curve, you can use **Path > Object to Path** first (see p. 73).

 You can select more than one node using **Shift-click**, or you can rubber-band more than one node by dragging the node arrow to form a box around the nodes you want. If you then drag on one of these nodes, the curve will change in a different way.

68

Using the node control bar

Dragging on nodes or lines is not all you can do by any means. Notice the control bar for the node tool, just above the horizontal ruler where a control bar always appears when you are in a tool. As usual, pointing at each option gives you an explanation of what the option does. Most of these will be sufficiently explanatory, but you may need a little more information for a few of the options.

Let's skip along the control bar for a moment to the next to last option ⎇ . If you have one or more nodes selected, clicking this will show the blue Bezier handles. Dragging on the handles is another way to alter the line—often the smoothest way.

Next to this option, just to the left, is the option ⁘ to show transformation handles for the nodes you select. This will insert a box with little double arrows around it, just like the transformation arrows you are used to when you select with the regular selection arrow (see p. 30).

The little arrow-handles work the same way. The difference is that they surround only the portion of your drawing controlled by the selected nodes instead of the whole drawing. You can use the arrow-handles in the same way you already know, to stretch, resize, deform, or twist the lines in the box. As usual, you can toggle the arrow-handles between the resize handles and the rotate handles by clicking on the selected lines or nodes.

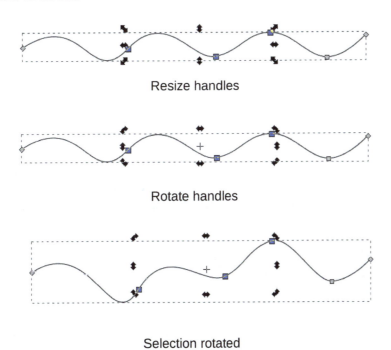

Resize handles

Rotate handles

Selection rotated

Let's go back now to the beginning of the control line and look at some of the other commands.

⁜ The first option in the control line adds nodes. When you click on a spot on the line segment where you want a new node, the nearest nodes on either side will be selected. Then clicking on the add symbol will insert a new node, usually about halfway between the surrounding nodes. Continuing to click will continue to multiply the nodes. Actually, if you want to specify where you want a new node, you will be better off double-clicking the spot on the line where you want it. That will add the node. Holding down **Ctrl-Alt** while you click on the line will do the same thing. Another trick if you want a new node halfway between two others is to select both nodes and then click the add-node symbol. You can keep clicking if you want more nodes halfway between the others.

For even more control, just to the right of the add-node symbol ⁺ is a little down arrow ▾ for a drop-down menu. The choices below it allow you to add a node at the left-most point (min X) or the right-most point (max X) or the lowest point (min Y) or the highest point (max Y) between two selected nodes.

You may be wondering why you would want to add nodes. New nodes allow you to produce a new curve or point or even a straight section in your old line. Remember the double Bezier curve we started with above? Suppose we want to change it so that the big initial curve becomes two little "hills." To follow along, use one of the copies you have made. First, let's add a node just before the top of the big "hill."

Next, drag the new node down to a position you like.

If, say, you don't really like the shape of the second "hill," you could add another node and make further adjustments. You can proceed in this way until you are satisfied with your line. Click somewhere outside the node selection box and the node symbols disappear.

The remaining options in the first three sections of the control line enable you to delete nodes, join nodes within a path, split a path into two separate paths, join two paths with a new segment, or delete a segment between selected nodes. If you point your cursor at the symbol, you'll learn what the command does.

The next section of options allows you to change the type of node.

There are basically two types of node, <u>angle</u> (for a corner) and <u>smooth</u> (for a curve), the first two choices above. In addition, two more choices produce <u>symmetrical</u> nodes or <u>auto-smooth</u> nodes. To experiment, use another of the copies of the double curve that you made earlier.

First, let's change that central node to a corner node. Select the node with the node arrow and then click on the corner node  option. The node symbol on the line changes to a diamond.

Grab the line below the node and experiment with dragging it into different positions. You'll see that you can end up with a point at the node, producing, for example, a figure that looks a little like a child's shorthand for a flying bird:

If we now change the selected middle node to smooth  , we end up with the line below, shown with the node handles visible. The curve through the node point is now smoothly continuous, though the handles are not the same length. Handles always follow the tangent of a curve.

Remember, the line will not go back to the original figure because we have manipulated the lower lobe of the curve.

71

If instead we changed the center node of the "flying bird" to symmetric  , we would end up with almost the same curve, but the top and bottom Bezier handles would be the same length. That's what symmetric means in this context.

Symmetric does <u>not</u> mean you will end up with a symmetrical figure, because the adjacent curves may not be alike.

Auto-smooth 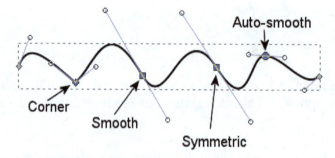 differs from **smooth** and **symmetric** in that once it is set, if you move <u>surrounding</u> nodes or line, the line will automatically be made as smooth as possible.

Notice that the little node symbols on a line will differ according to the node type.

Auto-smooth

Corner

Smooth

Symmetric

Back on the node control bar, the next two options are fairly obvious. The first 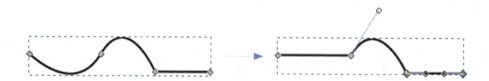 converts a curved segment to a straight one; the second option 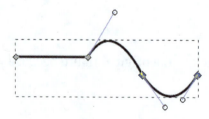 does the opposite.

Applying these to the first and third segments of the line on the left, below, we get the following:

A curve is <u>not</u> automatically produced for the third segment, but nodes and handles have been placed to allow for pulling the line into a curve.

72

Converting Objects and Strokes to Paths

The next two options on the node control bar open up new worlds of possibility: These are used to convert objects or strokes of objects to paths.

You might remember that in a vector program like Inkscape, everything is based on paths. Some paths are defined as shapes within the program, but these very same shapes can also be redefined as paths. That is what these options are for. If, for instance, you draw a square using the rectangle tool, Inkscape defines the shape as an object with dimensions, not points. That means we can act on it only in ways that will respect its dimensional aspects: enlarging it, skewing it, and so on. But we can tell Inkscape to instead define this square we've drawn as a **Path** made up of four points in particular positions and related to each other by straight lines. That means we can now mess with it in ways beyond the skewing or resizing we could do before.

Most lines drawn by line tools don't need to be converted to paths. They're paths already. Exceptions are the Spiro curve drawn by the **Spiro mode** of the **Bezier pen** and the **B-Spline mode** of the **Bezier pen**. Because of the particular constraints of these curves, you can't easily add or subtract nodes or do other path operations on a Spiro or B-spline curve until you convert it to a path. At that point it will no longer be a Spiro or B-spline.

To see how conversion works, let's start with a square (we could just as well start with an ellipse or star or spiral or a Spiro line or even text) and see what converting it to a path can mean. Once you've drawn a square, select it with either the **Select Arrow** or the **Node Arrow**. If you use the **Select Arrow**, you will find the conversion command under **Path > Object to Path**. Or you can do the conversion from the node control bar, clicking the symbol.

You will notice that the square has only four nodes, one at each corner, joining four straight segments.

You could, of course, turn one of those corner nodes into a smooth node, enabling other deformations if you play with the handles:

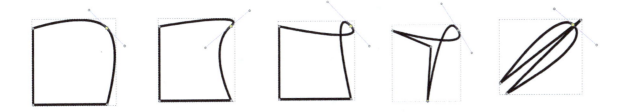

73

But why limit ourselves to one little rounded node, when, as you now know, we can add more nodes anywhere we want? Draw a fresh square, convert it to a path, select the two upper nodes, and start adding nodes using the first option on the left. As you click that option, one node will be added in the middle of the top line. Click again, and you'll get two more nodes. Again, and you'll get four more nodes. By adding nodes in this way, they will be evenly spaced.

Click to deselect the nodes. At the moment, since the line is straight, the nodes are all corner nodes. You could start selecting them alternately, dragging them down one at a time to form points.

You could, of course, change some or all of these nodes to a different type for a different result.

 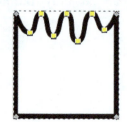

Now suppose that inspired by this craggy square, we want to make a stylized crown with equal points.

We'll start with the square again, with a number of nodes across the top.

We'll leave the nodes as corner nodes to produce the points. This time we'll select all the even nodes at once. To select, remember to hold **Shift** while clicking on each node. Grab one of these, drag straight down, and now you have an even row of points.

Perhaps we want to end up with a crown with sides that slant inward and a bottom that is slightly rounded to give a sense of three-dimensionality. One way to start is to change those two bottom nodes so that we can get an even curve. Select the two and change them to auto-smooth. You'll suddenly have a rather menacing-looking tulip shape.

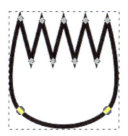

To re-straighten the sides, select the top left and bottom left nodes and click 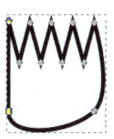, **Make selected segments lines.**

Do the same for the other side.

We could also slant the outer lines a bit by dragging the lower nodes inward.

Certainly, this little crown will earn no design awards. The point (!) here is the ease with which lines, figures, and even **Shapes** can be altered using nodes. **Anything** we draw in Inkscape can be altered with nodes.

More Node Controls

Before we move on from nodes, we'll look at remaining items on the node control bar, adding a couple of additional pointers.

We've seen that a **Shape** can become a **Path**. The <u>stroke</u> of any shape or other object can also become a path. You might think that this is what we've been doing, with a square that had a heavy stroke and no fill, but this is a different matter. Draw another square and select it. This time, click on **Path > Stroke to Path**, or on the node control bar, **Convert selected object's stroke to paths** .

If you look carefully, you'll see that this square now has <u>two</u> nodes in each corner, representing the corners of each side of the stroke. To test this feature, **Select** the two outermost nodes at the top of the square. Then drag upward from the middle of the top line. Mess around with pulling the stroke this way and that. You will see immediately that the stroke has become alterable in all sorts of new ways.

It will usually be better to give yourself more nodes to play with, depending on what you want to do. You can double click at either edge of the stroke to add a node. If you want equidistant nodes along the line, you can use the node tool to select the whole side of a rectangle or even the whole square. Then start clicking the **Insert new nodes into selected segments** command, the first command on the node control bar. Stop clicking when you have as many nodes as you want. Note that in the square below all of the nodes are double, one on each side of the stroke.

From there, you can drag the nodes as you like. You can pull a node so that the stroke bulges, or you can cross over to the other side of the stroke for a different effect. You can change the type of node for rounding or points. You can drag the nodes farther apart or closer together, sculpting as you go. Below are a few examples of what can be done. The last example is a tiling of the fifth example. All of these are based on a square. Obviously, you can do the same kind of thing on any object.

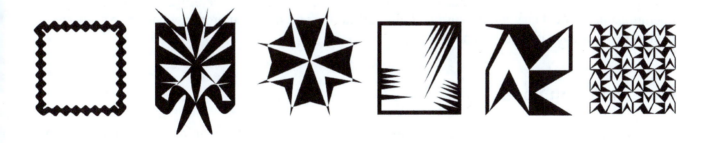

The last command on the node control bar to be mentioned here is **Show path outline** .

If you have a more complicated drawing with several components, especially if they are on top of each other, you may not readily see the node path. This option will provide a red line to show where a particular node path is. This one is a B-Spline path.

Getting your fill of lines: fill in odd spaces

By this time, you're aware that you can add fill to closed spaces like rectangles, circles, and arbitrary shapes. Many of the figures we've been drawing here have been given a stroke but not a fill, the better to see the lines. But you can add fill as you like.

Strangely enough, you can also add fill to open figures—lines like some of the wavy lines we've been drawing. Suppose we just draw a single wavy line like the one on the left. And then suppose we add fill. We end up with the figure on the right.

What has happened is that Inkscape has drawn an invisible straight line through the curves from one end-node to the other and has filled in the resulting closed spaces. If you select the figure with the node tool and check out the nodes, you will see that there are no additional nodes along that straight line. There wouldn't be on a straight line—just the end-nodes. Understand, then, that there is <u>always</u> a line that closes the end-nodes of a non-straight path, even though that line may be invisible.

You may be able to use this characteristic of Inkscape as a design option.

You will also want to bear this characteristic in mind when we discuss some of the special path operations in the next chapter, because knowing about this will help you predict what some of these operations will do to objects you have drawn.

More help with nodes

For more precision in your drawings, you may want to be aware of some additional aids. First, on the node control bar you'll find two drop-down white boxes that tell you the <u>X and Y positions of a selected node</u>. You can use this to keep track of where your nodes are, or you can set the position of a node.

Another helpful feature is the ability to move nodes slightly with the keyboard, sometimes better than dragging with the mouse if you want fine movement. Here's how much you can move a selected node (or any selection) up, down, left, or right with the arrow keys:

      1 screen pixel: **Alt + Arrow**
      2 screen pixels: **Arrow**
      10 screen pixels: **Alt + Shift + Arrow**
      20 screen pixels: **Shift + Arrow**

You can also move selected nodes closer together with < , or farther apart with > .

You can use **Snapping** with nodes. Hover your cursor along the snap bar at the right of your screen to note the possibilities. You may find it useful to use node snapping if you are using a grid for accurate placement. Conversely, if you are having trouble getting your nodes to behave—if they seem to have a mind of their own and you can't get them to stay where you put them—you may need to turn snapping off.

A very useful aid for node placement is the **Align and Distribute** menu, which has a special section for aligning nodes. Let's suppose that you want all the dragged points on the following figure to be at a consistent height.

First, rubber-band the nodes of all the upper points or select them with the node tool while holding down the **Shift** key. Next, be sure the **Align and Distribute** menu is open on the right side of your screen (**Object > Align and Distribute** or **Shift + Ctl + A**). With the nodes highlighted, the only choices available to you in this menu concern nodes.

Four different choices are available with the blue dot symbols: horizontal alignment, vertical alignment, horizontal distribution, and vertical distribution. The choices in the drop-down menu slot allow you to specify where and how the alignment or distribution will take place.

For the current problem of uneven points, we'll choose **Max value** to raise all the points to the height of the highest point. Press the first symbol for horizontal alignment. Now the points are even horizontally.

A similar process works for vertical alignment.

Distribute helps you to space nodes equally either horizontally or vertically. To illustrate, we'll use the following line with all the nodes selected.

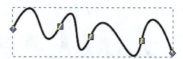

We'll choose the **Middle of selection** option in the drop down menu. Click **Distribute selected nodes horizontally**. This makes the nodes equidistant <u>across</u> the line.

If we were after curves of equal dimensions, we would need to add extra nodes at the tops and bottoms of the curves and use the horizontal alignment option to adjust the curves again.

A final trick to mention here is the <u>sculpting</u> of a group of nodes. If we select a group of several nodes and drag them, they will all move the same amount. However, if instead we hold down the **Alt** key while moving one, the selected portion becomes much more elastic: all the selected nodes will still move, but at different rates. The nodes farthest away from the dragged node will move less. This can produce interesting effects and will put lovely curves on a straight line, like this:

Nodes with the Pencil Tool and Calligraphic Tool

We've been using Bezier curves and square objects to illustrate node manipulation, but nodes are available for the **Pencil tool** and **Calligraphic pen** as well. Nodes for the **Pencil tool** work similarly to those of the **Bezier pen**; there will just be lots more of them—so many that it may seem daunting to know where to begin. This is where smoothing and simplification come in. As you smooth a line, there will be fewer nodes.

Nodes on a pencil line with a smoothing of 0

Nodes on a pencil line with a smoothing of 20

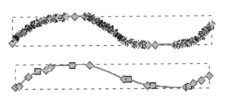

Mostly, you will just want to use **Pencil tool** nodes for minor tweaking. This is also true for the **Calligraphic tool**, but because the line for that tool is made up of the fill surrounded by two strokes, it works like the figures you get from converting a stroke to path, as we did above (see pp. 76). Thus, each side of the Calligraphic line can be altered independently.

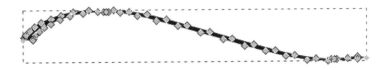

The **Pencil** line will remain a single line of nodes, even if you add a shape before you draw, whereas the **Calligraphic** line will always show two lines of nodes.

Chapter 7
Getting Things Together and Taking Things Apart

Each object you draw in Inkscape remains separate until you decide to join it somehow with another object. This is true even if you are drawing one item on top of another.

I count five ways of putting objects together in Inkscape, three of which you already know from earlier chapters. These range from very temporary to permanent.

Method	What it works on	How to join	Purpose or result	Duration
Multiple selection	Any objects	(**Shift + Select Arrow**) or rubber-band	Momentarily move, scale, rotate or skew, or copy items together.	Until another selection or mouse click elsewhere
Group	Any objects, including any groups	**Group (Ctrl + g)** or **Line 2:**	Move, scale, or skew items together until ungrouped	Until **Ungroup** command (**Shift + Ctrl g**)
Combine	Only ungrouped paths, not shapes	**Path > Combine (Ctrl + k)**	Put multiple paths together in order to use other path operations on the whole collection	Until **Break Apart** (**Shift + Ctrl k**) or until another path operation is used on the combination.
Joining nodes	Only two open paths	Node tool > **Join selected end nodes with a new segment** or **Join nodes** if one end lies on top of the other	Make one path out of two by adding a segment, however short or long; or make two paths continuous	Permanent. Can immediately use Edit > **Undo** (**Ctrl + z**)
Union	Only ungrouped and overlapping paths	**Path > Union (Ctrl + +)**	Make one continuous path from multiple paths. Closes open paths, sometimes in unforeseen ways.	Permanent. Can immediately use Edit > **Undo** (**Ctrl + z**)

The **Combine** and **Union** commands are the new options for you. Both of these are path operations and are sometimes used to prepare for other path operations such as **Difference**, **Intersection**, **Division**, **Exclusion**, and **Cut Path,** which will be considered in the next chapter.

How do you choose whether to use **Group**, **Combine**, or **Union**? Each has specific purposes and results.

Group is the command you want if you are looking for something to hold objects together in your desired configuration while you change the stroke, fill, scale, or orientation of the whole collection or when you want to copy and paste or clone the whole combination. You may want **Group** as insurance to make sure you don't accidentally move things out of alignment or delete a tiny piece while working on other items. **Group** will work on both shapes and paths, no matter whether they are overlapping or spaced apart. It will hold things together until you deliberately **Ungroup** them again. You can usually tell what's in a group by the unified bounding box around all the objects when you click on one. The notification line will also tell you how many objects are in the group.

You can easily add other objects to a group by simply selecting all the objects or sub-groups and clicking **Group** again. When you do that, Inkscape preserves the hierarchy in which you joined things. Suppose we start with this mishmash of shapes, select them, and group them:

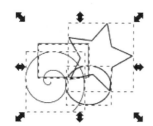 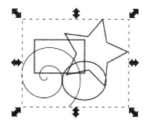

Four separate objects selected.   Objects are grouped.
Four bounding boxes appear.   One bounding box appears

Now suppose we want to add a frame composed of two rectangles we've already grouped:

We resize the frame to fit the shape-mishmash we grouped above, and then group the whole combination:

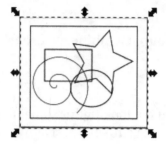

As you would expect, we now have one bounding box around the whole thing. But notice what happens if we **Ungroup** this figure:

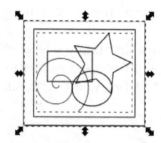

Ungrouping doesn't break the figure into all its components. Instead, it just goes down one level to the two compound items we last grouped. Thus the process of **grouping** is preserved according to exactly what was **grouped** together at each stage. This will help get back to an earlier **grouping** if you change your mind. If you want to **Ungroup** all the way to individual pieces, you can.

Grouping is the enemy of the **Combine** and **Union** commands. When you start using either of the latter commands, it's especially helpful to keep an eye on the notification area at the bottom of the Inkscape screen. There you will be reminded about what is happening and warned about what may not have worked. If you **Combine** something you've already **Grouped**, it may look as if the process has worked. But if you try to perform any of the path operations on the new combination, they won't work, and you'll probably get the notice, "One of the objects is **not a path**, cannot perform Boolean operation." A **Group** is not considered a path, no matter if all its components are paths.

We'll see what to do with **Combine** in the next chapter.

Tip! A number of the more complicated functions of Inkscape (e.g. some of the **Path Effects** and **Extensions**) use **Combine** to hold elements together. If you think you should be able to take elements apart and you're not being successful, try **Break Apart**, which you will meet again in Chapter 9 (see p. 122, 125).

As for **Union**, using it converts two or more paths into a single path. That usually means making the path continuous unless some part of the collection doesn't overlap and is <u>outside</u> the other(s). In that case, it just remains by itself, a permanent fellow-traveler. The objects that overlap become one path. Sometimes this means that Inkscape closes open paths in such a way as to produce a maze-like figure. Most of the time it means reducing the objects to their outlines.

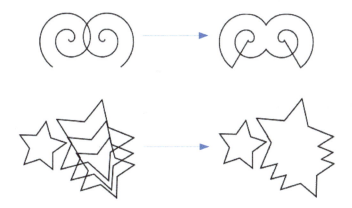

Union can be useful if you need an outline of an odd shape and you prefer to use the **Shape** tools to construct it. For instance, I've drawn a teddy bear from circles and rounded rectangles:

The figure above admittedly looks more like a robot muscle-man than a teddy, but notice what happens when I select the whole, apply **Object to Path,** and then press **Union**.

Apply a few features, and *voila!*

I won't try to incorporate the features into the **Union**. They would disappear. That's what happens to stray objects inside, rather than outside, the collection of paths.

> **Tip!** For most of your joining needs, **Group** will be your best choice. You can always use **Ungroup** if you need the components. Only use **Combine** or **Union** if you have a specific objective in mind.

Chapter 8
Making Patterns by Cloning and Tiling

In this chapter we'll move on to a more automated way to make patterns than simply duplicating or pasting.

Reminder: Anything in a bounding box can be copied or cloned.

A clone is a copy of an object that is linked to the original object. Changing the <u>original</u> object will change the clone or clones. You will find the **Clone** command under the **Edit** menu.

A clone can be moved, skewed, resized, or rotated without changing the original, but its attributes, such as fill or stroke can only be changed to differ from the original's by using the **Unset** command indicated by the **?** sign in the **Fill and Stroke Dialogue**.

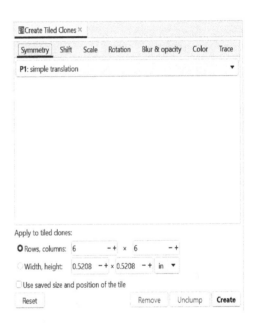

By itself, the **Clone** command doesn't do much for us that **Copy** and **Paste** wouldn't, except when you want to make changes all at once to several copies of an object.

If you point at the **Clone** command, you will also see **Create Tiled Clones**. Clicking that will bring up a dialogue like the one to the right. It appears in the large box on the right side of the Inkscape window.

When you **Create Tiled Clones** of anything in a single bounding box, the contents of the box will be copied and arranged in a pattern. The pattern can be chosen from various <u>symmetries</u>, and you may also choose such attributes as <u>rotation</u> and <u>distance between clones</u>.

To the left is a simple tiling of a 12 pointed star with a stroke of 2.

I have used 6 rows and 6 columns with the most basic symmetry, **P1: simple translation**. All this does is clone the original star 36 times, placing the stars in even rows and columns. While this kind of arrangement may sometimes be useful, it doesn't begin to exhaust the possibilities tiling provides.

By the way, the original object is sitting on top of the first star, the one on the top left, as you can see by the bounding box and the x in the middle that indicates the rotation point. If you alter this original, you will alter all the clones, too. Try that out by selecting, say, a black fill. All the stars should turn black. The original can be moved away from the tiling. Clones can be unlinked from the original with **Edit > Unlink Clone**. That turns clones into independent objects.

Illustrators and web designers will often use tiling by first constructing a blank base tile of the shape and dimensions desired. Then this tile is cloned. And finally, the base tile is decorated as desired, changing all the clones at once. In this chapter we will take a different approach. We'll begin with a simple drawing and see how the positioning of clones, and thus the overall design, will be affected by changing the controls.

Exploring the "Create Tiled Clones" Dialogue Box

The dialogue box offers seven tabs for controls of various kinds. Of these, only the first four will be of interest to metal artists designing in unshaded black and white.

- **Symmetry** provides 17 different choices for symmetrical arrangements. Some of these are shortcuts for tiling you could also produce by manipulating the remaining controls.
- **Shift** controls the distances between cloned tiles.
- **Scale** provides a way to progressively increase or decrease the sizes of tiles.
- **Rotation** controls how the tiles are rotated around the rotation center, which is found in the center of the original, or base, tile, but can be moved outside of the tile for additional effects.

Someone well versed in geometry might be able to use these controls to exactly plan out the results. Most of us, however, will proceed by experimentation. I suggest that when you happen on a tiling that you particularly like, you write down the "recipe" for the controls you have used.

Tab 1: Seventeen Symmetries

Believe it or not, mathematicians and crystallographers have identified exactly 17 different symmetry groups for figures on a plane surface. They are called wallpaper symmetries for obvious reasons. The labels Inkscape uses for these symmetries (P1, CM, P3M1 and so on), are the standard labels of the International Union of Crystallography. Likewise, the terms (translation, reflection, glide reflection, etc.) are standard terminology. In the notes below, I will try to explain in lay terms what I see happening in these symmetries. The best explanation, however, is usually the visual one.

To try out the various symmetries, we will use the following figure. It has the advantage of being asymmetrical and will thus show the different symmetries much better than beginning with a figure that is already symmetrical, like a circle or star.

As you might guess, the figure above is simply a circle superimposed on an arc and grouped together using the **Group** command. The bounding box of the figure will become the tile.

You may wish to follow along as I describe the various symmetries, trying out each one in turn, watching how the patterns change. I have inserted the number of rows and columns that will give a good sense of each particular pattern, but you can use as many as you want. Remember that any of these seventeen symmetries can be further altered—a little or a lot—with the other controls, **Shift**, **Scale**, and **Rotation**.

The Seventeen Symmetries		
Symmetry Label	**Example**	**Notes**
P1: simple translation		3 rows, 4 columns shown. The original tile is simply repeated across all columns and down all rows.
P2: 180° rotation		3 rows, 4 columns shown. The tile in each subsequent column is rotated 180°. All rows are the same.
PM: reflection.		3 rows, 4 columns shown. Each column mirrors the tiles in the previous column horizontally. All rows are the same.
PG: glide reflection		3 rows, 4 columns shown. Columns are the same; each row mirrors the tiles in the previous row horizontally.
CM: reflection + glide reflection		4 rows, 4 columns shown. Both rows and columns mirror the previous tile horizontally.

PMM: reflection + reflection		4 rows, 4 columns shown. Each column mirrors the tile in the previous column horizontally; each row is a vertical mirror of the previous row.
PMG: reflection + 180° rotation		4 rows, 4 columns shown. Each row is reflected vertically; each column mirrors the previous tile horizontally and vertically (that is, the tile is also turned 180°).
PGG: glide reflection + 180° rotation		4 rows, 4 columns shown. Both subsequent tiles mirror the previous tile horizontally and vertically in both rows and columns.
CMM: reflection + reflection + 180° rotation		4 rows, 4 columns shown. The first two rows are just like PGG: Reflection + reflection. The next two rows mirror each column horizontally (rotate it 180°). The following two rows are like the first two, and so on.
P4: 90° rotation		4 rows, 4 columns shown. Each subsequent tile in a row and in a column is turned 90°.
P4M: 90° rotation + 45° reflection		4 rows, 4 columns shown. Tiles could be said to cluster in eights: 2 rows of 4 columns forming the cluster. Each row mirrors the previous row vertically. Each subsequent tile in a column is rotated 90° and then mirrored vertically, except that the figures overlap, producing a tight pattern.

		2 rows, 4 columns, spaced widely. Here tiles are spaced farther apart horizontally to show the rotations more clearly. To do this, go to the Shift tab. Write 50% in the Per Column slot of Shift X. Press Create.
P4G: 90° rotation + 90° reflection		3 rows, 8 columns shown. Each row clusters the tiles in the columns into fours. Each subsequent tile in a column is rotated 90°, forming a sort of pinwheel. After a pinwheel of four is formed, the next four columns repeat the pattern. All rows act in the same way.
P3: 120° rotation		6 rows, 6 columns shown. Tiles are clustered in threes in triangular pinwheels. (Remember, 120° is one third of a circle.) The odd rows begin at the "margin." The even rows begin at the lower right point of the first pinwheel in the previous row.
P31M: reflection + 120° rotation, dense		6 rows, 12 columns shown. Tiles are clustered in sixes in triangular pinwheels. Taking just a single cluster of 6 columns to describe, the second tile is mirrored vertically in place over the first tile and then rotated 120°, overlapping the first tile by 1/3. The third tile is reflected. The fourth tile is reflected in place and then rotated 120°, overlapping the third tile. The fifth tile is reflected. The sixth tile is reflected in place and then rotated 120°, overlapping the fifth tile. In the second row, the process begins about 1/2 a tile from the left margin, so that part of the pinwheel from

		the first row is overlapped and an alternating pattern is created. The third row goes back to the margin. You can see this pattern "exploded," with its elements moved farther apart, in the next symmetry, P3M1.
		1 row, 6 columns shown. A single cluster of both P31M and P3M1 is shown here for clarity.
P3M1: reflection + 120° rotation, sparse		6 rows, 12 columns shown. The pinwheel created by six columns is exactly the same as in P31M. What is different is the spacing. There is only a tiny bit of overlap between pinwheels, creating a looser lattice effect.
P6: 60° rotation		3 rows, 12 columns shown. Tiles are clustered in sixes. The tile in each new column is rotated 60°, forming a six part pinwheel where about a third of each tile overlaps. After the sixth column, the figure starts over. The second row is indented by three tiles, and the third row is back at the margin.

P6M: reflection + 60° rotation		3 rows, 12 columns shown. Tiles are clustered in twelves. The second tile is a vertical mirror of the first tile. It is then rotated 60°, leaving it to overlap the first tile. The third tile is a diagonal mirror of the second tile but is not rotated. The fourth tile diagonally mirrors the third tile and then is rotated 60°, leaving it to overlap all three previous tiles. The fifth tile mirrors the fourth but is not rotated. The other tiles proceed in the same manner, alternating mirroring and mirroring + 60° rotation. The second row is indented by half the pinwheel. The third row is back at the margin.

Tab 2: Shift

The shift controls determine the distance between tiles in the different dimensions. Positive numbers move the tiles farther apart, while negative numbers move them closer together. You'll note that the shift numbers are in percentages—the percentage of the tile.

Shift X moves tiles on the horizontal axis; Shift Y moves tiles on the vertical axis.

To show how this works, we'll use a symmetrical object, a circle. We'll tile 4 rows and 4 columns.

Before shifts:

Suppose we want a healthy space between each circle and we want to maintain the overall square array. We want space between columns on the X axis and space between rows on the Y axis. Let's make the distance half the size of the circle tile, that is, 50%. Thus the Shift X will be 50% per column and the Shift Y will be 50% per row. We end up with this:

```
O O O O
O O O O
O O O O
O O O O
```

Suppose instead we want to overlap all the circles by the same distance, 50%. This time we insert -50% in the same slots as above.

Let's go back to the positive numbers but use the opposite axes. Put 50% in the slots for Y axis per column and the X axis per row. What happens is that the rows shift to the right by 50% each subsequent row, while the columns shift down by 50% each subsequent column. They are close enough to overlap.

You can also experiment with <u>Alternate</u> and <u>Cumulate</u> for either rows or columns or both. You can probably guess what these control. You may even want to try <u>Randomize</u>.

<u>Exponent</u> multiplies the distance by the size of the tile. Here I've used an exponent of 2 per row and per column:

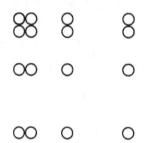

The final control, <u>Exclude tile</u>, is useful for certain circular designs when you want all the rotation centers to be in the same place and don't want one or more clones moved away from the original. We'll look at circles shortly.

Tab 3: Scale

The <u>Scale</u> tab allows you to gradually increase or decrease the size of your tiles along the various dimensions. As in the <u>Shift</u> tab, we have options for X and Y axes, plus <u>Exponent</u>. This time <u>Base</u> has been added for use with logarithmic spirals, which will be explored later. You can also <u>Alternate</u> or <u>Cumulate</u> your sizes.

Here's the effect when we increase <u>Scale X</u> and <u>Scale Y</u> in both rows and columns by 20%.

You'll notice immediately that while we've increased the size of the tiles, we haven't increased the spacing, which is calculated on the center of the original tile. Thus the tiles now overlap.

If we want the tiles to have some space between them, we will have to mess around with the Shift tab. Here <u>Scale X</u> and <u>Y</u> are both kept at 20% for rows and columns, but the <u>Shift X</u> and <u>Y</u> have been changed to 40% for rows and columns and the <u>Exponent</u> has been increased to 1.2 for both rows and columns.

Changing only one of the X or Y dimensions when we scale results in a flattening of the tile one direction or the other and then a re-rounding as the other dimension catches up. Here we have set <u>Scale X</u> at 20% per column and <u>Scale Y</u> at 20% per row:

Negative numbers decrease size. Here we've set both <u>Scale X</u> and <u>Scale Y</u> at -20% per row—the eye-chart effect!

Tab 4: Rotation

We've already seen rotation at work in some of the seventeen symmetries. It is also possible to adjust rotation by this tab. Just remember that the rotation will affect the individual tiles, one after the other. If, for example, using P1 symmetry, we set the rotation at 20° per column, each tile in a row will rotate 20° more than the last.

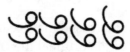

Some results will be more pleasing with a tile of the same width and height, others with more elongated tiles.. Here's a star tiled at P1 symmetry, 15° per column and row:

You can also alternate the action. Here the star is rotated at 30 per column and row, with <u>Alternate</u> checked on both.

Or you can <u>Cumulate</u>, as in this example of a rectangle rotated at 5 per row and column. Each movement increases the effect.

Using the Rotation Center: adding another type of tile rotation

You might recall that objects can be rotated around a center point or rotation point. The little + sign that marks this rotation point appears when you first draw the object. When you have clicked on an object twice with the **Selection Arrow** and can see the double arrows that allow you to rotate or skew the object, the + changes to a more visible symbol: ✛.

What makes the rotation point especially useful for tiling is that it can actually be moved around. It can even be moved outside of the object. This can be used in conjunction with the **Rotation** tab to produce interesting results.

Here the rotation center has been moved straight down out of the center of the star. If you hold down the control key while you drag the ✛, it will be constrained to vertical or horizontal.

Next, the P1 symmetry, 2 rows, 4 columns, and a rotation of 20° per row and column produces this little array of falling stars.

You will notice that two kinds of rotation are happening at the same time. The individual tiles are rotating, but in addition, the entire array of star tiles is rotating around the rotation point which has been moved outside of the original star. While this design is not especially thrilling, you may begin to see a glimmer of possibilities. We are starting to see an arc of stars forming. Can we go further?

Tip 1! Sometimes if you wait to move the rotation point until after you've pressed **Create**, it will be hard to see. It's easier if you move the point first and <u>then</u> press **Create**. You can usually find it then and can further adjust it as you like, pressing **Create** again.

Tip 2! If you have moved the rotation center marker ✣ and you want to return it to its original position, press shift while clicking on the ✣.

Spiraling out of controls

If you're wondering whether tiling can be used to form spirals and circles, the answer is yes! In the following pages we'll try out a few recipes to get you started on a vast world of designs.

We'll begin with a logarithmic spiral, which happens to be the kind of spiral often found in nature. Pine cones and seashells, spiral galaxies and corneal nerves, hurricanes and unfurling fern fronds present us with examples. Each turn of a logarithmic spiral looks like the last one proportionally; it's just bigger.

Here's one recipe for such a spiral:

Set the center of rotation (✣) outside of the object or tile (see the previous page).
Symmetry: P1: Simple translation
Shift: per column, Shift X, -100
      per column, Shift Y, 0
      Exclude tile: unchecked
Scale: Scale X, per column 4.00%; Scale Y, per column 4.00%
      Base 4 on both row and column
Rotation: Per column, 25°
Rows, 1; Columns 30

Applying the recipe to the four-pointed star, we get these patterns:

Star spiral based on recipe above.   Same spiral showing rotation marker.   Same spiral, tighter rotation marker placement

Most of the numbers can be changed and you will still end up with a spiral, so you'll want to experiment. Here's how it will work.

- The farther from the original object you set the center of rotation, the farther apart the tiles (the stars, in this case) will be.
- You <u>must</u> use -100% in the **Shift** tab. This will initially keep the tiles from shifting—spacing— as they normally do. If you had not changed the center of rotation, at -100% all the tiles would

be piled directly on top of each other. A -100% setting now allows you to control the spacing via the center of rotation so that you get a curve as well as spacing. (Yes, that's <u>minus</u> 100%.)

- **Scale X** and **Y** can be set to whatever you want, but at 5% the size of the tiles will increase very quickly. It's unlikely you'll want to go bigger than that, and even that may be too much. You can also use negative numbers. That will put the largest tile in the middle of the spiral, and the size will decrease from there. Use the same number in X and Y unless you want to gradually elongate the tiles.
- A **Base** setting must be used to attain a spiral. Negative numbers can't be used. A number below 1 will again make the tiles decrease in size from the center out, while numbers above 1 will make the tiles increase from the center out. The closer to 1.000 the base number is the tighter the spirals.
- Using negative numbers in **Scale X** and **Y** at the same time as using a base setting less than 1.000 simply cancels out, so size will increase from the middle out.

By the way, reversing the settings for row and column will produce the same spiral as the settings above. You're just operating on the rows instead of the columns:

Shift: per row, Shift X,   0
            per row, Shift Y,   -100
Scale: Scale X, per row 4.00%; Scale Y, per column 4.00%
            Base 4 on both row and column
Rotation: Per row, 25°
Rows, 30; Columns 1

Multi-row Spirals

You may be wondering whether it's possible to add rows to your spiral. The answer is yes, but with some caveats. The special kind of logarithmic spiral that allows for multi-rows is called a Fibonacci spiral, or Golden Spiral. Without the exact proportions of the Golden Spiral, the various arms of the spirals would begin to overlap in irregular ways and the results would not be pleasing. Thus care is needed in the recipe. There's no harm in experimentation, though. The yellow **Undo** arrow is always there!

Another consideration for Inkscape tiling is the presence of the original tile. When we press **Create** in the **Create Tiled Clones** dialogue, another tile is duplicated right on top of the original tile. You might remember that this original tile can be moved away from the cloned tile array you have created, but that's often not even necessary for most clonings we have done so far. For this and other circular cloning, however, the original tile—in fact, an *extra* tile—can throw a monkey wrench into the calculations. Inkscape has a way to compensate. **Exclude tile** under the **Shift** tab will exclude the original tile from the calculations. Some of the recipes in these pages will require **Exclude tile** and some won't.

Here's the recipe for a pinwheel of Fibonacci spirals given by Tavmjong Bah in his *Inkscape: Guide to a Vector Drawing Program.* His shaded 5-pointed stars have been replaced by solid 4-pointed stars.

Shift: per row , Shift X,   0
           per row, Shift Y,   -100
           Exclude tile for row and column
Scale: Scale X and Y, per row 39.3%; Scale X and Y, per column 24.2%
           Base 2.7 on both row and column
Rotation: Per row, -11.5°; per column 20.6°
Rows, 8; Columns, 21

Because the size of these tiles increases so rapidly that the large stars overwhelm if you zoom out enough to really see the pattern, I actually prefer this alternate recipe:

Shift: per row and column, 0
        Exclude tile for row and column
Scale: Scale X and Y, per row 13.1%; Scale X and Y, per column 8.667%
        Base 8 per row and column
Rotation: Per row, -11.5°; per column 20.6°
Rows, 8; Columns, 21

Tip! If you lose the original tile (probably because it has another tile on top of it), you can easily find it again. Use **Edit** > **Clone** > **Select Original,** or **Shift +D.**

A satisfying multi-row spiral is this one. Try it first with stroke but no fill until you get a feel for how far you want to drag the rotation center from its original position. The farther you drag, the less overlap you'll get. The recipe follows:

Shift: per row and column, 0
    Exclude tile for row and column
Scale: Scale X and Y, per row and column, 3%.
    Base 10 per row and column
Rotation: Per row, 11.5°; per column -20.6°
Rows, 8; columns, 36

Rolling Spiral

How about a rolling spiral that looks a bit like a roller coaster? This one is very sensitive to the placement of the rotation center.

Shift: per row and column, 0
    Do not exclude tile for row and column
Scale: Scale X and Y, per row 0%; Scale X and Y, per column 1%
    Base 4 on both row and column (You can raise these numbers for larger loops.)
Rotation: per column 25°
Rows, 1; Columns, 60

Other spiral-related arrays

Here are a few other recipes that yield interesting tiling patterns.

A Ribbon of tiles

Depending on how far down the center of rotation is dragged, the effect varies.

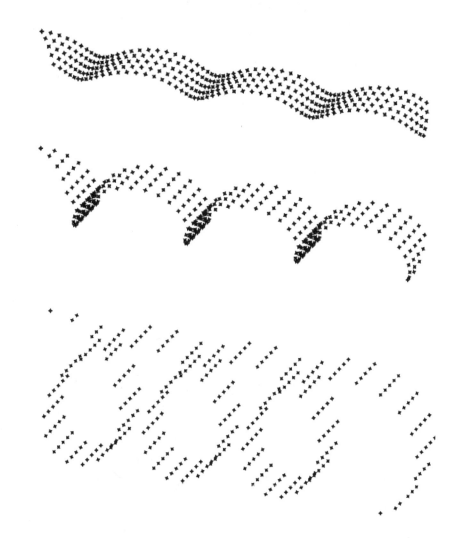

Shift: X and Y 20% per row and column, 0
         Do not exclude tile for row and column
Scale: Scale X and Y, per row and column, 0 or 1%.
         Base 0 per row and column
Rotation: 20° per row and column
Rows, 3 or more; columns, 60 or whatever you like

Pinwheel manqué with seven vanes

Shift: X and Y per row and column, 0
　　　Exclude tile for row and column
Scale: X and Y per row -3 %
　　　X and Y per column 0
　　　Base .3 per row and column (Also try .3 base on row only.)
Rotation: Per row, 50°; per column 0°
Rows, 30; columns, 1

Twelve-spoked wheel manqué

Use tiles with stroke and no fill at least until you see how far you want to drag the rotation point. As you can see, it makes a big difference.

Shift: X and Y per row and column, 0
　　　Exclude tile for row and column
Scale: X and Y per row and column 3%
　　　Base 0

Rotation: per column 30°
Rows, 1; columns, 100

You may notice that the last two recipes produce arrays that are not quite symmetrical. That's because they are actually spirals, with tiles increasing in size. *There even appears to be a missing tile, hence manqué* in my title. The slight skew is not very noticeable because the increase is slight. Nevertheless, if you want symmetry, these arrays may not be for you.

Dual overlapping circles

Here two circles of tiles overlap vertically.

Shift: X and Y per row and column, 0%
        Exclude tile for column only
Scale: X and Y per row and column, 0%
Rotation: per row and column, 20°
Rows, 2; columns, 40

Adding Shift Y per row moves the circles apart vertically. Try 50%.

Three ovals overlapping on diagonal

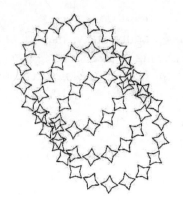

Shift: X per row 100%
        Y per row 50%
        X and Y per column, 0%
        Exclude tile for column only
Scale: X and Y per row and column, 0%
Rotation: per row and column, 20°
Rows, 3; columns, 20

Or, 4 or more rows with the rotation point dragged far enough will achieve a sort of barrel shape.

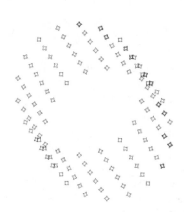

Other symmetries and the rotation point

Ever since we began looking at what happens to tiling arrays if the rotation point is moved, we have been using the P1 symmetry. However, even some of the other symmetries can be altered with good results by moving the rotation point. For example, the P4M symmetry has been used here on our old arc and circle combination with 6 rows and 12 columns. The rotation point has been moved only slightly until it touches the outside lower right of the bounding box.

This setup produces the following tiling pattern:

Beyond the recipes

Do keep experimenting, for you will discover favorite arrays of your own. Keep in mind as well that we have been tiling only simple objects. A tile can consist of much more complicated drawings. Also, once you have found an array you like, you can group the tiles or turn them into a path and then use the unified whole as one component in a larger design. We will be learning about paths in the next chapter —after we have some fun with circular tiling.

Be sure to make a note of the "recipes" you develop for yourself.

Reminder: If you have moved the rotation center marker and you want to return it to its original position, press shift while clicking on the ✦ .

Going around in circles

For those who love symmetry, what could be better than a circle? How about a complex circle—one made up of a bunch of repeated objects? In other words, tiling in a circle, like this wreath of 12-pointed stars:

Here's one recipe:

Symmetry: **P1: simple translation**
Shift: X and Y per row, 0%
         X per column, -100% (This places all the clones directly on top of the original,)
         Y per column, 0%
         Do not check Exclude tile
Scale: X and Y per row and column, 0%
Rotation: per column only, 30°
Rows, 1; columns, 12

Handle the creation of this circle much as you have previous figures. Move the rotation center before clicking **Create**. Here's a refresher on the steps.

- Use the **Selection Arrow** to click on the object twice to get the double rotation arrows around the bounding box.
- Notice the ❖ rotation center marker in the middle of the star. Grab that with your cursor, hold down **Ctrl**, and drag the ❖ straight down away from the star 3-4 star-lengths.
- Once you have all the right numbers in the dialogue box, press **Create**.
- You should get a circle of stars. You can adjust the distance between stars by dragging up or down on the rotation marker ❖. Press **Create** again for the new spacing to take effect.
- If the object you're cloning has fill or a pattern or is a group of objects, you may have trouble seeing the little ❖. It may be more readily visible before tiling.

Adding more stars or other objects

You can vary the number of objects in the circle, as long as the number can be evenly divided into 360, the number of degrees in a circle. You will change the degrees of rotation accordingly:

360° ÷ number of objects = degrees of rotation

Reminder: How to find the rotational center of an object or a group of objects
- Select the object or group with the **Selection Arrow**.
- Click on the object again to get the rotational arrows. The ✚ sign for the rotational center will appear. The rotational center can be moved, even to outside the bounds of the object or group.

Tip! Changes can be made to the original of a tiled group and that change will apply to all of the clones. For example, you can change the stroke width or the fill. For the change to take effect, click **Create** again.

With this technique, you can produce unlimited variations on the circle of objects. Here are just a few examples:

One-row circles based on single shapes made with shape tools:

One-row circles based on groups of shapes made with shape tools:

One-row circles copied and pasted into each other to form concentric designs:

Use the **Alignment** dialogue to get the pieces properly centered.

You can also experiment with adding additional rows to produce concentric circles from whatever object or group of objects you choose, but that will require changes in the **Shift** and **Scale** tabs. For instance the figure below is produced by using an arc with the following settings:

Symmetry: P1: Simple translation
Shift: Shift X, Per column   -100
Scale: Scale X, 50%; Scale Y, 50%
Rotation: Per column, 30
Rows, 5; Columns 12

Keep in mind that tiling can be done with complex drawings, including lines and paths. Think of the possibilities!

Chapter **9**
Taking Out the Trash:
How to ~~Erase~~ Crop, Clip, Delete, Nudge, or Tweak

For the novice Inkscaper, excising parts of a drawing can be frustrating, especially for someone who is used to a raster graphics program. In Inkscape, deleting whole objects is no problem. Just select an item, press **delete** or **backspace**, and the object disappears. It's eliminating <u>pieces</u> of objects that can seem like an impossible puzzle. In practice, though, taking out the trash can be very easy, once you learn a few key approaches.

This chapter will begin with a go-to solution you'll probably use for 90% of your trash-removal issues: **Clipping**, which is really just a sophisticated way of covering up those areas you don't want to show. Next, for those instances when cover-up just won't do and you actually want to delete bits and pieces, we'll move to methods of manipulating and deleting nodes. We'll need to look at a little more background on the difference between raster and vector programs to help you understand why you can't get rid of things by running something like an eraser over your drawing and how you have to mess with the nodes instead. Then we'll move on to using some automated commands that Inkscape provides for doing this node-based change. Along the way we'll explore a couple of additional tools.

In case you don't want to wade through everything in this chapter to find a fast answer to a specific need, you'll find a quick guide to the various processes on the next page.

Taking out the Trash: Which Process Do You Want?

Your objective	Solution	Deletes scraps forever	Can undo once saved & closed	Closes or deletes open lines	Good on multi-line drawings	Alters number or position of nodes	Optimal file size	Ease of use	Page
Crop or trim edges using any outline you can draw	Clipping	no	yes	no	yes	no	no	easy	112-4
Crop a single line	Node manipulation or Cut Path	yes	no	no	—	yes	yes	medium	115-8
Crop a multi-line drawing that has open paths.	Combine + Cut Path	yes	no	no	yes	yes	yes	medium	126-9
Cut a void out of one or more shapes or paths. (Get rid of what you surround.)	Difference	yes	no	yes	no	yes	yes	medium	123-4
Keep only what overlaps between two objects. (Keep what you surround.)	Intersection	yes	no	yes	no	yes	yes	medium	124
Fill alternate spaces of a multi-line drawing	Exclusion	yes	no	yes	okay	yes	yes	medium	125
Cut an object into pieces with another object or path.	Division	if desired	no	yes	no	yes	yes	medium	125
	Eraser Tool	if desired	no	yes	no	yes	no	easy	129-33
	Calligraphic Pen + Division + Break apart	if desired	no	yes	no	yes	no	medium	132
	Bezier Pen + Stroke to Path + Division + Break apart	if desired	no	yes	no	yes	yes	harder	132
Delete interior lines and keep a unified outline of more than one object	Union	yes	no	yes	only for outline	yes	yes	easy	85-6
Gently move a line, round a corner, or take a small bite out of a closed edge	Tweak tool	—	no	yes	no	yes	maybe	easy	133-6

Clipping: An Answer to Most Cropping Needs

Clipping is covering up part of a drawing—one object or many objects—and making the covered parts invisible. Any shape or path you can draw can be used as the invisible container for the part of the drawing you want to keep. The rest is hidden.

Here, for example, I want to get rid of the left side of the drawing and that tree clump that seems to be leaning out of the picture. Easiest will be to use a shape to enclose the part of the drawing I want. I've used a black stroke here so I can tell how to place the rectangle, but it will disappear in the next step.

Next, select the whole and press **Object > Clip > Set**. That's all there is to it.

Here's the result with the rectangle gone. Now I can add other objects, including frames. If I wanted the same rectangle as a frame, I could have made a copy and set it aside to add later. Once the clipping is done, I can abut the drawing with other objects, group, save, and export the drawing just as I would any other drawing. If I should decide I want the rest of the drawing back, I simply select the clipped drawing again and press **Object > Clip > Release**. The whole drawing will reappear.

113

Rectangles certainly aren't the only outlines that can be used. As long as what you're using produces a single line of nodes around your drawing, you're okay. Don't use the calligraphic pen for **Set** because it produces a double stroke.

It is also possible to **Clip** a piece from inside a drawing. That is done with **Clip > Set Inverse**. You don't like that tree in the scenes above? Draw a pencil line around it, being careful to close the line, **Set Inverse**, and it's gone until you want it back.

Some graphic artists—namely Web artists—might have a little problem with Clipping. They might be looking for a drawing that has the smallest number of bytes possible for most efficient storage on the Web. Because the material trimmed by Clipping is really still there, along with additional commands to hide it, there are extra bytes. This is unlikely to be an issue for you as a metal artist unless storage on your computer is a major problem.

Patterns as a Method of Edge-Trimming

Clipping is such an easy way to get rid of edges that you don't need to use **Pattern** for this purpose. Save **Pattern** for times when you really do want a pattern to fill your outline, especially a repeating pattern (see pp. 38 ff.).

Other Methods for Trash Removal and Adjustment: Node-based Processes

Clipping is not for every situation. If you actually need to fully delete a portion of an object or drawing, or capture a portion of an object or drawing, you'll have to turn to some other methods. For that, it helps to have a little background in how a vector program like Inkscape differs from raster graphics programs such as Photoshop, Corel Paintshop Pro, and Gimp. Knowing some basics will help you understand what you can and can't do in Inkscape, so you'll run into fewer surprises.

Why Things Are Different in Inkscape: Raster Versus Vector

As you may know, in raster (bitmap) images everything is made up of little pixels—minute squares of color with a standard size. Hundreds of pixels are arranged next to each other to make up shapes. If you magnify a raster image enough to actually see the pixels, the borders between colors will look ragged on anything other than a straight horizontal or vertical line, because there are, of course, no curves in a pixel square. The shaded pixels fool the eye into seeing a smooth transition between colors.

Enlarged raster curve showing pixels

In contrast, an Inkscape drawing is made up completely of paths joining points in mathematical relationship to one another. Inkscape can maintain the same relationship between points while making everything bigger or smaller. The stroke and fill are "just" styles or attributes that get added on with brief notations in the program once the size is calculated. This means the clarity of the lines or fill remains the same whether large or small.

The differences between raster and vector have implications for deleting. If you delete a pixel or a hundred pixels in a raster image, they are gone for good. Period. Their disappearance has no effect on nearby pixels.

On the other hand, the lines of a vector image exist not in pixels, but in relationships among points (nodes). Get rid of one node or a couple of nodes and you may mess up the relationship with other nodes. This can radically alter the shape of a drawing.

An important principle: In Inkscape, all deleting involves moving or getting rid of nodes, but you have to realize how those nodes will impact the lines they control.

Manipulating Nodes

We'll begin by briefly reviewing how to manipulate nodes using the node tools, before getting to the more automated choices Inkscape offers. Two examples may help to explain how deletion of pieces has to happen in a vector program.

The first example involves a simple straight line:

Suppose we want to make the line a little shorter. We can't just use an ordinary eraser to cut, say, 1/4 inch off the end. That's because what looks like a line is really just two nodes at particular locations. If we turn off the stroke and click the node arrow, this is how our line appears:

What looks like a line to our eyes is actually the stroke, and that's just a style that has nothing to "hang on" if a node goes away. Thus "cutting off" an end would delete a node, and that would get rid of the line altogether. A single node does not a line make.

It's quite simple to make a straight line shorter. Just move the node.

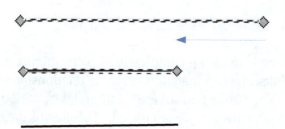

An alternative would be to click-add another node 1/4 of an inch from the end and then delete the resulting segment to the right.

Straight lines are easy. Curved lines are a little trickier. Suppose we've used the **BSpline** mode of the **Bezier tool** to draw the following line of curves:

And suppose we want to make the tails at the beginning and end the same height as the loops, but we definitely want to preserve the evenness of the curves. Should be an easy matter to get rid of these little bits, right? Applying the same method as on the straight line, we should be able to move the first and last nodes, right? Let's try it.

This line has quite a few more nodes than the straight line:

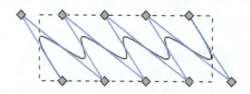

Let's set a couple of guidelines to help figure out where to move the nodes. Remember, you can just drag them down from the top ruler line.

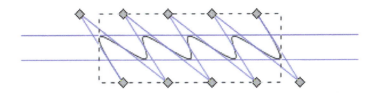

Now notice what happens if we drag the end node down to the guideline.

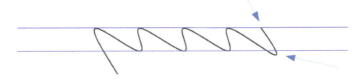

The bottom of the curve has shifted so that the last valley no longer matches the others. It might be possible to wrestle the line into place, but more likely, the symmetry will just keep getting more out of whack. What to do?

First, this figure was drawn in **BSpline** mode. Sometimes the nodes will be easier to manipulate if the line is converted to an ordinary path, using **Object to Path**. This puts the nodes right on the line.

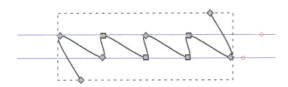

Next, it often helps to actually <u>add</u> nodes in order to hold the line in place and to make it possible to delete segments. Here three nodes have been added.

Now we remove the segment above the guideline by selecting the middle node and the node just under the top node, and then selecting **Delete segment between two non-endpoint nodes** on the node tool control bar.

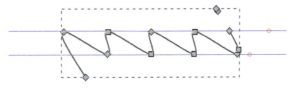

That leaves only the easy task of selecting and deleting those two remaining nodes at the top. Now we have this figure:

A similar process on the left end yields an even set of curves, ready to be used in further designs.

And here is a possibility:

Node manipulation may take some time and some planning, but if you need a clean line to combine with other components, it's an option.

To summarize what these examples demonstrate,
- All Inkscape objects are node-based.
- In order to alter an object or delete part of it, nodes must be moved or deleted.
- Sometimes to delete a node without losing or distorting other parts of the object, additional nodes must be strategically added before the deletion.

Discouraged? That, after all, was a lot of fussing. Now, wouldn't it be nice if Inkscape would do these operations for us automatically? It can.

Understanding Inkscape's Tools for Deletion and Node Manipulation

The desire for automatic ways to manipulate nodes brings us to some new tools, commands, and techniques which will be covered in this chapter:

- Path operations (Boolean operations):
  - Combine
  - Break apart
  - Cut path
  - Difference
  - Intersection
  - Exclusion
  - Division
- Eraser Tool
- Stroke to Path (or Calligraphic line revisited)
- Tweak Tool

Before we plunge into what these processes can do, we need to look at a two considerations that will determine which process to use when.

> **First question about deleting part of a drawing:** Does the drawing include open paths?

> **Second question about deleting part of a drawing:** How much does the file size of the drawing matter? Are you conserving kilobytes?

Open and Closed Paths

The first and most important consideration has to do with closed versus open paths. **This is key.**

A closed path is continuous. An open path is not—or at least looks as if it is not.

Examples of open paths:

Examples of drawings with several open paths:

Examples of drawings with a combination of open and closed paths:

Having seen the examples above, you probably understand that as a metal artist interested primarily in black and white images, you are likely to be making mostly line drawings and that many of these will have open paths.

But why is this difference between open and closed paths important to deletion processes? Notice that in the following line of figures, all of the open paths can easily be closed except for the straight line.

<u>That is exactly what is going to happen to open lines in all of the figures you draw if you choose the wrong automated process to remove some portion of a drawing.</u> In some cases, this won't matter to you, especially where the drawing is composed of a filled outline, like this:

After one of the path operations

On the other hand, suppose you've constructed a multi-line drawing using the same line we've been playing with above. (If you are following along, trying this, save a couple of copies of the multi-line drawing to use again later.)

If you wanted a circle with this scaly look, you would probably just use clipping. But suppose for a moment that you need a circle with the excess bits cleanly deleted for good. You decide to use one of the path operations, such as **Intersection**. You use a circle to do the cutting, and here's what unfortunately happens:

Once you put a circle outline around it, you get this:

You'll notice what has become of the scaly pattern. There are now additional diagonal lines as a result of the process automatically closing all the lines. It's possible you will like the "accidental" result of closing lines, but they may not be at all what you intended.

This brings us to an important distinction.

The following processes will **close** open lines:
- Union
- Difference
- Intersection
- Exclusion
- Division
- Eraser Tool

- Tweak Tool

The following processes will **not close** open lines:

- Combine
- Break Apart
- Cut Path

Tip 1! The only automated deletion process that does not close lines is Cut Path.

Tip 2! Sometimes you can get around unwanted line closing by using the **Calligraphic pen** or by using **Stroke to Path** on your lines. Both of these produce lines that are actually already closed. However, you may have to deal with other limitations.

Path Operations That Close Open Lines

Most of the time you will be using these processes on only two objects, but it is possible to operate on more objects with some of the path operations. I've tried up to five objects, but theoretically you could probably keep going, though I don't know why you would want to, except for **Unify**.

All these operations use the **Z-order** of objects to determine what object operates on what other object. Think of **Z-order** as a stack of cards. On the bottom is the first object you drew. The next object you drew is above that in the card deck, no matter where it appears on the screen. The third object is above that, and so on. You can move these objects all around on the screen, but if you try to put them on top of one another again, they will still stack in the same order. You may not have realized this because we've mostly been drawing objects with a stroke and no fill, so they all appear to be at the same level. Try **Z-order** out by drawing two or three objects and giving them each a different color fill.

You can change the Z-order of an object by selecting it and then choosing **Object** > **Raise**, or **Object** > **Lower**, or **Object** > **Raise to Top**, or **Object** > **Lower to Bottom**.

The **Z-order** will apply to the **Path Operations** if the whole group of objects is rubber-banded. However, if instead you select the objects one by one, the order in which you select determines the bottom to top order for Path Operation. The top always acts on the next object down.

Any time you use a **Path Operation** on an object, that object is automatically converted into a path, even if it began life as a **Shape**. If a path operation refuses to work, check that the objects are not grouped and that you have actually selected the whole collection. Remember to look at the notification area.

Because the **Path Operations** are sometimes only visible with <u>filled</u> objects, I have used shadings in some of the examples, even though they would not be useful for metal work.

How to Use Union

This has been covered on pp. 82, 85-86. **Union** will eliminate most interior lines in a multi-line drawing or combination of objects. It leaves the outline.

How to Use Difference

In short, **Difference** keeps what does <u>not</u> overlap.

Two objects   One object

 That's easy enough to remember if you are dealing with only two objects. More than that becomes complicated and is not recommended unless you **Combine** the objects first.

To do this, select all the objects except the "cutter", click **Path > Combine**, place the "cutter" on top, and then press **Difference. Combine** unifies the lower objects, gives the whole the same fill, and treats them all as one item to cut out. The "cutter" disappears, leaving a "cutter" shaped hole. Individual strokes disappear, leaving only the outline, if there is one.

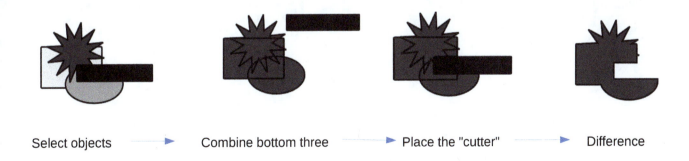

Select objects   Combine bottom three   Place the "cutter"   Difference

If a single curved line is used as an object, the line is closed before the cutting takes place.

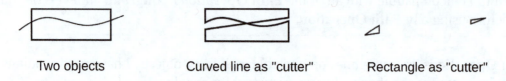

Two objects   Curved line as "cutter"   Rectangle as "cutter"

If a straight line is one of the objects, one or both objects will disappear.

For irregular shaped objects, you may find it useful to draw a pencil line around the portion of a drawing you want to disappear. Use care to connect the ends of the pencil line so you have a continuous line. Click **Difference**, and you're rid of the unwanted section. Just be aware that you will be closing any open lines. **Difference** can, in fact, be used to create unified donuts of whatever shape you want. **Difference** is as close as you'll get to the ability in a raster program to select a section of an object and then delete it.

I like a pencil line because it is the easiest line-drawing tool to control. It does, however, leave behind a border of many nodes, so it wouldn't be the best choice if you care about ending up with the fewest bytes. If you are going to use a pencil line, **Simplify** it before using it.

How to Use Intersection

The opposite of **Difference**, **Intersection** keeps only what overlaps with the top object. Though this technically works on more than two objects, there will probably be very few instances where more than two will be needed. The final result takes the fill of the bottom object.

Again, you can use a pencil line to grab an irregular portion of a larger drawing, with the same caveats —that open lines will be automatically closed and lots of nodes will be left behind unless you simplify the pencil line.

How to Use Exclusion

Parts that overlap get completely cut out, but all remaining pieces are left in place and will act on the next level down. So, the top object works on the next one down. That combination works on the next one down, and so on. The result is a sort of checkerboard. The final result takes the fill of the bottom object, but only in those areas where there is fill. This process appears to have no effect on unfilled objects, but using **Break Apart** allows separation of the pieces, whether filled or unfilled.

How to Use Division

Division works with two objects only. The top object is the "cutter." Its path cuts the lower path and disappears, leaving the segments of the lower path in place. Those segments are all closed segments. These segments can then be separated.

Again, you can use an irregular closed path, such as a pencil line, for the "cutter."

Tip! Another alternative if you're dealing with lines you don't want to appear closed by a cutting process is to select the lines, click **Path > Stroke to Path**, and then cut the lines. Just remember that they will no longer have a single line of nodes (see pp. 76 ff.).

Path Operations For Design

With some imagination, all of these **Path Operations** can be used in creating effective designs. They are especially good for relatively large areas of fill, rather than for lots of lines.

A Path Operation That Does <u>Not</u> Close Open Lines

How to use Cut Path

This is the **Path Operation** that is of most interest for multi-line drawings. To remind you, **this is the only automated deletion process that does not close open lines. Combine** and **Break Apart** are also **Path Operations** that don't close open lines, but they are not deletion processes.

In the discussion of node manipulation, you may recall that it took a bit of trouble to cut the extra tails off that figure we keep using:

We can accomplish the same thing with **Cut Path** without having to take all that care about the extra nodes and careful deletion of the right ones. Inkscape will do this for us accurately and automatically.

First, draw a figure to be the "cutter." We'll choose a rectangle because that will provide us with two horizontal straight lines we can use to cut off both tails at the same time.

Position the rectangle over the wavy line so that the upper and lower lines of the rectangle are just about, but not quite, touching the wavy line. Make sure the stroke on the rectangle isn't too thick, so you can get close enough.

Now press **Path > Cut Path**. You will see that the bounding box for the figure has become three bounding boxes: one larger box and two tiny ones at each end. The rectangle has disappeared. Click somewhere else on the canvas and then click one of the tails. You can now delete it. Do the same with the other tail.

That's the process for a simple one-line drawing. **Cut Path** can also be used for a more complex drawing with numerous lines. First, though, you must stick all those lines together with **Combine**. You cannot use **Group**.

To illustrate the use of **Cut Path** with a multi-line drawing, let's use yet another variation on the same old wavy line:

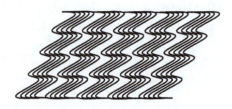

Before we do anything else, we'll select the whole thing and **Ungroup** a couple of times, just to make sure there are no groups at any level in the drawing. If all is clear, the notification at the bottom of the screen will tell you there are no groups in the selection. Next, we'll **Combine**. It will look as if nothing has happened, but the notification area will now tell you how many nodes are in the selection. Combining is necessary if you are going to use **Cut Path** on more than one path besides the cutter.

As you can see, **Combine** leaves all your lines intact and all the underlying nodes in the same places. Thus it differs from **Union**, which takes the simplest way to join all the nodes, usually eliminating lines and adding others in the process.

Now, suppose we want to cut a rectangle from this figure. The objective will be to even off the left and right sides. The top and bottom of the figure have the tails piled up and look a little ragged, so maybe we'll want to cut those off, too. First we draw a rectangle as a cutter. It will be most efficient to position a single rectangle over the image rather than cutting off the sides one at a time. I strongly advise making a copy of the rectangle outline for use in a subsequent step. Put that copy to the side.

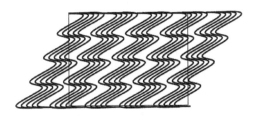

Next, rubber-band to select both the jagged drawing and the rectangle on top. Click **Path > Cut Path**. The rectangle disappears. In addition, the command not only cuts off the sides, it breaks apart the combination. Thus you end up with lots of little pieces. Be careful not to disturb the wrong ones.

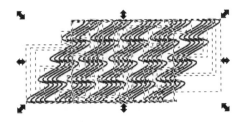

The little pieces are the big disadvantage of Cut Path. With rectangular shapes it's usually not too difficult to rubber-band the edges and pull them away to discard. I'd suggest the following process.

Rubber-band and **Group** the whole figure, ends and all, so that you can move the extra copy of the rectangle outline back into place to help you see what you are doing. Once that's done, rubber-band and **Ungroup** everything again. Zoom in so you can see the details. Rubber-band just outside the rectangle outline to select the rectangle and contents. **Group** all this. You should now be able to move the rectangle and contents away from the waste ends. You may have to clean up stray pieces.

Now you can **Ungroup** and move the rectangle away or keep it, as you prefer.

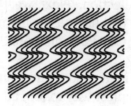

What if we want a circular cutout instead of a rectangle? Let's try that on the scale-like pattern we attempted earlier—this time using the **Cut Path** instead of the "wrong" path operation. Remember we started with this:

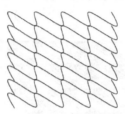

We complete the same steps presented in the previous example:

1. Rubber-band and **Ungroup** the figure down to the bottom level.
2. Rubber-band and **Combine**.
3. Draw a circle as cutter.
4. **Copy/Duplicate** and set aside an extra circle for a guide later.
5. Rubber-band to select the drawing with the circle on top.
6. Press **Path > Cut Path**. The circle disappears and the figure breaks into many pieces.

At this point, we find that the circular shape raises particular challenges. Instead of putting the spare circle on top, we'll rubber-band the scale-like figure without grouping it and move it onto the circle, because we need to be able to see where all those little dotted break-up lines are. Position the figure over the circle as accurately as possible.

Now we really have a problem. Bounding boxes are rectangular, so it's tricky to rubber-band an area that contains the circle and its contents but doesn't end up with strays. Better to stay a little further outside the circle than get too close. Turning on a grid may help. Perhaps the best option is to hold the **Alt** key as you drag the **Select Arrow** through the pieces. A red line will show what pieces are selected and will be deleted when you press **Delete** or **Backspace**.

Once we have the bounding box, we can **Group** and move that group away from the waste. If this isn't successful, **Undo** and try again or pick the strays off. This time we'll leave the circle as an outline.

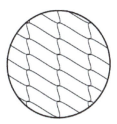

An Alternative

This is all a rather picky process, and you may be asking yourself whether it's worth it. Read on for an alternative for getting rid of all those little chunks after the cutting process.

The Eraser 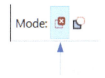 Tool: Not What You'd Expect

Once you get past the name Inkscape developers have given the so-called Eraser, it can be quite a useful tool. Just don't expect it to act like erasers in raster programs or the eraser at the end of your pencil. I think of this tool as drawing a red laser beam through objects, destroying and cauterizing as it goes. I'd rather call this tool the Zapper Tool, but I guess we're stuck.

Here's the command line for the tool:

The **Eraser Tool** has three modes. All work by drawing a red line through an object or series of objects. The red line becomes invisible once it has done its job. The first mode, the **Delete Objects** mode with the red X, is the one we want for the circle problem above.

If we once again try the first six steps on our scale-like design from above, we get the broken-up version of the figure that you saw previously:

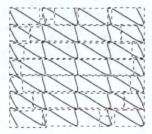

We may or may not need to put the extra circle guide back on top this time. Just make sure to zoom in far enough to see all the dotted lines. Now, with the whole thing selected and the **Eraser** in the first mode, drag a red line through all the broken bits on one side of the circle. The bits will disappear.

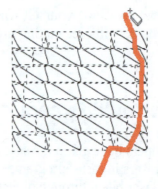

Do the same with the other side, once you've selected again. Then select once more and take a good look at the top and bottom. There may a couple of stray bits to get rid of. You may then want to put the extra circle on top as a border and group the whole thing again.

Eraser Tool: The second mode

The second mode of the Eraser Tool is actually much like the **Path Operation**, **Division**. This eraser mode is called **Cut out from Objects**.

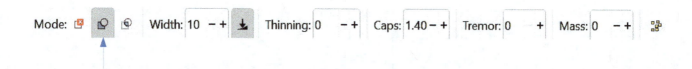

It works well for certain purposes. Think of it as zapping a highway of nothingness through an object, leaving a stroke on either side of the path—in other words, putting a berm along the highway on both sides. Select the figure first. As you draw, the line will be red. If you are cutting more than one object, the tool will only work on the topmost. **Combine** to cut several objects at once.

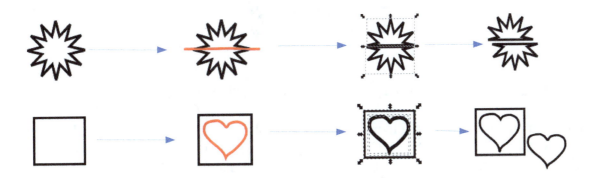

The result is rather like **Division** or **Difference**, only with a double line as the cutter, rather than some other object. If you want the pieces to come apart after you draw the line, make sure **Break apart cut items** is highlighted at the right end of the tool command line. Or you can use **Path > Break apart**.

Here's a caution about the second example above—tthe heart cutout. You can add fill to the heart that was pulled out of the rectangle, but if you try to add fill to the rectangle hoping it will act as a sort of "doughnut" with an empty heart center, it won't work. The whole thing will fill. Only if you have an opening to the outside will you end up with a hollow center.

Filling only the rectangle border doesn't
work when closed: the rest fills.

Filling only the rectangle border
does work when open.

If you want a "doughnut" effect, the way to go is to draw two objects and use one to "cut out" the other using **Difference**. I don't believe there's a way to end up with both the "doughnut" and the cut out piece except by making a copy of the top piece.

You can set the eraser's "highway of nothingness" to whatever **Width** you like. You can also set the **Mass**, just as you do in the **Calligraphic pen**. The higher the mass, the more "drag" on the line and the slower it draws. That helps in producing a less jerky line. Or you can go the opposite way and set a **Tremor** value to make your line rougher.

The **Caps** setting determines the shape of the end of your line of nothingness. This seems to matter only when the end of the line is <u>within</u> a filled object and not when you cut all the way through.

Cap settings from 0 to 10

Other ways to split an object into parts: Using the pens

As you can see, there's not much point to using the eraser tool in this mode except for quickly cutting off or cutting up parts of a closed object. The eraser tool generates lots of nodes, even when the Mass is set high. That will not matter to most of us, but you might want to know about a couple of other options that do exactly the same thing but can be smoother or more shapely. These options do take a couple of additional steps.

One is to use the **Calligraphic pen**, which also generates a double line of nodes. Once a line is drawn, just select everything and use **Path > Division** to split the parts. Then use **Path > Break Apart** so that you can pull the pieces apart.

Another is to use the **Bezier pen** in any mode. Draw the line, click **Path > Object to Path**, and then **Path > Stroke to Path**. Use **Path > Division** to split the parts. Then use **Path > Break Apart** so you can pull the pieces apart.

Drawn with Calligraphic pen

Drawn with Bezier in Spiro mode

Drawn with Bezier

Any of these pieces can, of course, be filled. This might be a great place to employ **Pattern**, by the way.

Eraser Tool: The third mode

This mode is a real fooler. Try it on lines with or without fill and you'll think you finally have an actual eraser that gets rid of parts of lines without closing them. Enjoy the illusion and use it to your heart's content. You won't run into potential trouble until you turn on the **Nodes Arrow**. Then you'll see that the lines you thought you erased are still there. What you've used is another way to Clip, which is why this one is labeled **Clip from Objects**. You are merely removing the stroke and fill of parts of objects rather than eliminating them, thus rendering those parts invisible.

In practice, this tool can be a real time saver. Just remember that if you try to alter nodes, you may get unexpected results, such as bringing the object back in full.

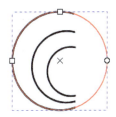

| Momentary red line traces the erasure path. | A clipped area appears empty but isn't. | A broader line turns a larger chunk invisible. | Pointing with the node arrow shows underlying forms. |

The objects above show stroke only, but the mode also works with fill. Objects can be Grouped or Combined. They can be Shapes or Paths. But as you can see in the last image above, the underlying Shapes or Paths are still there once the Eraser has done its job. If you were to click on the third image above, the bounding box would be the original bounding box. If you point with the Node Arrow, you get a flash of the full circle in red. If you click with the Node Arrow, the original nodes or Shape symbols appear (in this case, Shape symbols).

Because the result of this mode is really a clipped image, you can't break the pieces apart.

If you use any of the **Align and Distribute** functions, they will operate from the underlying bounding boxes, so the resulting visual spacing may not be what you'd want.

The Tweak Tool: a Versatile and Friendly Shaper

Here's a tool that does not deserve to be hidden away at the end of a long, complicated chapter. Think of it as the *pièce de résistance* of node manipulation tools. Color graphics artists are probably twice as in love with this tool as I am, but even in black and white the uses are exciting.

The Tweak control bar offers thirteen different modes, the last three of which are for colors or blurring and do not pertain to our needs as metal artists. Of the remainder, the first six operate on whole objects, offering another means of moving, scaling, rotating, or duplicating. These probably are best used with collections of objects (not groups). However, the modes of greatest interest to us are the node manipulation modes:

Push parts of paths in any direction

Shrink parts of paths or use with **Shift** to enlarge parts of paths

Attract parts of paths towards the cursor or use with **Shift** to move parts away from cursor

Roughen parts of paths by adding tiny bits (creates many more nodes)

As you can see from the control bar, there are three drop-down menus to determine how the tool functions.

Width: sets the size of the orange circle-cursor. It's a circle to represent the smooth and gradual effect it will have on a path. The circle does not grow and shrink as you zoom, so often it's easier to zoom than to be continually changing the width.

Force: determines how strongly the parts of the path will be affected.

Fidelity: determines how much the entire path retains its shape. Remember that action on one node may mean other nodes are adjusted. If fidelity is set high, the other nodes will be less likely to move much, but that may mean additional nodes will be added. If the fidelity is set low, other nodes will be adjusted and the path smoothed more. Low fidelity is good for more rounded forms.

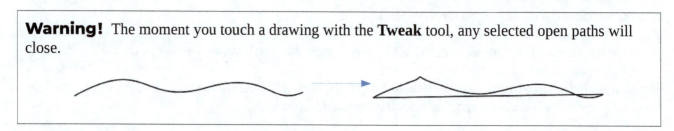

Warning! The moment you touch a drawing with the **Tweak** tool, any selected open paths will close.

The **Tweak** tool allows you to adjust a path a little or a lot in a highly intuitive way. First **Select** the path or paths you want to mold and then click the **Tweak** tool. You can use it like a brush to stroke or push the path into different shapes, or you can spot-click it to grow or shrink areas. The effect will be distributed over an area of the path to keep it smooth.

Here are examples of how a path can be modified by pushing and pulling.

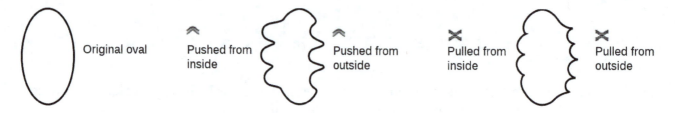

Original oval   Pushed from inside   Pushed from outside   Pulled from inside   Pulled from outside

Here's an example of growing and shrinking parts of a path.

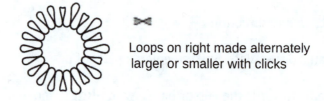

Loops on right made alternately larger or smaller with clicks

The **Tweak** tool doesn't work well, if at all, on straight lines—think about the lack of nodes to act on. If you want to tweak a straight line, try curving it slightly first by using the node tool command **Make selected segments curves**. Or you can add nodes. The **Tweak** tool is best for big, blobby, organic curves or for small adjustments.

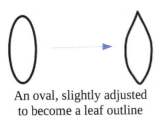

An oval, slightly adjusted
to become a leaf outline

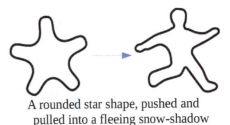

A rounded star shape, pushed and
pulled into a fleeing snow-shadow

Experimenting with the **Tweak** tool can be amusing. Here are a few doodles starting with a spiral:

With the **Tweak** tool, you can make subtle changes to regular shapes to make them look more organic. The petals of this cherry blossom, for example, were produced by tweaking an ellipse. First the bottom of the ellipse was narrowed. Then the ellipse was duplicated. Finally, each petal was tweaked differently to produce a more natural effect, and the petals were filled with white so they would overlap properly.

The **Tweak** tool cannot be used on a **Group**. You'll remember that <u>no</u> **Path Operations** can be used on a **Group**. However, you can select several objects and tweak all of them together. That brings us to another place where the **Tweak** tool can be quite useful: making hatched lines for shading. Below, for

135

example, is a series of duplicated lines made with the **Calligraphic tool**. Since a **Calligraphic** line is a closed figure with two strokes and fill, it doesn't have the annoying habit of closing when you don't want it to close (see pp. 63 ff.).

Here, the shrink and grow mode of the **Tweak** tool, run up and down all the lines selected at once, helps provide the illusion of three-dimensionality in this collection of lines.

The push mode has then been used to provide a further curve on all these lines:

Tip! If you're having trouble getting the **Tweak** tool to work, you may have forgotten to select the drawing first. The other reason it won't work may be that you are trying to operate on a straight line without internal nodes.

Chapter 10
Using Text

Adding text to your designs offers a whole new world of possibilities. You can add words to your designs. You can design an entire piece with letters, decorated or not. You can modify letters and words by stretching or rotating, or by adding pattern. You can fill shapes with letters or words. You can flow words onto a path, such as a circle, spiral, or curvy line. You can play with dingbats, the little pictures that replace letters in some fonts, and you can further modify those little pictures as decorative elements. You could even create your own fonts.

First Things First: Cautionary Notes

Before we get into the details of using type, we need to look at some legalities. Fonts are intellectual property subject to copyright. That means that fonts that came with your favorite computer programs are likely to be copyrighted. You may be surprised to learn that well-meaning people have even run into legal trouble when they have self-published an e-book using a popular font that came with their text-writing application.

 The bottom line? If you are planning to sell your jewelry, you need to pay attention to copyright. That doesn't mean you shouldn't use fonts. It does mean you should check the license on any font you use commercially. That's true for fonts that show up automatically in Inkscape, because these are just all the fonts that have been installed on your computer. And it's true even for free fonts you download from the Internet. A further complication is that the license can specify different uses. Some uses are okay, while others are not, even if you actually paid for a font.

How do you check the license? If you bought or downloaded the font from the Internet, there will probably be license information appended to the download. If it's a font that came with another program, you may have to search for it by name on the Internet to see if you can find the licensing information.

There are a number of reliable sources for fonts that are free for the purposes you are likely to need. Just be sure to look for fonts in the public domain or free for commercial use. Here are four sites to explore:

- Google Fonts (https://fonts.google.com)
- Font Library (https://fontlibrary.org)
- FontSquirrel (https://www.fontsquirrel.com) For fonts from this site, you still need to check the license to make sure it's good for your jewelry purpose.
- DaFont (https://www.dafont.com) offers both copyrighted and copyright-free fonts, so be careful. This site allows you to search for only those fonts that are public domain. You must first click on a category, then find the line just above the first font. At the end of the line, click More options. That will bring up check-boxes, including Public domain.

An Organizing Suggestion

Because you probably already have many fonts on your computer and because a number of these will not be legitimate for your commercial purposes, you might want to keep a list of those that <u>are</u> okay so you don't have to look up the license every time you want to use a font. Another possibility would be to download the license information (usually a text file) along with the font, and accumulate all those license notations in a folder somewhere on your computer.

Downloading and Installing Fonts

Remember to use reasonable precautions with anything downloaded from the Web.

If a font you want to use (legitimately) is not already installed on your computer, here are some steps to get it into Inkscape.

- Download the font and maybe the description with its accompanying licensing information. There will usually be a download button in or near the font description. The exact procedure will vary according to your browser. Save the font file to your computer somewhere you will be able to find it, such as the download folder of your computer.
- Unzip the font file if zipped. These days, unzipping is usually obvious and rather automatic. Save the unzipped file where you can find it, again probably in downloads.
- To install on a Windows machine, simply right-click on the font file. Then click on Install. That should do it. Be sure to install all of the files of a font to get the regular type face, the bold, the italic and whatever else is offered. You want either the TTF files (True Type Font works on Windows) or OTF (Open Type Font works on both Windows and Mac).

If you're not using a Windows 10 operating system, you may need to look for directions online, but they should be easy to find.

Once the font is installed on your computer, it should show up in Inkscape the next time you start the program.

Warning! If you choose an uncommon font for a design and you or someone else tries to read the text on a different computer which does not have that font, your text may not be visible or may be changed to a different font. To avoid this problem, you can convert the text to a path, but then you can no longer edit it as text. As a jewelry artist, you are unlikely to be putting files on different computers very often, so you probably won't have to worry about this much.

Two Ways to Enter Text in Inkscape

Text is defined in Inkscape as an object or set of objects with dimensions, in the same way that rectangles, ellipses, and other shapes are defined. **Text** can be converted to a **Path** like any other object, but it does start life with dimensions.

Just as you create any other object, you can enter text anywhere on the Inkscape canvas. Once you click on the bold **A** text tool on the left of the window, you can start the text in one of two ways.

1. Regular Text. Just click on the canvas and start typing. A dotted bounding box just like those you are used to will appear with the text inside, expanding to accommodate the text you type. You can make manual line breaks as you go. This is usually the best way to enter text.
2. Flowed Text. Use the text tool to draw a rectangular text frame first, and then start typing text within it. The text will flow into the frame, creating new line breaks automatically if there is enough room. If there isn't, you can resize the box by dragging on the little corner squares. The only advantages of this mode are the automatic line breaks if you are writing a long text and the ability to justify the text (which is sometimes quite important to design). Otherwise, regular text is the way to go.

In both cases, you can come back to the text to edit it. Just click again on the **Text** tool and click within the text you've written to get a cursor as you do in other text programs like Word or Open Office. Then you can add text, or highlight the whole text sequence and change fonts, or italicize, or justify, or do most of the operations with which you are probably familiar from other programs. You do these operations via the **Text Control Bar**.

The Text Control Bar

Like the controls for other tools, the **Text** control bar can be found just above the ruler line when you have clicked the **A** in the tool bar. As usual, when you point at the options on this control bar, you will see explanations for each item. Explanations are also given here to help you familiarize yourself with the options.

Overview: the Entire Control Bar

This graphic is split in half below so that it can be more easily seen.

> **Tip!** Because the **Text** control bar is crammed with possibilities, your bar may be too long for your screen. If so, you can click on the tiny ▼ symbol at the far right to see the additional options.

The First Half of the Control Bar

Liberation Sans ▼	Bold ▼	40 ▼	pt ▼	↕ 1.25 − +	lines ▼	≣▼	xˣ xᵧ
1	2	3	4	5	6	7	

1. Font-family (name of font)
   Here you can choose from all the fonts installed on your computer, using the drop-down menu. A font-family is made up of all the styles (italic, bold, etc.) of that particular font.
2. Select all text with this font-family.
   If you have used several fonts in a drawing, you can select those from a particular font-family. You might want to do that if you decide to change the entire family to another font-family.
3. Font style (e.g., normal, bold, italic, condensed).
4. Font size.
5. Unit of measurement of font size.
6. Spacing between lines.
   Line spacing is for the whole text object.
7. Unit of measurement for line spacing.
8. Align left, center, right, justify.
   Justify (spacing words evenly across the whole line) is only available for flowed text.
9. Superscript, subscript.
   Makes characters 65% the size of other characters and raises them above or below the line. Best done by selecting the text to raise or lower and then clicking the icon.

The Second Half of the Control Bar:

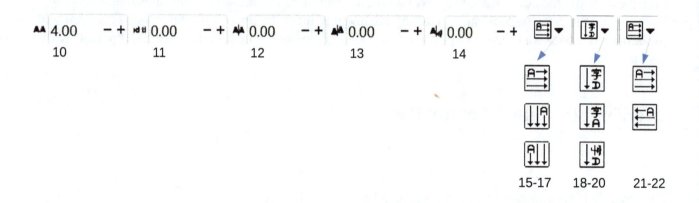

10. Spacing between letters.
    Adjusts the spaces between all letters in the text object unless you have made a selection.
11. Spacing between words.
    Adjusts the spaces between all words in the text object unless you have made a selection.
12. Horizontal kerning.
    Slightly shifts all letters to the right (or left with minus numbers) after the cursor.

140

Or, shifts only those letters selected.

13. Vertical shift.

   Slightly shifts all letters upward or downward after the cursor.

   Or, shifts only those letters selected.

14. Character rotation.

   Slightly rotates a character or characters. Each letter rotates independently.

15. Horizontal text.

   The ordinary default setting.

16. Vertical text with lines right to left.

```
l i h M
a t a a
m t d r
b l a y
  e
```

17. Vertical text with lines left to right .

```
M h l l
a a i a
r d t m
y a t b
    l
    e
```

18. Auto-glyph orientation.

   Determines the orientation of the characters automatically.

19. Upright glyph orientation.

   To get letters to sit horizontally in vertical text, use this.

```
M  h  l  l
a  a  i  a
r  d  t  m
y     t  b
   a  l
      e
```

20. Sideways glyph orientation.
21. Left to right text.

   The default orientation in English.

22. Right to left text.

The Text and Font Dialogue Box

In addition to the **Text** control bar, there is a **Text and Font** dialogue box that appears to the right of the canvas when the bold **T** on the line <u>above</u> the control bar is selected or when the first option under **Text** in **Line 1** is selected. This dialogue contains some of the same options as the control bar. There, if you wish, you can set a default font. You can sometimes change the font size and a few other details more easily in the dialogue box because you don't have to select the text. You will also see a preview of what the font looks like.

Manipulating Text as a Graphic Element

The first commands covered here are found under the **Text** command in **Line 1** of the main menu.

Text along a path

Putting text on a path is so easy you won't be able to resist trying it.

First, type some text.

Next, draw a path. You could use the pencil tool or the Bezier pen.

Select both the text and the path.

Go to **Text > Put on Path** and click. The text should now be on the path. You may have to adjust the font size and the spacing between letters and words.

Now, what if you want to get rid of the line and just leave the text? You have a couple of options. First, you could just make the stroke invisible. Instead, you may want to get rid of the line altogether. For that, you have to select only the text. You can usually get hold of the text at the top, click to select, and move it away.

Stop! Before you click the line and delete it, you need to make sure the text doesn't turn straight again when the curvy line disappears, which is what will happen if you don't give the text its own curvy identity. With the text selected, go to **Path** along the top menu and click on **Object to Path**. That turns the curvy text into an object on its own.

Now you can select the line and delete it.

Each day that goes by well is a feast.

Once the text is a path, you can no longer use the **Text** tool to make changes. If you want to keep that option, make a copy before converting it to a path.

Using Shapes as a Path for Text

As you might expect, Shapes can also serve as paths for text.

We'll use a circle to illustrate the process. Draw a circle. Remember that holding down **Ctrl** while you draw helps get you a perfect circle.

Write some regular (not flowed) text with the text tool.

Santa's North Pole Workshop
Elf-Owned and Operated Since 1822

We'll want the first line on the top of the circle and the second line on the bottom.

Use the arrow and the shift key to select both the <u>first line</u> of the text and the circle. Go to **Text** on the top horizontal menu. Click on **Text > Put on Path**. Your results will <u>not</u> be what you hoped!

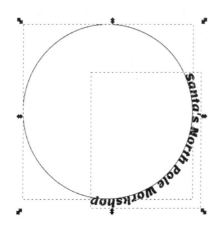

Not to worry. If you want the text on top of the circle, you'll need a double-arrow handle at the corner, like the one below:

Remember, you get these handles by clicking again. <u>Be sure both the text and the circle are selected</u>. If you don't select both, the process won't work.

Now grab this little double arrow and rotate it counter-clockwise around the circle. As you go, you'll see the text warping off the circle. Never fear. When you let up on the mouse button, the text will snap back to the circle. You may have to move the text by stages to get it exactly where you want it.

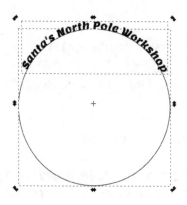

You can go back to the text tool and edit the text and spacing until you're satisfied.

What about the text for the bottom of the circle? We'll do that on a new circle. You'll see why in a moment. We'll draw the circle, write the line of text, and select both. Once again, we click on **Text** > **Put on Path**, and once again, we see the text is <u>not</u> exactly where we want it.

For the moment, keep the text upside down. Grab the corner double-arrow handle, making sure both the text and the circle are selected. Rotate the text until it is even across the bottom of the circle.

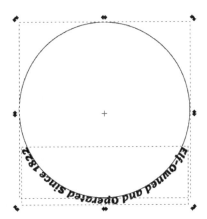

Next we're going to flip the text. In the control menu for the **Select Arrow** right above the ruler, you'll see some icons. The sixth icon from the left has two vertical triangles and is labeled **Flip selected objects horizontally**. Even if that makes no sense, it's the command that works. Click it.

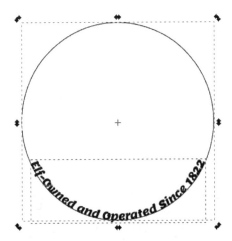

Now the text runs along the inside bottom of the circle.

Unfortunately, we have two circles, not one. That's the way this construction works. If we want text on both the top and bottom of a circle, like the print on a coin, we're going to need a work-around. Otherwise we'll get the top print on the outside of the circle and the bottom print on the inside. To solve the problem, use two circles, one inside the other. The top-text circle will need to be smaller than the bottom circle.

Fit the two circles together as accurately as you can, resizing as you go. When you have the circles as accurately sized and placed as you can make them, you can further align them with the **Align and Distribute** dialogue box to the right of the canvas. If that box isn't visible, bring it up with **Shift + Ctrl + A.**

In the little drop-down box in the **Align** dialogue, choose Align **Relative to <u>Page</u>**. Be sure you have only the two circles selected or you'll throw the center off. Now, under **Align**, find and click on the icon **Center on the vertical axis.**

Warning! It's possible that the circles and their text will seem to disappear. If so, they may have jumped to somewhere else on the canvas. Just zoom out to where you can see them and bring the wanderers home. This seems to be an occasional glitch in the program.

Next, make sure the two circles are selected and click on the icon called **Center on the horizontal axis**. The circles should now be concentric.

If you want to get rid of the circles and leave only the text, you first need to make each line of text its own object, rather than have it depend on the circle for its curve. You may have to zoom in quite a bit to select <u>only</u> on the text and click on **Path > Object to Path** to make the text a stand-alone curved text. Next you can delete the circles or move them out of the way.

To make sure the top and bottom text stay together, **Group** the objects together. Now all the text will function as one object. I've added an outer circle around the whole thing, aligned it and grouped it again.

Now it's ready for the addition of some clever illustration in the middle.

Using Other Shapes as a Path for Text

You can do the same kind of thing with other shapes. Just remember that if you want text with a line on top and a line on the bottom, both running left to right, a circle is by far the easiest.

Text on an oval: tricky but possible

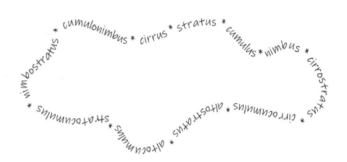

Text around an abstract shape: easy

Text around a spiral: easy

147

Putting Text Into a Shape

It's possible to flow text into any shaped object you can create. To illustrate this, I've drawn a heart, using a half-circle arc and a Bezier curve, copying and flipping the arc and curve, and joining the pieces by joining nodes.

Here's the process for getting text into the shaped object. Make copies of everything as you go!

- Get your words into one long line of regular text. (Some people recommend flowed text in a text box for this, but I find that does not work well.) Start with a smaller font size than you think you will need.
- Justify the text (the fourth choice of the text alignment drop-down buttons). Justifying will make a big difference to the fit of the text in the frame.
- Some situations will call for centered text rather than justified. You will have to experiment.
- Select both the text and the shape you want to flow into.
- Click on **Text** > **Flow into frame**.
- The text will appear in the frame.
- Adjust the size of the text and/or frame. Be sure to click outside the designs before doing this or you will be resizing everything and may find everything hopelessly out of sync. Often it's easiest to shrink or enlarge only the frame until the words fit within it and then resize the whole thing to your chosen dimensions.
- Make fine adjustments to the word and letter spacing.

Once you're completely done with whatever the **Text** function can you for you, I recommend lassoing the whole thing and using **Path** > **Object to Path** to get rid of whatever odd connections are tying the text and frame together. Then you can get rid of the frame and leave just the text to indicate the shape or fit it into your jewelry piece.

If you prefer to keep a frame, you may find that the frame you started with is too tight a fit for your liking. A solution is to make a copy of the frame, enlarge it slightly, and use it to frame both the frame and words. Then select the inner frame and delete it or make the stroke transparent.

Text flowed into frame, re-sized, justified, and further adjusted

Frame removed to let the text carry the shape

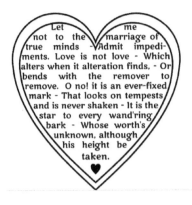

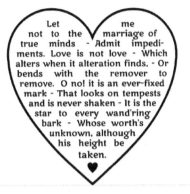

| Outer frame added to produce a margin | Stroke of the inner frame is made transparent |

Once you have things as you like, be sure to **Group** the whole. This is especially necessary if you are going to copy and paste the drawing. If you try to copy and paste without grouping first, you may throw the whole design into chaos.

The Shakespeare heart example above has text that will be too small for most jewelry applications. You will probably want fewer words and perhaps a more interesting font.

It's also possible to flow text into various doughnut shapes. You will first have to join the shapes into one with **Exclusion** (see p. 125).

Flowing text into multiple frames

Text can be flowed into more than one frame. Just select the text plus the objects to be filled and then press **Text** > **Flow into frame**. This will first fill the **first** object selected, so if you want the text to read from left to right, select the objects in order from left to right.

In the example below, centered text seemed more satisfactory than justified text

Unflowing Text

Below the **Flow into Frame** command is **Unflow**, which does what it says. If you click a frame or a text box that contains flowed text, that text will be moved elsewhere in a single line. Sometimes you'll have to zoom way out to find it on your screen. You won't be able to put the text back into a text box, but you will be able to put it into a frame.

Filling Shapes with Text: Pushing the Envelope

Text (and other objects) can be enveloped by nodes and pushed this way and that to deform whole words or groups of letters. Here's a name deformed to fit in an oval:

Here's the same thing with the guide oval removed and a bigger frame added:

The means for doing this kind of distortion is a **Path Effects** option called **Envelope Deformation**.

We'll illustrate this process with the steps for the following drawing:

I've drawn a silhouette of a hawk in flight, but you could experiment with any silhouette. Mostly horizontal figures are easier than diagonals or heavily curved shapes. You also need to think about the shape of the letters and what distortion will do to them. In the "Billy" drawing, the central letters are narrow. That may work better than rounder letters like the "G" in "Flight," which dominates the word as a result of the distortion.

These were my steps for drawing the hawk:

1. Draw a Bezier curve for the top of the wing.
2. Draw another for the bottom.
3. Join the two at the left nodes.
4. Duplicate the wing.
5. Flip the second wing horizontally (**Ctrl H**)
6. Draw a straight segment for a tail side.
7. Duplicate the tail side and flip it horizontally.
8. Draw an arc for the tail end.
9. Join the sides to the end at the nodes.
10. Position the wings and tail.
11. Draw the body and head with the pencil tool with smoothing, making sure to connect at the wing and tail nodes.
12. Use the **Tweak tool** to refine and to poke scallops into the trailing wingtips and the tail.

To prepare the hawk silhouette, select no fill and a thin black or gray stroke to make things easier to see. To insert and deform the text, write the individual words with the **Text** tool. I used a font called "Spicy Rice" in all upper case to keep the tops of the letters consistent. Fit the words fairly tightly into the wings and tail. I have inserted extra spaces between letters in "FOREVER," knowing that the curve will crunch letters together at the tops.

Tip! You'll find this whole process easier with **Snapping** turned off in the menu to the far right of the Inkscape screen.

We'll start with "FLIGHT."

Select the word.

Click **Path** > **Object to Path**. **Path Effects** work only on **Paths**, not shape or text objects. "Flight" will become a **Group** of paths. **Path Effects** can work on groups.

Click **Path** > **Path effects**. A **Path Effects** dialogue comes up on the right side of the canvas. It will be mostly blank to start with, but there will be **+** and **-** signs to the left just below the white space. If you have your path(s) selected, these will turn blue, indicating that you can add or delete an effect.

Click the plus.

A little box entitled **Add Path Effect** will pop up. We'll look at some of the other choices in a later chapter. For now, choose **Envelope Deformation**. This will add a further dialogue in the right hand box with choices about what you'll be able to warp. If you want to warp the top and bottom while keeping the sides somewhat stable, check only **Enable top & bottom paths**. If you want to warp the sides while keeping the top and bottom somewhat stable, check only **Enable left & right paths**. If you turn on both the options, the warping may not be what you'd expect. You might want to try out a deformation with, for instance, the **Enable left & right paths** checked, versus not checked, to see what difference the settings make. Use **Undo** (**Ctrl Z**) in between your experiments to get back to the original.

For our deformation, we'll check only **Enable top & bottom paths.**

Click on the node arrow to the right of **Top bend path.**

A special node bounding box will enclose the word. A thin green line will follow the top of the word. That's the warp line. You can pull it this way and that. You can also use the node handles to pull a smooth curve. Pay attention to the corner nodes while positioning. Keep adjusting until you are satisfied. By the way, I have changed the stroke of "FLIGHT" to a light gray to make it easier to see.

Note that keeping the side bend paths turned off has curved the vertical strokes of the letters more, especially at the far ends. If we had turned the side bend path option on, the verticals would remain straighter, but the tops and bottoms of the letters would be heavier.

Do a similar process on the **Bottom Bend Path**.

And then similar processes on the top and bottom of "DREAMS."

The tail is our last text problem. You'll have to take a guess at how to size the word and where to position it so that once it is curved rather sharply it will still fit decently.

This distortion will definitely look better with the left and right bend paths turned off. Start with the **Bottom bend path**, clicking on the node tool. Position the two end nodes along the sides of the tail. Change the stroke to a light gray so you can see the letters more clearly against the black line of the tail.

Bend the bottom line. Start by pulling down the center of the green line a little. Then you can start pulling the curve handles, which will give a smoother arc. Work back and forth between the handles until the line is where you want it. You can also change the length of the handles for a different curve.

We'll move on to the top line. You can always come back to the bottom line later to refine it. Click on the node tool of the **Top bend path** and position the nodes over the tail lines.

Now work on the bend for the top line. Pull down a little on the center of the line until you see the handles and then work on the arc. If you have trouble getting handles, click on an end node. They should come up.

Here's the entire thing to this point.

You can always go back and rework any positions or curves that don't satisfy you. The body and tail are not exactly symmetrical because the head is cocked slightly. Consequently, the letters will not be exactly symmetrical either.

Once you're done with adjustments, you can change the colors.

Rubber-band the entire drawing. Click **Path > Object to Path** to make sure none of the words will re-straighten. Change the stroke to gray. Click outside the drawing. Select all the words and turn the fill white (<u>not</u> X for no fill). Select just the hawk. Turn the fill black.

You may want to **Group** the whole thing.

It is also possible to go several steps further to end up with the following drawing, which lets the letters carry the shape of the wings and tail.

155

This can be achieved by ungrouping, creating short arced lines across each of the cut points, and then using **Path** > **Division** repeatedly to sever the parts and close the open paths. Once that is done, the lines surrounding the words can be carefully deleted. The whole thing should then be grouped, the stroke set to nothing, and the fill set to black.

Turning Text into a Path

Sometimes your project will go better if you abandon the peculiarities of text, which is subject to changes in font, kerning, alignment, and so on, and simply use characters as little graphics or groups of graphics. In other words, you might want to turn your text into a path or paths. If, for example, you want to use someone's initials in a design, and you want to further manipulate some font's characters for this purpose, you might need to turn the characters into paths to edit with the node editor.

Turning text to path is easy enough. Select the text with the **Select Arrow**. **Click on Path** > **Object to Path**. Each character is now a separate path, <u>but the paths are grouped</u>. If you want a single character or two, you must **Ungroup** before acting on them as individual paths. Once a character is a path, you can skew, enlarge, recombine with other elements, and so on. You cannot turn it back into text or use any of the text commands with it.

Some Other Useful Text Commands

Remove Manual Kerns

This could be a handy little command if you have some lines of text you've carefully adjusted for such things as fine spacing between letters or lines, directions of the letters, and so on. Suppose that you want the text back in its original form and you (Oh, horrors!) have not kept a copy. You can use this command to get rid of all those little changes.

Unicode Characters: More Type to Play With

Clicking **Unicode Characters** under the **Text** menu in **Line 1** will bring up another dialogue box in the area to the right of the canvas. There you will find additional characters that are not found on the normal keyboard. The exact characters available will vary with the font.

To familiarize yourself with what's there, click on a common font, like the Liberation Sans that I was using in the examples above. The font you've chosen should show up as highlighted in the Font family portion of the dialogue box. Next, choose **All** in the drop-down slot for Script and **All** for the drop-down slot for Range. Below this you should notice a large number of characters in the box. At the top will be familiar characters, but as you scroll down you'll see characters that are not on your keyboard, including those from a range of the world's languages, as well as symbols commonly used in math and commerce.

As you point at a character, you'll get a magnified version in white on black, making it easier to see. You may find some of these symbols useful at times, such as the copyright symbol © or the French **é** acute. To insert a character into your text, highlight it in the list and then click the **Append** button at the bottom of the dialogue. In some cases, the symbol appears in the list along with a dotted circle as a stand-in for the letter the symbol normally accompanies, as in this German umlaut:

To the left of the **Append** button, you will also see the Unicode number for the highlighted character. That presents an alternate way of inserting characters into your text. You may be familiar with the Unicode system, an international system of four-character codes for every computer character, meant to work across all countries and platforms. In theory, you should be able to get into Unicode in any program and then enter the code, which will then cause the character to appear. The little glitch is that getting into Unicode differs from program to program. In Inkscape, the way in is **Ctrl + u**, then the code, then **Enter**. Case doesn't matter to entry. However, there <u>is</u> a different code for each upper case and lower case letter.

Most of the time this entry method works. However, since most of us don't carry Unicode sequences around in our heads, it's easier just to use the Unicode dialogue unless you use particular characters frequently.

If you know what specific Script or Range your target character is in, you can limit your choices to that Script or Range so as to make your character easier to find. Or do as we have done above and choose **all**.

Using Dingbats and Other Odd Characters

Dingbats are little drawings that have been made into characters. They come in a wide variety of subjects, from floral frames to animals, from cartoons to traffic signs, from human faces to birds. The free license variety can be found with little trouble, and they can be installed just like other fonts, all ready to use as you would use any other text. Remember also that there are already additional characters on your keyboard that can be employed as easy design elements, such as the tilde ~ or the asterisk *.

Here's an example of arrow dingbats on a spiral.

Remember too that if you turn a text object into a path, it's available for any of the Inkscape techniques you can think of, though you will no long be able to use it as text. For instance, you could no longer use the **Text** > **Put on Path** command. There are, however, other ways of putting objects on a path, which we will get to later (see pp. 231-3, 258-9).

SVG Font Editor

This command is found under **Text** in **Line 1** of the Inkscape screen. It allows you to create your own fonts. Font creation will not be covered here since this is an advanced topic deserving of its own book and an author with the special expertise to write it.

Spell Checker

Once you click **Check Spelling** and click the **Start** button at the bottom of the dialogue, Inkscape will check <u>all</u> text on the canvas, whether it is highlighted or not. It functions similarly to other spell checkers, offering you replacement guesses or a chance to ignore the word. You can easily add words to the dictionary, as well.

Still More Text Odds and Ends

Other miscellaneous text utilities remain to mention, few of which will be of much interest to metal artists. Still, one never knows what will be needed. All the utilities in this list are found under the **Extensions** > **Text** menu on the top line of the Inkscape screen.

- **Change Case**
  This command allows you to change the case of a string of text in several different ways. It will operate on the entire text string.

- **Convert to Braille**

  This is a neat little utility that changes a string of text to Braille.

- **Extract**

  This will extract selected text blocks but not merge into one text block. You can choose the order of the text blocks in different ways. Original styles, such as font, will be maintained. When the chosen text blocks are extracted and strung together, they are no longer in the old positions. This extension seems to be a bit buggy.

- **Lorum ipsum**

  This replaces flowed text with Latin nonsense to act as a space filler for laying out text. If no flowed text box is selected, it will generate text on your page.

- **Merge**

  This will merge selected text blocks into one text block. You can choose the order of the text blocks in different ways, and you can decide whether to keep the original styles, such as font. The new text block will be pasted on top of the old. Just move it away. This extension seems to be a bit buggy.

- **Replace font**

  This allows you to find and replace fonts in your entire document.

- **Split text**

  When you enter text, you are creating a single text object that maintains certain characteristics of spacing, font, and so on. This utility allows you to split the text into pieces by lines, words, or letters. All of the parts will then be piled up on top of the original—if you have checked the box to preserve the original.

Chapter **11**
Tracing Images

So far, all the vector drawings produced in this book have originated with the drawing tools of Inkscape. That's not all you may want to do with Inkscape. What if you have an image you've drawn with a pencil or pen on actual paper? What if you took a photo that you'd like to turn into a drawing suitable for a piece of jewelry? What if you've found a public domain drawing in a nineteenth century magazine or a raster drawing in a copyright-free Internet collection? Is there a way to turn these into vector drawings you could manipulate for use in your jewelry projects? The answer, as you might suspect, is yes—but there is no one recipe for success.

One thing we can say for sure is that the **only way to vectorize a raster** (bitmap) **image is to trace it**. Furthermore, any image brought into Inkscape from outside the program (including a hand drawn one) starts as a raster image unless you happen to have found a copyright-free vector image online.

The process you choose for vectorizing will depend on the characteristics of the source image. We'll briefly mention the two processes available to you after the source image is actually in the Inkscape program, and then we'll look at how the source image will influence your choice of process. Once that outline is done, we'll examine the processes in more detail.

Processes in Inkscape

- Bitmap tracing
  Bitmaps are the computer "maps" underlying all raster graphics. In Inkscape, bitmap tracing builds paths out of the contrasting colors of the pixels. This automated process for converting a raster image to a vector image can work wonders—but not miracles. For those of us seeking clear black and white results, success will always depend on the contrast in the source image.

- Hand tracing
  Once you've brought any source image into Inkscape, you can use the drawing tools of Inkscape to trace over the source image. Often the pencil tool works best. While somewhat time consuming, hand tracing is a good choice when there is too little contrast in an image to use Bitmap tracing or when you want to simplify the detail in the original.

How Your Source Image Will Determine Your Process

Photos or drawings with strong lines and boldly contrasting colors, especially light and dark, will work best for translation to black and white vector images. Since you'll be shrinking your image down to jewelry size, simplicity helps. An abundance of little lines will just become confusing blobs when miniaturized. Some of these can be edited out later, but that could be time consuming.

160

For our purposes, the very best raster images would be those you may not even want to bother to convert to vectors, namely, stark mono-color drawings like this one:

Most of the time, your original image will have shading or colors or complexities that make using it in its raster format problematic for our purposes. Some of these are still close enough to a black and white image that bitmap tracing will be simple.

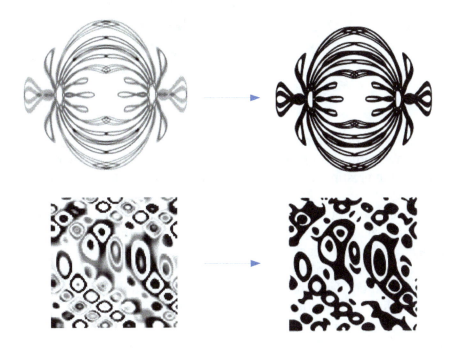

Even a fairly complicated landscape can be a good candidate for bitmap tracing with a little manipulation and persistence.

On the other hand, if the source image is made up of relatively large swatches of colors that, while very different, are nevertheless similarly pale or deep, it may not be a good candidate for bitmap tracing. You'll need to hand trace instead.

Remember that everything I say is based on the assumption that you're aiming for stark black and white. A goal of color vector images would call for entirely different strategies. With that in mind, consider the following digital photograph.

On the plus side, the image is fairly simple, with bold colors and not too much background mess. The curves of the dark green leaves produce a nice strong contrast with the flower shapes. With some cropping, the piece might be interesting, though the leaf on the lower right feels a bit unbalanced.

On the minus side, the flowers present relatively large expanses of one color, blue, which has a color saturation similar to the background. That is not likely to get us good lines. In addition, the image is a little blurry and the area at the center of each flower is muddy except for the bright yellow stigma. Ideally, what we want is a clear outline of the petals, perhaps a bit of veining, and good spots for the stigma, in addition to a leaf outline. Unfortunately, bitmap tracing is unlikely to achieve that. Here's the best I could do with bitmap tracing, although I tried various tactics.

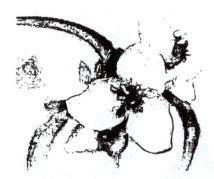

In this case, the best option is tracing by hand, which we'll look at shortly.

As you can see, your strategy for vectorizing an image will depend on a number of factors, and you may have to use trial and error before you will know how to proceed.

162

Getting the Image into Inkscape

No matter what method you are going to use to vectorize your image, the first step is to get it into Inkscape.

If you have a drawing or photo on paper, you will need to scan it yourself or have it scanned at a copy shop. A technician there will put the scanned file onto a USB stick or a CD, depending on what your computer can use. If you are given choices, have them save the file as a .PNG or .TIFF or even .JPG, and ask for at least a 300 dot resolution or higher. Try to avoid a .PDF file, which is trickier to work with. You might also ask if they can set the contrast higher. An alternative to scanning is to take a photo of the drawing with your phone or camera, although it is often difficult to avoid distortion and lighting problems. However you capture a digital image, save it to a folder on your computer.

Once the image is on your computer, you can import it into Inkscape. Inkscape can import nearly any image file format you are likely to meet. First open a new Inkscape file. Then, to import, you have several choices:

1. Open the file in another graphics program, copy it, and paste it into Inkscape, or
2. Open the file in the computer's photo view and take a screen shot:
   in Windows, **Shift + Windows button +S**; then draw a rectangle around the part of the image you want; paste it into Inkscape from the clipboard.
3. Drag the file into Inkscape from wherever it is on your computer, or
4. Use Inkscape's import command: **File** > **Import**. Follow the usual procedure for selecting and opening a file. Your picture should show up on the Inkscape screen.

If offered options for import parameters, just go with the defaults until you have reason to do otherwise.

Tip! Before you import into Inkscape, consider another possible step. If you know how to use a photo-editing program like Photoshop, Paintshop Pro, or Gimp (a free, open source graphics program), you may be able to improve the image for Inkscape purposes though it will definitely not be an improvement for photographic purposes. Be sure to work on a copy, not the original! What you want is as much contrast as possible and as little distracting background as possible. You may even want to do some erasing in your raster program, since erasing is relatively easy there.

Whether or not to use the photo-editing program to turn the image to gray-scale is another question. It's all a matter of line and contrast. Sometimes going gray-scale will help and sometimes not. You might even want to import two copies of the image into Inkscape, one in color and one in gray-scale, so you can experiment with each.

Bitmap Tracing

Find or make a raster graphic—or two or three—to use for practice and import them into Inkscape. To import, go to **File > Import**, select your file, and **Open**. Or you can just copy the image and paste it into Inkscape.

Always trace on a <u>copy</u> of your image. Remember to save often!

Select the image. In the notification box at the bottom of the Inkscape screen, you will see a description of what you've selected. It will say, for example,

Image 600 x 400: embedded in Layer 1.

This lets you know that what is selected is a whole image, probably a raster image, and tells you how big it is in pixels.

Tip! If you ever get mixed up about which image on your Inkscape screen is the original pixel version and which is the traced image, the Notification Area at the bottom of the window will tell you. The selected <u>traced</u> version will say "Select an image to trace" or "Path 480 nodes" or something similar. The <u>raster image</u> will say "Image."

Select your raster image and open the tracing dialogue by clicking **Path > Trace Bitmap**. The pop-up box will contain a number of tabs and settings.

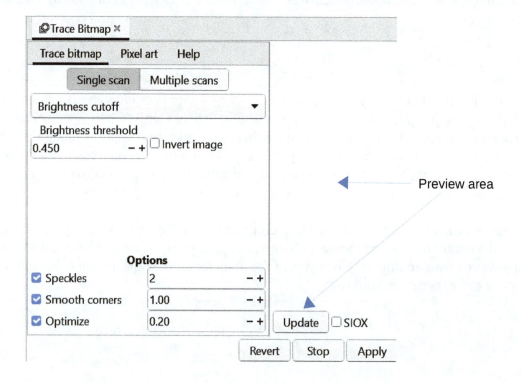

Preview area

The default choice is **Trace bitmap**, and that is what you will always want, unless you would like to check the **Help** section.

> **Warning!** Ignore **Pixel art**, unless you happen to be a gaming art enthusiast. Pixel Art is actually a relatively new art form based, as the name suggests, on pixels—that is, making the pixel squares extra visible, blowing them up so that each takes up a significant percentage of the drawing. Trying a pixel art trace on a normal size photo like the one above will win you a warning that such a large file will take a very long time. <u>It will absolutely hang up your computer</u>. Unless you have a need to scan a file that is only a few pixels in size, avoid this command.

To the right is a preview area. If you have selected an image to trace and if you click on **Update** at the bottom of the blank area, you will see a small version of what will result from the current settings. As you change the settings, you can press **Update** again to see the preview of the new result. Be aware that the preview probably won't look as good as the actual tracing. It will give you only a vague idea of what you would get.

If **Single scan** is selected, these choices are available with the drop-down menu:

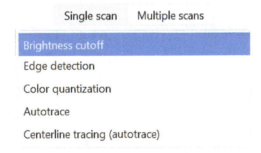

If the Multiple scans tab is selected, these choices are available:

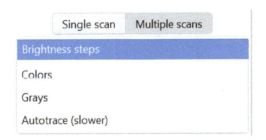

For our purposes, we will want **Single scan** > **Brightness cutoff** most of the time. This is the simplest approach to an image, although you will want to experiment with the other choices as well. Once you have had some experience you be able to better predict which of the choices will work best for your image and what you are aiming for. You may also encounter an element of surprise, sometimes serendipity, as you play with the variations.

The bottom left portion of the dialogue, **Options**, applies to all of the modes above. These options help to get rid of artifacts of raster images and minimize the number of nodes that will be generated—which in any case is likely to be very large. It's usually a good idea to use all of these, at least to some extent. They don't make a great deal of difference, but they're worth trying.

Options

☑ Speckles	2	− +
☑ Smooth corners	1.00	− +
☑ Optimize	5.00	− +

SIOX foreground selection at the lower right of the dialogue is meant to allow you to draw a line around the object you want to trace, add fill, and get rid of extraneous background. If you have the ability to erase around the edges in a raster program like Photoshop or Gimp, it's probably easier. If not, follow these steps.

1. Before you check the SIOX box, determine which mode and settings will likely work best for the part of the image you want to keep. You can try out and **Undo** various settings. Then make sure your best settings are on.
2. Use the **Pencil** tool to draw a line around what you want to keep. Adjust the nodes for a tighter fit if necessary.

Outlined with Pencil	Fill added to outline	End result after SIOX

3. 3.

4. Add a fill.
5. Lasso both the image and the penciled overlay.
6. Check **SIOX** and click **APPLY**.

SIOX will eliminate everything else and keep the part of the image you want, applying the trace in the process. If the unwanted background of your image is white or light colored, SIOX is an unnecessary step.

As you work with the settings in **Trace Bitmap**, experimentation is key. No image is likely to require the same settings as another, although as you gain experience, you may be able to guess what will work on which original.

Bitmap Tracing Modes

In this section, we'll use the same colored butterfly image above to look at the various tracing modes.

The first decision to make about modes is whether you want a single scan or multiple scans.

Tip! For all the bitmap tracing modes except Centerline Tracing, the result you get will be the <u>fill</u> of a path or paths, not the stroke. This is true even if you have chosen the edge detection mode. Once you have done a tracing, see what happens when you choose transparent for the fill and black for the stroke. You will clearly notice that tracing depends on the fill.

Single Scans

If you're aiming for stark black and white, wouldn't you always opt for the single scan? Not necessarily. The best bet, however, is <u>usually</u> going to be **Single Scan** and **Brightness cutoff**. You will need to play with the threshold number. The higher number, the darker the result.

Here is the photo of a butterfly we've been using.

This time I've edited out the background in a photo editor rather than using SIOX, so that we can consider the qualities, including color, of the butterfly itself. It's a high contrast photo, which is good. The right antenna is probably not going to show up, but that is easily fixed with an extra line.

To begin a scan, choose the mode and threshold, if applicable. Under the second tab, decide whether to **Suppress speckles**, **Smooth corners**, and **Optimize paths**, and how much for each of these. I've gone with the default for these. **Update** the preview. Make adjustments as necessary. Then click **OK**. The scan should take a second or two. The **Stop** button will fade out and the **OK** will come back to normal. The larger the original image in bytes, the longer the scan will take.

The original won't look much different—maybe a little darker. That's because the scan is sitting on top of the original. Just drag the scan to a blank spot on the screen and take a look.

Here's the result of a **Brightness cutoff** scan with a .530 threshold. You can see that neither antenna made it, but I'd rather have some white on the body, which would be lost at a higher threshold. The antenna can be added later.

If, instead of the **Brightness cutoff**, I try the **Edge detection** mode, I can get quite a different look.

Here, the lower the **Threshold** number, the darker the lines.

A nice feature of the single scan is that the black and white can be inverted. This, of course, makes a difference to a metal artist interested in which lines will be etched in the metal. In the image below, I have even added a white stroke to the fill of the image to make the white stand out more.

The third of the **Single scan** modes is **Color Quantization**. This works for color or gray-scale originals only, but produces a black and white image. Each adjoining color is assigned a value of either black or white alternately, with colors being defined by how many scans are chosen. This can produce interesting variations, somewhat different from the results from the other modes.

A few of the variations resulting from Color Quantization scans at different numbers of colors

Results from the **Autotrace** mode seem to be much like **Brightness Cutoff**.

Centerline tracing will be considered later. It is <u>not</u> a good mode for an image with large blocks of color, unless you are trying for an unusual effect.

Multiple Scans

Occasionally **Multiple scans** can produce a better result than single, but the process will require some fiddling. The advantage of multiple scans for those of us seeking clear black and white is that they can be taken apart and the parts isolated or reconfigured.

The four multiple scan options each have their uses. For example, if you have a color original and you want to get rid of a particular color, scanning in the **Colors** mode can isolate it so that it can be deleted or changed to a different color. In the butterfly example, I could extract the orange layer, delete it, and end up with holes (white) where the orange would be. Here's the extracted layer:

To demonstrate how "fiddling" might improve the results of tracing, let's consider a landscape that might be usable in a piece of jewelry. No attempts at applying a single scan were very satisfactory, so I will resort to a cut and paste process.

What I would want would be the tree, the mountains, and some foreground texture. The sky, though appealing, might not translate well into an etched or metal clay piece: the cloud lines might be confusing above the mountains. Instead, perhaps a moon, a flock of birds, or something similar could be substituted. It's possible to take elements of more than one tracing and combine them into something more satisfactory than a single tracing could yield.

Here is a summary of the process I will use:

1. Chose trace options: Mode is **Multiple scans**, **Grays**, **Scans** 6, check **Smooth**, uncheck **Stack scans**, check **Remove background.**

2. Click **OK**. Wait for the scan. Close the trace dialogue.
3. Turn off Snapping.
4. Drag the trace off the original.
5. **Select** the trace.
6. **Ungroup** the trace (all multiple scans are initially grouped).

7. Click outside the trace.
8. Click on the trace again and start dragging the layers apart. Since I checked Remove background (usually the lightest layer), there will be five layers, which are numbered here.

1   2   3

4   5

Layer 1 is mostly sky. I will delete it. Layer 2 has some mountain outlines, which I would like to preserve. The rest can go, because I like the more skeletal tree in Layer 5. I will use some Path operations to delete unwanted lines. Similarly, in Layer 3, I want the mountain lines but not the rest. In Layer 4, again I want the mountain. Layer 5 I will keep.

The next step is editing the layers I want to change a little. For Layer 2, I draw a pencil line around the mountains I want, rubber-band the whole drawing, click **Path** > **Object to Path** to make sure everything is a path, and then click **Path** > **Intersection**, to excise only the mountains and delete the rest.

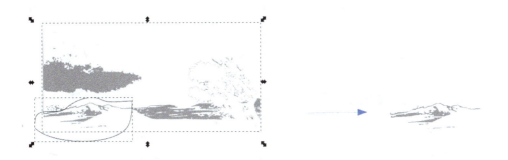

171

I do the same sort of editing on the other layers. Next I carefully put them back together and turn the fill black on the entire drawing. Then I **Group** everything so pieces don't migrate.

Now, if I wish, I can add a sky focal point and perhaps a frame.

When I am splitting layers apart, I prefer not to **Stack scans**. Stacking scans means that each layer is made up of its own paths plus the paths above it in the Z-order. I find it easier to deal with the layers individually, but this may be something for you to experiment with.

It is also possible to break each layer into its tiny component paths. To do that, select a layer, make sure it is **Ungrouped**, and then select **Path** > **Break Apart**. I assume that these tiny pieces must have been **Combined** by the program when traced, and thus the **Break Apart** command works. Deleting at this level could be another way of getting rid of unwanted bits and pieces, but be warned, the bits are many and easily misplaced.

A Special Use for Multiple Scans: Stencils

If you have a drawing composed of interwoven lines like the one below, you might have looked at the white/transparent spaces and wondered whether it would be possible to somehow turn those spaces into the holes that comprise a stencil.

If the spaces are big enough and if you make the stroke wide enough to separate those "hole" spaces sufficiently, the answer is yes—with a little fiddling.

We'll start with a very simple drawing with a row of horizontal waves and columns of intersecting straight lines. Those strokes will become the plastic or cardboard framework of the stencil. Depending on how large the final stencil will be, you may have to widen the stroke for strength. We'll leave this stroke for our example. Don't worry about the tails on three sides. If you don't want them, they will be easier to deal with later.

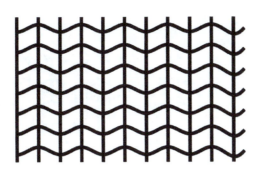

Next, we need a contrasting color rectangle to put under the drawing—an easily identifiable color. Just draw it over the black and white grill, and then send it to the back (**Object > Lower to Bottom**). We'll use red, since that is the color used by the popular cutting machine, Silhouette, for cutting lines.

 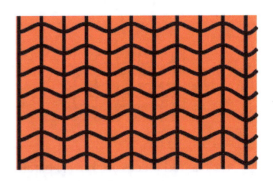

To make this procedure work, we next have to turn the two-color drawing into a bitmap/raster image so that it can be traced. By far the easiest way to do this is to use the snipping tool built into your operating system.

- First, make sure that the drawing is on white space in Inkscape, with no grid or guidelines behind it
- In Windows, press **Shift + Windows key + s**. After a pause, the screen will darken and the cursor will turn into cross hairs.
- Drag a rectangle around the drawing and release the mouse.
- In Mac, the command is **Shift + Command + 4**.
- The raster image is now on your clipboard. Immediately paste the image back onto white space in your Inkscape window.
- Select it.

- In **Trace Bitmap**, choose **Multiple Scans**, and beneath that, choose **Colors**. Under **Scans**, choose **2**, since we have only black and red. The rest we can leave at the defaults for now.

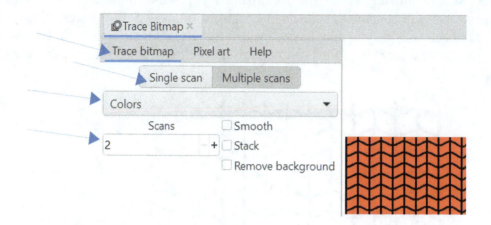

- Click **Apply**.
- Drag the new scan and the bitmap apart. Remember to look at the bottom notification line to know which is which.
- Select the scan and **Ungroup** the two colors.
- Click in white space. Drag the black off the red. You can delete the black or save it to use for some other purpose.

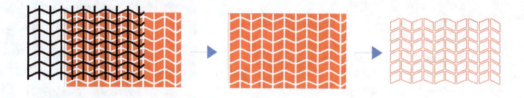

- The red pieces are now separate objects held together with **Combine**. If you wish to delete the extra bits around the three sides, first **Break Apart** the whole thing. They should now be easy enough to surround for deleting. With some designs, selecting with **Alt + Select Arrow** and dragging may work best.
- Add a thin red stroke and transparent fill for cutting.

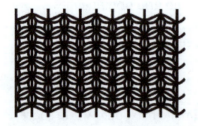  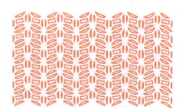

A slightly more complex design based on the same wavy and straight line grid

Centerline Tracing

The only bitmap tracing mode that yields a single line rather than a double line and fill is the **Centerline tracing** mode under **Single Scan**. If you have an image that is made up mostly of lines rather than fill, this may be the right mode for you, though the result will not necessarily produce crisp lines from many raster originals. Suppose we have a two-color image and want just the black lines. The Blackness Cutoff mode would work fine for the particular image below, but if we want to be able to play with the line thickness, we might be better off with Centerline, which traces down the center of any lines it detects. The lines are quite broken up, and the accuracy isn't perfect, but the mode does allow for easy alteration of the stroke.

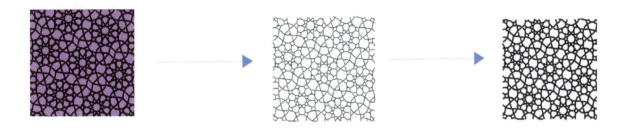

Cleaning Up a Badly Pixelated Original

Sometimes you'll find or make a charming design in a raster program, and it will be disappointingly blurry or ragged because edges are not pixelated properly. Tracing in Inkscape might (though not always) be a way to solve that problem.

Here, for example, is a pattern made in an intriguing little app that was created for Windows XP and hasn't been updated:

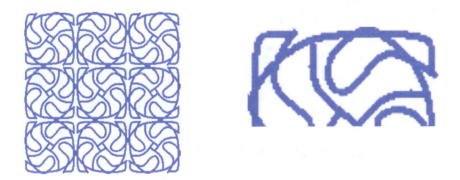

While it looks pretty good in the size on the left, if I wanted to use just one panel, or even four panels, it wouldn't make the best texture plate because of the ragged lines visible in the closeup on the right.

Also, the lines are blue, and in this bare-bones app, there is no black option. What to do? I might be able to fix some of the problems in a raster program.

Here I've used a raster program to blur the lines a bit to get rid of the ragged edges. But now, of course, the image is (surprise!) blurry and still not optimal.

Now, if I trace in Inkscape, single scan, brightness cutoff, this results

Very clear, if a little angular. With this setting, the color turns black and white. However, it's not possible to change the thickness of the lines easily.

If, instead of the single scan, I use the Centerline scan option, the result is this, once I've changed the lines to black:

One advantage to Centerline tracing is that the width of the stroke can be changed:

We now have a good, clear image, although a few irregularities remain.

Hand Tracing

There are two ways to hand trace an image to use in Inkscape. Hand tracing is used when the colors and lines of the original just cannot give you a good bitmap tracing.

- Trace the original paper image on tracing paper or plastic (such as a report cover) and then scan the newly traced image into your computer for Bitmap tracing.

> Or

- Trace on top of the raster image of the original in Inkscape using the drawing tools.

Let's return to the photo of the blue flower we looked at earlier in this chapter.

Tracing on Paper or Plastic

I have hand traced over a printed copy of the original on plastic and then scanned and imported it into Inkscape with a regular scanner. Printers often have a scan function you could use for this purpose.

Now all that remains is to **Trace Bitmap**. I've used a **Single scan** with **Brightness cutoff**, which works very easily on line drawings.

Now I can make whatever further adjustments I want, using all the tools of Inkscape.

Tracing with Inkscape Drawing Tools

Assuming the photo or other artwork is already in Inkscape in raster format as described at the beginning of the chapter, the question is how to trace over it by hand using the Inkscape tools. Here are a few suggestions.

- Use two **Layers**, one for the original and one for your tracing. **Layers** allow you to keep parts of a drawing separate, but they can also be used to lock an image or parts of an image so you don't move them around accidentally. I find it highly annoying when I want to manipulate a line I have just drawn on top of the original and I move the original instead of the line. The solution is to <u>lock</u> the layer with the original. To do this, bring up the **Layers** dialogue by clicking on the little layers symbol ⬓ in the second line of the Inkscape screen or by clicking **Layer > Layers** or **Shft + Ctrl + L.**

- Presumably, the original is already on Layer 1. You will see a tiny padlock symbol to the left of Layer 1 in the dialogue. Click it to lock. Now nothing on Layer 1 will move, nor can you add to or subtract from this layer until you unlock it. Add another layer. This can be done with the + sign toward the bottom of the dialogue. A floating dialogue box will come up. You can give your new layer a name, like "Lines" or "Top." Draw the lines on Layer 2, just as if you were drawing directly on top of the original. But now the original won't move around. If you ever wanted, you could make a layer invisible by clicking on the eye symbol to the left of the padlock symbol. You can also turn down the **Opacity** of a layer, making it partially transparent. If you are planning to use lines with different stroke widths, you could put those of one width on a layer and those of another width on a different layer. You can make as many layers as you want. Right-clicking on a layer in the dialogue will bring up a menu of possibilities.

- Work large. Use the zoom function to fill your Inkscape screen with all or part of the original. That way it's much easier to get detail—if you want it—and shrink it down later. You may find that the **Pencil tool** is the easiest to use. Remember to set the smoothing to 20 or more so that your lines will not be so shaky.

- Work with fairly short lines so that a sudden sneeze or shake of the hand doesn't mess up too much. You can easily continue a line by starting again at the little dot left by the old line.

- Set the stroke to a color that contrasts with the original to make it easier to see. You can change it later.

Once the lines are done, you can group them and move them off the photo layer. Then you can turn the lines black and decide whether you need to do further editing.

Tracing by hand within the Inkscape program is about as easy as tracing on paper with a pencil, even if using a mouse, and the advantage is that you don't have to scan or **Trace Bitmap**. If you want more natural looking lines, you might try the **Calligraphic pen** or the **Pencil tool** with a shape so that there is some variation in line width.

Another Process to Consider for Tracing

The **Paint Bucket Tool**

This handy tool found on the left hand tool menu will be a neat addition to your Inkscape toolbox. You'll find out more about how to use it in the next chapter, but you might want to be aware that some people use the **Bucket Tool** instead of **Trace Bitmap** to trace certain kinds of raster images. For our purpose of stark black and white images, I find **Trace Bitmap** to work better, especially on more complex photographs. Where the **Bucket Tool** shines is when the original is made up of only one color or a very few colors or where you want to end up with a line drawing composed of single lines, rather than the double lines produced by a bitmap trace's **Edge Detection**.

Here's an example of the **Bucket Tool** being used to trace a simple drawing pulled from the *Open Clip Art* website. This bird with a laurel twig was created by Netalloy in 2014.

First, the drawing is imported into Inkscape. The drawing is then zoomed to its maximum while still keeping the whole thing visible on the canvas. Try **View > Zoom > Zoom Selection** for this. Next, the **Bucket Tool** is applied by clicking over the body of the bird. The body outline will appear slightly larger because I have made the stroke of the new image visible as a red line, and that stroke takes up space. I've ignored the circle.

Once I've moved the original away and removed the stroke from the new version, I'm left with a pretty good vector version of the original, although a few of the laurel leaves have gotten lost.

We'll see more uses for the **Bucket Tool** coming up next, but for now, consider it as an alternative way to trace.

Chapter **12**
A Miscellany of Tools, Dialogues, and Settings

This chapter will be devoted to three tools not yet covered, as well as a few other features previously ignored.

The Bucket Fill Tool Revisited

In the last chapter, we looked briefly at using the **Bucket Tool** as a tracing device. Here we'll dive into the bucket a little more deeply. To work, the **Bucket** needs a boundary and that boundary must be complete—no openings—though it will likely be made of more than one intersecting path, like the circle and square on the left in the figure below. If we just had one path, we wouldn't need the **Bucket**; we could just use regular fill. When used, the **Bucket** actually draws another path inside the boundary, and that is where the fill goes.

Two objects intersect, making a fillable space.

Bucket fill creates an extra path within the space (no fill)

Fill added to new path

The **Bucket Tool** should work in any bounded space, whether there is another fill under it or not. The tool will fill the space with whatever current fill has been selected and that fill can be changed like any other fill. You are actually creating a new object.

I say "should work" above, because the tool is occasionally stubborn. The notification area at the bottom of the screen will tell you what is going on with the tool. If there is a "leak" in the boundary, the message will be, **Area is not bounded, cannot fill**. Rarely, you will get such a message even when you know the area is bounded. In that case, you might try fooling around with the settings and the fill, trying the tool after zooming in or out, or saving your work, closing the program down, and opening up the page again.

The tool will work at any level, no matter how many items are stacked on top of one another, and no matter whether the source of the bounded area is a raster or vector image.

To understand more about how the tool works, however, it is necessary to know a little more about what *bounding* means. *Bounding* is defined by by the difference in <u>color</u> between the bounded area and the boundary. When the **Bucket tool** encounters a color or shade or lightness that is different enough from the area being filled, the filling stops. You can set how much difference will be noticed by the tool.

When you click the **Bucket tool**, the tool controls will show up in the usual place just above the horizontal ruler line.

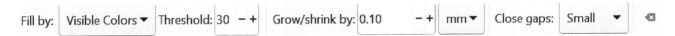

Fill by and Threshold

The first setting is **Fill by**. That controls what the tool will look at in determining where to draw the new path for the fill. The default is **Visible Colors**. That will cover most situations. As you gain experience, you may need some of the other options, but for black and white situations, you will likely only need them if you are filling over a raster image with fine color gradations.

The next drop-down menu is important. That is the **Threshold** number. To illustrate threshold numbers I'll trace over the blurry little raster pattern below. I will be attempting to fill the white areas, since they are interconnected. I could do the black areas, but since they are not connected, I would have to do them individually, and I surely don't want to do that! Since the white areas "leak" into the outside, I will have to put a box around the pattern.

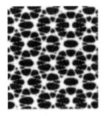
Unbounded

Bounded

Now, if I set the **Threshold** number low, say 2, the **Bucket tool** is very quickly going to run into a shade of light gray that will halt the process. All I get is a tiny blotch of white. Here is the little blotch enlarged with the stroke in black.

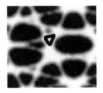

183

If I set the **Threshold** to the opposite, say 99, the Bucket tool will ignore all those grays until it runs up against something it will have to call black.

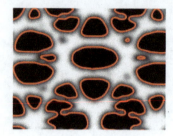

Here again is a magnified portion of the original with the Bucket result on top and the result's stroke changed to red, the better to see it. You can see that the tool has now ignored a halo of grays around the blotches. The process isn't perfect though, and for some reason a few of the smaller gray-black splotches have been missed. In this case, turning down the threshold a little did not help.

Now the result can be dragged off the raster original and filled, if it hasn't already been filled. The red stroke has now been reset to transparent (X).

Since I bucket-filled what had been the <u>background</u> to the splotches, that part is now black and the splotches white. If I want the same scheme as the original, I can fill the image with white and move the pattern onto a black rectangle.

Another thing that influences how an area will fill is how big or small you make the original <u>on the screen</u>. If you zoom it up until it fills the visible page, the fill will come closer to the edges of the shapes. If the original is small, there may be some gaps near edges. Take the squiggle below on the left, for example. It has been bucket-filled at two different zooms. Number 2 was small—zoomed out—when filled. Number 4 was large enough to fill the screen—zoomed in. In numbers 3 and 5, the filled result has been moved off the original. Note the filling gaps in 2, resulting in 3 not being true to the original.

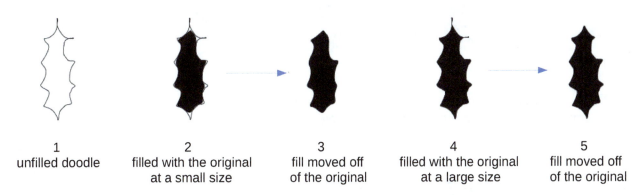

| 1 | 2 | 3 | 4 | 5 |
| unfilled doodle | filled with the original at a small size | fill moved off of the original | filled with the original at a large size | fill moved off of the original |

If you have only a gap or two, you can also just zoom to a higher size and click the bucket again in the omitted space. If you decide to do that, select the old fill result, and **Shift**-click with the bucket in the new area. That will smoothly join the new area to the old in one set of nodes, instead of having one image lying on top of the other.

Tip! To get the largest possible drawing on your screen, **Select** the drawing and then click **View > Zoom > Zoom Selection**.

Grow/Shrink by

This setting moves the stroke of the new bucket fill farther inside or outside of the boundary line. In graphic design this is known as inset and outset. Below is a simple rectangle drawn with a red stroke for visibility. Outside the red line is the black stroke of a bucket fill at 10 mm in the Grow/shrink option. Inside is the black stroke of a bucket fill at -10 mm.

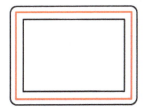

You will immediately see uses for this feature. First, **Grow** can sometimes be used (with positive numbers) if there are some unfilled spots and if your original lends itself to the rounding that will result. More intriguingly, **Grow/shrink** can be a fast way to construct concentric figures—certainly faster than duplicating and then shrinking or growing some and then aligning all of the results.

One design possibility is to use **Grow/shrink** with text. Here it's used repeatedly with a stroke but no fill.

Below, **Bucket Fill** has been used a second time to fill resultant cavities alternately, providing nice dark lines that would be better for photopolymer or etching.

Close gaps

The final drop-down menu in the **Bucket Fill** controls is **Close gaps**, and it is meant to do just that. Where there are tiny gaps in the boundary that may provoke the dreaded notification, **Area is not bounded, cannot fill,** this option may help. If you have used a geometric shape, the problem is unlikely to be tiny gaps, but if you are tracing a raster image, you may not be aware of some small gaps. Try these settings before resorting to other corrections.

The Reset

At the end of the drop-down menu is the **Reset** button. As usual, clicking it wipes the settings clean, resetting all the options to the default.

Filling More Than One Object

If you want to bucket-fill more than one object at a time and these objects are all touching, you can drag the bucket through the objects while holding down the **Alt** key.

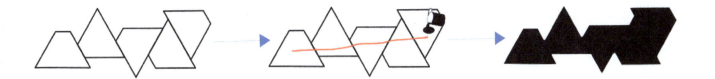

Turning Several Objects into a Single New Object

In the example above, you could consider the all-black figure to be a single new object. You will find the new object on top of the old pieces and can move the new object away from the old. The **Brush** tool can thus be used to create new shapes that you could save for yourself in a repository of shapes. The **Bucket Fill Tool** can be a quick way of joining components into a new whole. Consider this method of creating a simple silhouette flower:

Draw a circle, holding down **Ctrl**. For now, leave these unfilled so you can see what you're doing. Duplicate the circle four times to get a total of five circle petals. Arrange these in a circle so that their edges are just overlapping slightly. Don't worry about being exact, but as you move them around be careful not to skew them. If you do, use **Undo**. Now, over this figure draw another circle bigger than the others with the circumference running approximately through the centers of the other circles—or a little smaller.

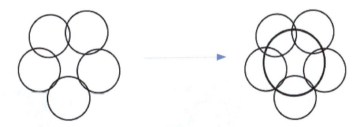

If you want to end up with everything nicely symmetrical, there is another menu we haven't considered yet that will help with this problem. Go to **Object** > **Arrange** (at the very bottom of the **Object** menu) to pop up another dialogue to the right. Choose the tab for **Polar Coordinates**. Click **Objects' rotational centers**, **Last selected circle/ellipse/arc**, and **Rotate objects** (not really necessary for this instance, but necessary if you have, say, ovals). Move the larger circle off the others so you can select it last, and then select all the circles, making sure the big one is last, since that's what you checked. Then click **Arrange**.

187

The circles should end up in this configuration, which will be symmetrical:

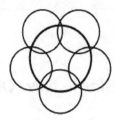

What has happened is that the program has used the large circle as the object on which to arrange the other circles. There has to be something to arrange the other items around. The larger the circle at the center, the farther apart the others will be. Conversely, the smaller the circle, the more the others will overlap. Overlap can be used to nice effect.

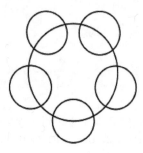

But what does any of this have to do with the **Bucket Fill Tool**? We were aiming for the first figure in this section. To get it, return to the five slightly overlapping circles and remove the center circle. Add a black fill. **Group**. Add a white circle and center it by selecting the group first, and then the white center circle. Click **Arrange**.

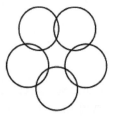  

To get the black part of the flower to be one shape forever, usable as such in other drawings, click with the **Bucket Fill Tool**. Add black fill and no stroke. Move the filled object off the original. You can test which is which: you won't be able to **Ungroup** the new object.

This process was made more complicated by learning to use the **Arrange** feature to produce symmetrical objects, but the basic principle of **Bucket Tool** filling to unify a new shape is really quite simple and can be useful if you want to accumulate some custom shapes.

The Spray Tool

This is another non-essential tool that is nevertheless very useful at times. It is used to "spray" copies of objects just as you would spray paint from a can. You can specify the width, density, rotation, randomness of the spray, as well as other parameters. What are you spraying? Any object that can be copied, meaning just about anything!

Suppose you want seven-pointed stars to show up in a random swath across a shape—maybe even the same shape, only bigger. Just draw a seven-pointed star, copy it, and spray by dragging.

The control bar for the tool is straightforward. As usual, pointing at each menu item will get you an explanation.

If you want more overlap of the objects, turn **Offset** down.

I have not found a way to keep parts of sprayed objects from overlapping boundaries of a shape. We would have to find a work-around, such as clipping.

Stars overlap the outline   Outline has been clipped

If you spray clones of an object, you can apply changes to the original and change all of the clones at the same time.

What you spray can be composed of complex objects:

Each sprayed object remains independent, so you can edit such things as position, size, and rotation if you don't like how or where an item landed.

The Measurement Tool and Other Measuring Tricks

Inkscape has various ways of measuring lengths and angles. One is the dedicated tool that looks like a stubby orange ruler.

If you hover the little ruler over an object, the basic measurements of the object's path appear in gray boxes. Length is the length of the entire path, wherever it may wander. Height and width are the vertical and horizontal measurements. X and Y tell the position on your page, measured from the top left-hand corner of the page. If you are hovering over a group, the ruler measures the group. If you want to measure just one item of the group, hover and press **Ctrl**, but don't click.

To explore the Measurement Tool further, draw a circle on your canvas. I have given mine a gray stroke so that we can see the little red measurement x's more clearly. Click the **Measurement Tool**. Let's start the measurement well outside the circle, dragging a diagonal line through it. The bold black numbers have been added so we can discuss what you are seeing.

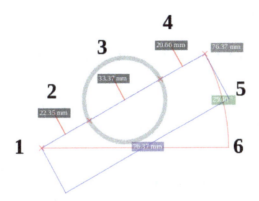

1. The measurement line started here at the x and was dragged to the red x beyond the circle at the top right, where there is a gray box giving the length of the measurement line in millimeters.
2. The number in this gray box is the length in millimeters between the start of the measurement line and the path of the circle. The tool ignores the width of the stroke. The red x's mark the beginning and end of this measurement.
3. The number in this gray box is the distance between the two "sides" of the circle. It may or may not be the diameter because I may not have drawn the line quite through the center of the circle.
4. The number is the distance between the circle and the end point of the measurement line, with red x's marking the beginning and end.
5. The number in the green box shows the angle between horizontal (3 o'clock) and the measurement line. You can pay attention to this number while drawing a measurement line to place the line at the angle you want. Angles always start at 3 o'clock unless you reset the preferences.
6. The measurement line between 1 and 6 is the radius of the angle being measured in 5. It is the same as the length of the original measurement line.

Those are the basics, but of course the tool control bar offers more.

Font Size: 11.00 − + Precision: 2 − + Scale %: 100.000 − + Units: mm ▾   Offset: 5.00   − +

Font size may be the first thing you'll want to change, so you can actually <u>see</u> those tiny numbers in the boxes. The only problem is that if you raise the font size, the boxes may start overlapping each other. Compromise may be required.

Precision refers to the number of places after the decimal you want to measure. Just how picky do you want to be?

Scale allows you to see what would happen to all of the measurements if you were to scale the size of the drawing up or down to a specific percentage. You can check this without actually changing the size of your drawing on the screen.

Units allows you to change the unit of measurement.

Measure only selected. When you measure with click and drag, this lets you measure only the selected objects and not others on the page.

Ignore first and last. This tells the tool to ignore the first and last points of the measurement. This allows you to let the program do the work of figuring out where a figure begins and ends. In the circle above, for instance, what you're likely to want to measure is the distance across the circle. But where are the points of beginning and ending? Placing those is made even harder by the width of the stroke. By starting the measurement line outside of the circle a ways and ending it beyond the circle, the program automatically figures out the points where it crosses paths. This **Ignore** feature just eliminates measurements that won't be relevant to what you really want to know.

Show measures between items. Suppose you have several figures in the line of measurement, as we see here. Do you want to measure all the distances on your measurement line, or only the distance between the first and last points of the drawing? This allows you to turn the internal measurements on or off.

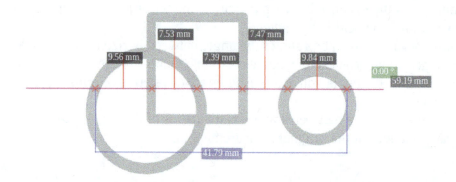

In the figure above, the internal measurements are turned on and the first and
last points are ignored. The measurement line is horizontal, so no angle is shown.

Show hidden intersections. This odd little symbol is supposed to be a closed eye. If you have a filled object on top of another object, you can choose whether or not to include hidden intersections in the measurements. In the first figure, the hidden edge of the circle is not measured. In the second figure below, it is.

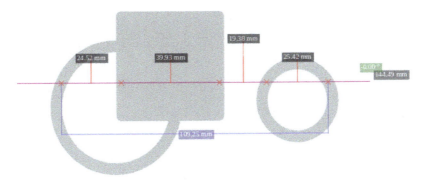

Hidden circle edge is ignored

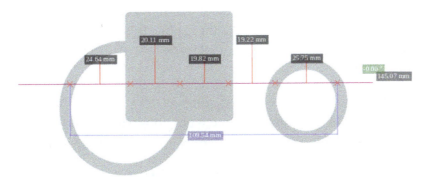

Hidden circle edge is measured

Measure all layers. This allows you to measure all layers or only the current layer.

Reverse measure. This reverses the starting and ending points of the measurement.

Phantom measure. This produces a grayed-out version of the current measurement. Then a new measurement can be applied on top, and presumably choices can be compared.

193

|/| **To guides**. This adds guide lines based on all the measured points in your drawing. It is especially helpful for positioning diagonal lines. The guidelines will persist even if the original figure is removed.

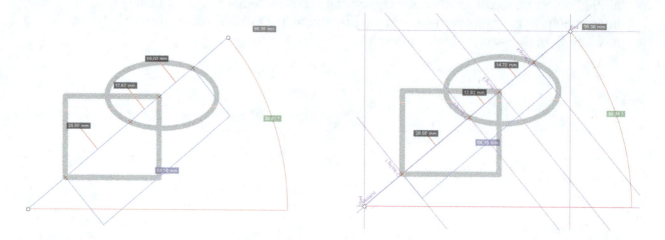

Any guidelines, no matter how they were created, can be removed with **Edit > Delete** all guides.

Convert to item. This turns a measurement into an object. If you don't use this, the measurement will go away with each new click. It can sometimes be useful to have the measurement as an object so that it can be reused later, or perhaps used in instructions as I have done in this section. You might even be able to use a measurement as a design element. Create some gears (see pp. 222, 279-80), add some measurements, *et voilà*! A steampunk hybrid?

Mark dimension. This turns a measurement line into a line object plus a measurement label object. You can do all the usual things to these objects, such as copy, rotate, enlarge, and so on.

If you draw a measurement while pressing **Ctrl**, you can draw a level horizontal or vertical line or a line that changes by 15 degree increments from the previous pause. There is a snap action like the action that occurs when you draw a perfect circle or square by pressing **Ctrl**.

The Arrange Dialogue

We looked briefly at the **Arrange** dialogue in considering a use of the **Bucket Tool** above. You will find some additional features of the dialogue useful in other situations where you need to exactly arrange various elements of a drawing. Most often, you will instead be using the **Align and Distribute** dialogue, but that won't allow you to put things neatly into circles or multiple rows or cause objects to abut directly or by a given measurement.

To try out some of the features, draw some objects and call up the dialogue by clicking **Object >
Arrange** (at the bottom of the list). There you will find two sub-dialogues: **Rectangular Grid** and
Polar Coordinates. The first puts objects into rows; the second puts objects into circles or arcs.

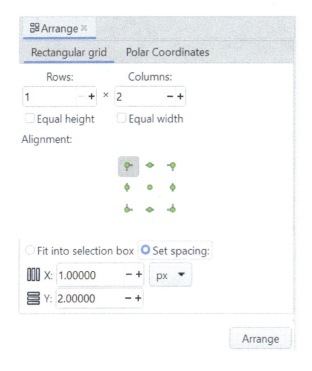
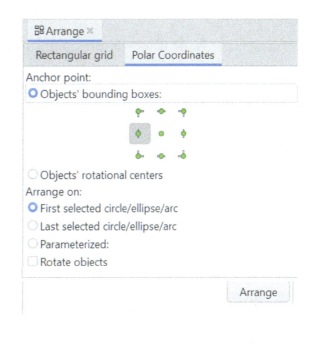

Rectangular Grid

Rubber-band all your objects and decide how many rows and columns you want and whether you want
them of equal height and width or not. If you have too many rows or columns for the number of
objects, Inkscape will correct you.

Alignment presents you with a grid of little green circles. These allow you to choose which part of
each object will serve as the point of measurement when the objects are arranged. If your objects are all
circles, this really won't matter; if the objects are irregular, and especially if they differ from one
another, it will matter. The easiest way to get a feel for how the alignment works is to draw a number of
irregular shaped objects with different orientations. Then try aligning them, first clicking on one of the
little green circles and **Apply**. Next, click on a different green circle and **Apply**. Repeat with a different
green circle. You will see the differences as the objects align slightly differently.

In the bottom third of the dialogue, you have a choice between **Fit into selection box** and **Set spacing**.
Let's say you have six objects. If you rubber-band all of them, there is a selection box around them,
indicated by the eight double black arrows surrounding the items. This is true even if there are
individual selection boxes around each item, indicated by the dashed lines. **Fit into selection box**

195

refers to that larger invisible box with the black arrows. If you choose this option, all the items will shift in relation to one another, but they will still be bounded by the same selection box.

Set spacing, on the other hand, allows you to choose the distance between objects horizontally (X) and vertically (Y).

You must click **Apply** before the program will operate on the objects.

Polar Coordinates

This second tab of the **Arrange** dialogue is for arranging objects in circles or arcs.

Let's start with the last half of your choices—Arrange on.

- You can put your objects on a circle, ellipse or arc—a control line you draw that the other objects will adhere to. Then you can keep that line or delete it. For this option, click either **First selected circle/ellipse/arc** or **Last selected circle/ellipse arc**. You select your control circle or arc first (or last) and then select the other objects before clicking **Apply**.

- Instead of using a control line, you can use numbers to exactly define how you want your objects to arrange. For this option, click **Parameterized**. This brings up another sub-dialogue.

  Center X/Y allows you to put the center of your figure exactly where you want it on your page. X and Y both start at the upper left corner of your page. Raising the X number starts the figure farther to the right; raising Y starts the figure farther down. This option will be largely irrelevant to you since you will be likely to moving figures around on your page anyway.
  Radius X/Y sets the radius of the figure, which will also determine how close the individual objects will be to one another, as well as the size of the figure.

  Angle X/Y sets the beginning and end of your arc (or circle). In Inkscape, an arc begins at 3 o'clock. If you put 360° in either box (not both), the objects will arrange on a circle. If you want a perfect half-circle arc, put 180° in the first box and 360° in the second.

Rotate objects should be checked if you don't want the objects to remain in their original vertical orientation. Here's the difference, using simple lines as objects. If the objects are circular, this command won't matter.

Not rotated   Rotated

Now, back to the first section of the Polar Coordinates dialogue. Here we have a choice between arranging objects on some point on the bounding boxes or else on the center point of the objects. If we choose the bounding boxes, we have the familiar grid of little green circles to choose from. Each of the nine points will result in a slightly different orientation. The middle circle will be essentially the same as checking the box for <u>Objects' rotational centers</u>. To illustrate what happens with three different orientations, I've drawn a simple stylized leaf using an elongated Star shape plus a line to indicate a stem, the better to show results on a non-radial drawing. I've duplicated it repeatedly. Since I'm going to arrange the leaves on a control circle, I've drawn that as well.

Here are the results when three different little green circles are chosen. I have removed the control circle so the "stems" and tips are more visible. **Rotate objects** is checked.

Bottom middle green circle   Top middle green circle   Middle green circle, left-hand column

In the first figure, the leaf stems start at the outside of the control circle. In the middle figure, the leaves are completely encompassed by the control circle. In the third figure, the circle ran through the left side of each leaf and the leaves are therefore skewed slightly.

Finally, here are the same leaves arranged on a control arc.

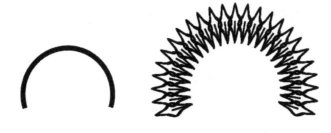

The Transform Dialogue: Using Exact Numbers to Change Drawings

Most of the time when we move, resize, rotate, or skew objects, we rely on the **Select Arrow** and our eyes. We can add the benefits of the **Measurement tool**, as well. If more exact changes are ever needed, however, there is a dialogue that will allow you to do everything by the numbers: the **Transform** dialogue. To open it, use **Object > Transform** or **Shift + Ctrl + M**. There you will find five tabs: **Move**, **Scale**, **Rotate**, **Skew**, and **Matrix**. All these should be self-explanatory except for **Matrix**, which we will ignore. Note that you can apply changes to objects in a group together or separately and that you can clear all the numbers you have entered with the **Clear** button.

Different Strokes

You've learned how to change the color and width of the lines you draw. You can also change other style elements of your strokes. Like stroke color and width, these style elements are available in the **Fill and Stroke** dialogue (**Object > Fill and Stroke** or **Shift + Ctrl + F** or on line two of menu symbols).

Look under **Stroke style**. **Select** the line to alter and click one of these possibilities.

Dashes: ──────── ▼ | 0.10 − +

Dashes: Choose from a variety of dot and dash sequences. The drop-down menu allows you to move the dots and dashes along the line. This will only matter where you need to change how the spacing or dot-dash combination begins or ends:

— ▪ — ▪ — ▪ — ▪ — ▪ — ▪ —

versus

▪ — ▪ — ▪ — ▪ — ▪ — ▪ — ▪ —

Markers: | ▼ | ▼ | ▼

198

Markers: These are little symbols attached to the beginning, middle, or end of the line <u>at the nodes</u>. If you need more markers to appear along the line, you may need to add more nodes for them to attach to. The size of the marker is dependent on the width of the stroke, so if the stroke is fairly wide, the marker may be larger than you want. The only difference between the lines below is the width of the line. The choice of marker size is the same. Extra nodes have been added.

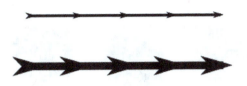

It is possible to add your own new custom markers, using **Object > Objects to Marker**. Simply draw a simple or complex object, select it, and click the command. You may have to shut down and reopen the **Fill and Stroke** dialogue to get the new marker to show up.

Warning 1! Make your custom marker quite small for starters. You can add larger versions after you see how the marker shows up.

Warning 2! Once you have created a new marker, there is no easy way to delete it from the list. You will have to go into the XML code.

Join: Corners can be drawn in different styles, rounded, beveled, or mitered, as shown in the options. The drop-down menu pertains only to the third option, mitering. If you had two lines joining at a very acute angle, it would be possible to have quite a long miter. This gives you a limitation option that so that the miter is cut off after a certain length. The higher the number, the longer the point can be.

<table>
<tr><td>Round</td><td>Bevel</td><td>Miter</td><td>Miter limited by
drop-down</td></tr>
</table>

Cap:

Cap: This determines the way the line ends. The cap has to do not only with the actual shape—squared off or rounded, but with where the node appears at the end. The round and square caps have a little extra shaping beyond the nodes; the butt cap, as the name implies, ends abruptly.

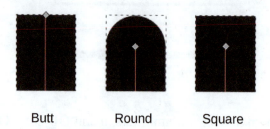

Butt   Round   Square

If lines are narrow, the type of cap may not matter much to your design, but as your lines get wider, they might be a significant element.

Order:

Order: Three different style elements. **Fill**, **Stroke**, and **Markers**, have to be layered in some order when you use them together. Do you want the fill on top of the stroke (especially when the stroke is wide) or vice versa? Do you want the marker to lie behind the stroke? The three elements make for six different possible orders. Most of the time, the first will be most desirable, but occasionally you might want to make a different choice.

Options for Fill

While we're on style options, let's take a look at an odd little setting that might easily be missed. Click on the **Fill** tab in the **Fill and Stroke** dialogue (**Shift + Ctrl +F**).

To the right of all the little square patches are two tiny horseshoe-shaped symbols. These control how the fill will appear in a figure made up of a path crossing itself one or more times.

Consider, for example, this doodle:

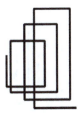

If we add fill, what will happen? The solid horseshoe on the far right below is the default: for <u>this</u> doodle, <u>all</u> the spaces will be filled.

You might recall that because the figure above appears to be an open line, when you add fill, Inkscape automatically closes the line so you end up with a diagonal between the two ends. Then Inkscape fills all the spaces, using a fill rule called **Non-zero**. Don't worry about this terminology unless you're a stickler for detail.

Now see what happens if you choose the fill option second from the right:

Inkscape has applied an **Even-odd** fill rule.

This option always gets you **Even-odd** filling if you have a single line. However, the default **Non-zero** option doesn't always end up with solid fill.

If the line reverses, then the esoteric **Non-zero** formula kicks in and you get a result like this:

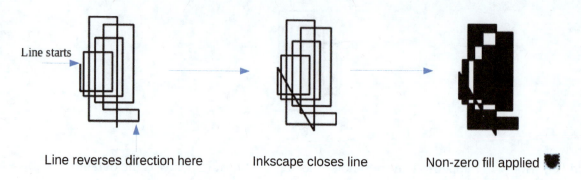

Line starts

Line reverses direction here   Inkscape closes line   Non-zero fill applied

Chances of your ever needing the **Non-zero** formula are probably nil. You're safe to leave the default at non-zero; just be aware that you have the rather neat **Even-odd** fill option when you want it.

Inset, Outset, and Offset

Inkscape offers four commands for offsetting your original image. These can be especially useful if your drawing needs a cutting margin for metal clay. They can also be used for designing with concentric lines. All of the commands produce only closed paths, whether the original was closed or not. If lines of the original cross, spaced shared by two or more crossing lines will <u>not</u> be offset. Use the **Bucket Tool** instead.

The first two commands replace the original drawing. That drawing disappears and you are left with the new path. If you want to keep both the original and the new outline, make a copy of your original first and then align and group the copy with the new outline after you inset or outset.

- **Path > Inset** draws an outline 2 pixels <u>inside</u> the original drawing.
- **Path > Outset** draws an outline 2 pixels <u>outside</u> the original drawing.

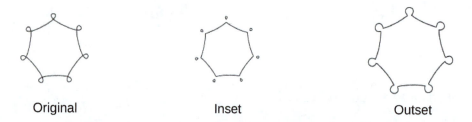

Original   Inset   Outset

These commands work on both shape objects and paths, but not on groups. If you want an outline around the outside or inside of several objects, use **Path > Combine** first.

The two commands above will be somewhat more faithful to the original than the next two commands. Both of the following commands work only on closed paths. If there is more than one element in the drawing to be offset, use **Path > Combine** first. Both of these commands will give you a node arrow, as well as a tiny white diamond handle at the top of the drawing. You can drag this handle outward or inward to outset or inset the drawing. The two commands produce somewhat rounded corners.

- **Path > Dynamic Offset** replaces the original with the new line(s) as you drag the handle.

- **Path > Linked Offset** produces new line(s) as you drag the handle but also leaves the old.

Dynamic Offset (Inset)

Dynamic Offset (Outset)

Linked Offset (Inset)

Linked Offset (Outset)

Depending on how much you drag the handle, you can get figures very different from these.

If you want a Linked Offset to become a separate object, use **Path > Object to Path.**

Tip 1! All of these commands will produce figures more faithful to the original if you size the original so it is large on your screen. The smaller the original, the more distortion you will get.

Tip 2! If it's stencils you're after, offsets have limited use. **Linked offset** works well if you need to produce more space between independent objects. It also works well when lines of objects do not cross. If lines cross, the results will be disappointing. If you had hoped to convert the spaces between lines into objects that would become the holes of a stencil, you will be better served by the **Bucket Tool**, which may be tedious, or by a tracing process (see pp. 172 ff.).

If you need to control your offset numerically, you can use the Live Path Effect **Offset**, treated in an Live Path Effect chapter coming up (see pp. 230-1).

On-Canvas Alignment

An alternate and rather limited way of aligning objects is meant to be constantly accessible from the bounding boxes of objects right on your canvas. By default, this feature is turned off. To turn it on, open the **Align and Distribute** dialogue and click the bounding box symbol in the upper left corner so that it is highlighted in gray.

Turning On-Canvas Alignment on

Once on, the feature is available if you select more than one object and then click through to a third type of **Bounding Box** with these double arrowheads around it:

Best for lining up objects along a vertical or horizontal line or piling objects on top of one another, the feature doesn't help at all for even spacing.

Don't try it for a group of objects like those on the left below. Note what happens when the center symbol is clicked. The objects are lined up horizontally through their center points.

Better suited are the following items, which all have a vertical orientation. They can be successfully lined up through the center points of each object by clicking the center x symbol. The spacing between objects doesn't change.

Clicking the center top symbol will line the objects up along their top points (their outside points), whereas clicking the center bottom symbol will line objects up along their bottom points (also their outside points).

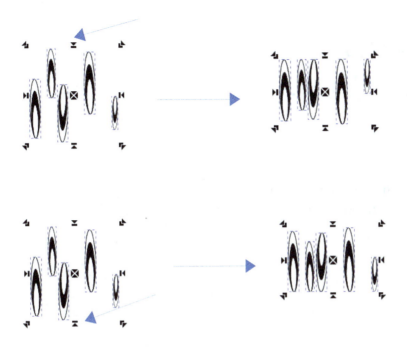

Clicking the center side symbols will just pile all the current objects on top of one another in a line down the side, but if the objects were horizontally oriented, then the side symbols would be the ones you'd want to use.

Shift-clicking adds other options. **Shift-click** the center x to arrange horizontally-oriented items in a line through their center points. **Shift-click** a center-side symbol to line items up by their inside points rather than their outside points.

The center x and corner symbols can be used for overlapping configurations. Here are a few simple shapes which could be nested to make a design:

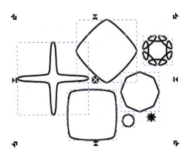

Clicking the center x once will line the objects up horizontally through the center points, as we have seen. If we then **Shift-click** the center x again, all the center points will be dumped on top of each other. In other words, all the objects will be concentric, resulting in this figure:

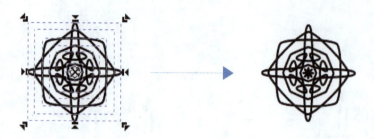

The corner symbols can be used for corner nestings. Clicking on the top right corner symbol of the grouping below yields the figure in the middle. **Shift-clicking** produces the one on the right.

Keeping Track of Objects

Often you may have a number of objects on your screen—perhaps even more than one layer. If you ever lose track of what layer your objects are on, whether they are clipped or not, or what the Z-order of your objects may be, there's a handy feature for discovering basic information about each object. **Object > Object** opens a dialogue that lists all objects on your screen in their Z-order. You can move objects up and down the Z-order list with the arrows at the bottom. The same list will tell you about any layers, and whether the layers are locked or visible, as well as whether any object is clipped.

Object > Object Properties allows you to attach extra information to any object. If, for instance, you want to remember details about how you created an object, you can add that information in this dialogue. You can also give the object a title that might be more descriptive than the path number which is automatically supplied.

Symbols

If you explore the odd nooks and crannies of Inkscape, you may stumble upon **Symbols** under **Object**. Unless you happen to need a National Park symbol or a word balloon, this feature will probably be of little use. It is possible to draw your own symbols and add them to the feature, but unless you take the extra step of putting them into the **User Symbols** folder of Inkscape's System folder, they will disappear when you close your document. This extra process will not be covered here, but it is analogous to the process used to preserve Paint Servers (see pp. 328 ff.). If you don't do this, using Symbols for your own drawings has no advantage over simply saving a copy of the symbol/drawing you have devised.

Filters

Accessible in the first command line, filters are used mostly to achieve a variety of shading effects on the fill of objects in a raster setting. Because they don't lend themselves to stark black and white, they won't be covered here.

Select Same

Occasionally you may have the need to pick objects out of an array by color or shape. I've done this when I've created a tiling in a different .SVG program that uses colors to produce patterns. If I only want the part of the pattern made up of objects of a particular color, I can, for example, select and copy only the blue objects and paste them onto the canvas as a new array. I can then turn them black if I wish. This has been useful in creating stencils.

Be sure everything in the array is **Ungrouped**. Select one of the target items. The command is **Edit > Select Same**. The drop-down menu then allows you to choose by fill or stroke color or both.

There's also an option to choose the same object types out of an array, meaning that you could pick out all the polygon Shapes or all the closed paths. A polygon Shape and a polygon path would be read as different. A four-pointed star Shape and a five-pointed star Shape would be read as the same.

Chapter **13**
Path Effects I

Inkscape now has more than 40 different effects for altering paths in some way, some more useful than others. **Path Effects** are also known as **Live Path Effects.** If you are seeking additional explanation online, you will often find these called LPEs. You have met a few of these in earlier chapters. All of the effects can be accessed with the command **Path > Path Effects** or **Shift + Ctrl + 7.** You will need to **Select** an object first. Now the **Path > Path Effects** command will start a dialogue in the usual area at the right of the screen. Clicking the + sign at the bottom of the dialogue will bring up a large new floating menu with an icon for each path effect.

Greatly reduced Path Effect window without experimental LPEs

Click on the down arrow below any of these LPEs. You'll see a blue box, at the bottom of which these icons appear:

Clicking the first icon brings up a very brief summary of what the LPE does. The star allows you to construct your own list of favorite LPEs while ignoring the others. The check mark opens the LPE in

the Dockable Dialogue box. You can also open an LPE simply by clicking on its icon. Some LPEs give you complex choices, others none at all.

If you would like to see the LPEs that have not yet been accepted fully by the Inkscape developers, move the slider button next to **Show Experimental** to the right until the button's background turns blue. Some of these LPEs may be of interest even though glitches are possible.

You can rearrange the icon menu so that it has larger or smaller icons or appears as a vertical list. The arrangement is controlled by the checkerboard boxes at the top of the menu. You can also star LPEs as favorites if you use them often.

As you work, be sure to **Save** often, since some of the LPEs are unstable. It's also a good practice to make several copies of the original path you want to work on, just in case. Sometimes the **Undo** command won't work or will produce unexpected results. So to repeat: **Copy** and **Save** often!

A few of the **Path Effects** work by changing the stroke to a path to add fill to it behind the scenes. These thus make it impossible to add further fill to what you might have thought was a fillable cavity. In those cases, you will have to use a work-around, such as the **Bucket Tool**. With the black and white images we're interested in, these instances will likely be few.

Path Effects are "Live" because many of them produce objects that retain the ability to be altered until they are stabilized with **Object to Path**.

In this chapter and the next, you'll find explanations for the **Path Effects** I consider might be in any way useful for the black and white images metal artists are looking for. The others may be useful for color art, but they will be ignored here. Even a few of those covered here might fall under the category, "Yes, but why?"

The user interfaces (the control dialogues) for some **Path Effects** may change with new versions of Inkscape, so if your version doesn't look just like the one in this book, don't worry. The changes will probably be slight enough that you will be able to figure them out.

Tip 1! If you're having trouble getting an effect to work, try **Path > Object to Path** and then run the effect again. Most LPEs work with shapes now, but there may be a few lingering problems with objects drawn with unconverted shapes.

Tip 2! Since these path effects are live, your drawing may continue to be subject to change even when you think you're done with an element. To stabilize an object and prevent further changes from an LPE, use **Path > Object to Path**.

An Index to All of the Path Effects as of Inkscape Version 1.11

Includes experimental LPEs labeled with a warning symbol because of possible instability

Path Effect	Page	Path Effect	Page
Pattern Along Path Turns an object into a series along a path, or a single stretched object along a path, retaining the curve of the path.	231-3	**Simplify** Reduces the number of nodes on a path, thereby smoothing it.	241
Perpendicular bisector (experimental) Draws a line through the center of another line.	233	**Sketch** Replaces a path with parallel "sketched" lines.	242
Perspective/Envelope Deforms an object along the straight lines of a rectangle or parallelogram.	233-4	**Slice** Cuts an object in two.	242-3
Power Clip Not covered.	–	**Spiro spline** Produces a curved line based on circles. Can be applied to a pencil line after drawing.	243
Power Mask Not covered.	–	**Stitch Sub-Paths** Adds paths perpendicular to two original paths. Good for hatching, duplicating lines, producing complex linear patterns and basket-weaves.	244-7
Power stroke Allows smooth bulging or tapering of a path.	234-5	**Tangent to curve (experimental)** Draws a line touching a curve.	247
Rotate copies Copies an original and rotates those copies around an axis. Good for making kaleidoscopic figures.	236-40	**Taper stroke** Allows tapered but straight widening of a path.	247
Roughen Makes a smooth path irregular.	240	**Transform by 2 points** Allows stretching or contracting of an object along a line.	248-9
Ruler Adds ruler ticks to any path.	241	**VonKoch** Produces some fractals and complex cloned images.	249-53
Show handles Produces a vector copy of nodes and handles visible when in node mode.	241		

Angle bisector (experimental)

Of minimal usefulness, this path effect draws a line through an object, using the angle formed by the first three nodes as the starting point. There will be a tiny circle near the new line—a handle that can be used to drag the line in other directions. This LPE deletes the original object, so if you want to keep this object as well as the line, be sure to **Duplicate** the object first (**Ctrl D**).

Attach Path

Perhaps an animator might find this LPE useful, but most users will find this a novelty rather than a convenient option.   Before you use this method, ask yourself if you can achieve the same result with considerably less trouble by grouping, layering, or combining.

Paths with a T or Y branch are not native to Inkscape. Currently, the only way you can join a branch to a path at the node level is with this path effect—and it's pretty unstable, with the connection easily broken.

Here's the process.

1. Draw the paths you want to join. These can come from shapes turned into paths, if you wish. One path will be the main line (the receiver line); the other will be the branch that the path effect will control.

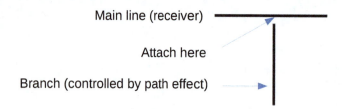

   Path direction matters for where the branch line will attach. Here the main line was drawn left (start) to right and the branch was drawn top (start) to bottom. If you need to reverse the line direction, use **Path > Reverse**.

2. Copy the main line (receiver) to the clipboard.

3. Open the Path Effects dialogue (Shift +Ctrl + 7). Select **Attach Path** from the menu. Throughout the dialogue, "path" always refers to the branch, not the main line.

4. Add a Start path number. This is the point on the main line where you want the new branch path to start. Here's how to figure out the number. In our example, the main line has only one segment. The first node at the beginning (left) of the segment is numbered 0. The node at the end of the segment (right) is numbered 1. If we want the branch to intersect halfway in between, that's .5. Enter that number as the Start path number. If there were more nodes in the main line, the number would be counted accordingly. Alternatively, you could add a new node to the middle of the main line exactly where you want it. In that case, the number would be 1.

5. The dialogue assumes that the branch line will have a curve, and the join may actually be more stable with a curved line. The angle is how the branch line attachment will be curved. We'll keep the angles at 0.

6. The distance of the curve seems to affect the distance of the gap between the point of contact and the start of the branch line. If the lines are close, as in our example, too long a distance will make for a convoluted join. I have left both distances at 0. If you insert a distance that is impossible, Inkscape will crash.

7. To execute the join, click the little **Link to path** icon next to **Start path**:

To test that the join has happened, you can drag the receiver path around. Don't do that with the branch path: it will detach.

It's also possible to link to a third path at the other end of the branch path. That's what the **End path** part of the dialogue is about. The process is exactly the same.

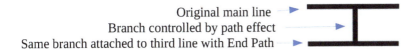
Original main line
Branch controlled by path effect
Same branch attached to third line with End Path

Bend

Use this to bend a path into pleasing curves. While the menu allows pasting of a curve from the clipboard onto the path you want to curve, it's much easier to use the node bending tool.

First click the path you want to curve, and then click the node arrow symbol in the dialogue.

A green line though the path will appear. This line can be moved this way and that to curve the line as you wish. Once the line begins to curve, handles will appear to help with the adjustments. The figure below is a single path.

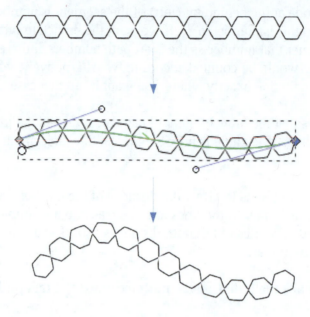

The effect will even work on grouped or combined paths, though the distortion may be worse. The node method will work on a single vertical path; the only time you need to check the vertical option is when you are using the paste method or targeting a group.

Boolean Operations

You've already met these operations, also called **Path Operations**, in Chapter 9. For most of your needs, those commands under **Path** will do the job simply and quickly. This recent LPE, however, does offer some new features you might like.

The major advantage is that the operations are "non-destructive." That is, once the operation is complete, you can still go back and edit the original objects. You can also move the "cutter" around to experiment with other configurations. Even after you've moved on to drawing or editing another object on your screen you can still go back and drag the cutter or edit the nodes. The trade off for this increased flexibility is a slightly more complicated menu.

You'll need two and only two paths or shapes. For all the operations except Union, I like to think of one as the "cutter" and the other as the "target," though that is not accurate in mathematical terms.

Copy the "cutter" to the clipboard before you go to the LPE. (With Union, it doesn't matter which you copy.)

Select the "target."

Choose **Path > Path Effects**. Click + for the menu, and then click **Boolean Operation**. From the first drop-down menu, choose the Operation you want: Difference, Division, Intersection, Symmetric Difference, or Union. Symmetric Difference is called Exclusion in the older Path Effect menu.

Next, click the yellow clipboard symbol above this menu. The operation will occur.

As mentioned, you can move the "cutter" around if to try out different positions. If you can no longer see the "cutter," click on the little "Select original" icon in the "Operand path" line. That will bring back the bounding box of the original object, so you can see what to move around.

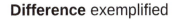

Difference exemplified

 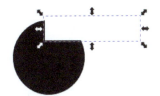 

Two objects: white will be "cutter" and be copied to clipboard.

Operation is complete after clicking on yellow clipboard symbol

Move "cutter" around as desired.

Switch operands if desired. Circle becomes "cutter."

You can also change from one operation to another simply by selecting it in the list of operations. If you want to switch which object is the "cutter," check "Swap operands."

The "Remove inner" option is only relevant for those who are being careful about bytes. The "File type" options would be relevant for more complex figures with varied fill.

Bounding Box

Not covered here.

BSpline

This effect was covered on pp. 55-8 in the discussion of the Bezier pen. The effect can also be applied to a pencil line after creation.

Circle (by Center and Radius) (experimental)

This LPE draws a circle based on two nodes of a path you have selected. The center of the circle will be at the first node of the path. The circumference of the circle will pass through the last node of the path. The original path will disappear, so if you want it preserved, duplicate it. The LPE does not work if the path is closed, as in a square or circle.

Circle by 3 Points (experimental)

Like the previous LPE, this draws a circle, this time based on the first three nodes of the path. Again, the original path disappears: to preserve the original, duplicate it. Unlike the previous LPE, this one works on a closed path.

Clone original path

This is handy if you haven't kept a copy of an original path before you started adding path effects.

1. To use it, copy the target path—the present path with its path effect(s)— to the clipboard.

2. Next, draw a simple path to be a sacrificial path. It will disappear when the action is complete.

3. Select this new path and add the **Clone original path** effect to it. No change will be visible.

4. Choose **Without LPE's** from the drop-down menu if you just want a copy of the original object.

5. Now click the first symbol next to **Linked path**. This is labeled, amazingly, **Link to path**. A clone of the original will now be found somewhere on the canvas. Most likely it will be on top

of or under the target path. However, if you've duplicated the target path or moved it around quite a bit on the canvas, the clone could be elsewhere on the canvas.

Target path with path effect   Sacrificial path   Original path dragged away
from target path

Construct Grid

A convenient way to construct a grid with as many squares across (X) and up and down (Y) as you want. Start with a sacrificial path with at least three nodes. The resulting grid may initially be skewed toward a parallelogram, but it's easy enough to straighten it out with the bounding box arrows. Unlike the grid you set with your page (**View > Page Grid**), this one is visible when printed.

Corners (Fillet/Chamfer)

Here's a handy way to make decorative changes to the shape of angles. *Fillet* and *chamfer* are terms used in engineering and woodworking. A *fillet* is a rounded corner; a *chamfer* is a corner that has been sliced off or beveled with additional oblique angles. This Inkscape LPE offers fillet and inverse fillet, chamfer and inverse chamfer.

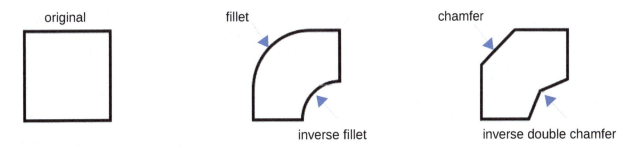

original   fillet   chamfer

inverse fillet   inverse double chamfer

Select an object and click **Path > Path Effects**, click the + as usual, and then choose **Corners (Fillet/Chamfer)** from the menu. Click the **Node Arrow**.

Once the path effect is active, you could actually operate it for fillets without making any changes to the dialogue at all. That's because the effect works by using the Node Arrow to drag the little "knots" that have appeared at each corner.

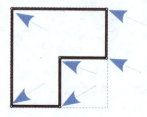

Tiny control knots at
each corner

A knot dragged with
node tool

Corner arc after
releasing node tool

By dragging a knot without altering the dialogue, you will automatically get a perfectly symmetrical arc, producing a rounded corner, or fillet. However, to produce a chamfer or inverse fillet or inverse chamfer, you will need the dialogue. The dialogue will also allow you to produce Bezier curves on the fillet and inverse fillet.

The dialogue initially looks like this. If you decide you'd prefer to set other defaults that would better suit your work, you'll find a command at the bottom to change these default values.

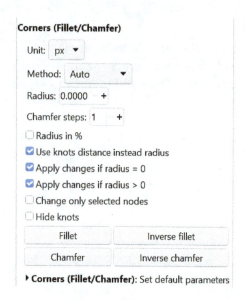

You can set the **Radius** of your fillet or chamfer if you need exact measurements. If you do that, consider changing the **Unit** from **px** to **mm** or some other unit: pixels are awfully small and may not show up until your numbers are high.

The easiest way to use the LPE, however, is by dragging the knots with the **Node Arrow**. If you want to fillet or chamfer more than one corner, **Shift + Select** the relevant knots. Be sure to select **Fillet** or **Chamfer**, etc., in the bottom boxes. You can switch from one to the other.

Method controls the kind of fillet line you will get. **Auto** produces a balanced line, as does **Force arc**. **Force bezier** makes a bezier line possible. It will not be as rounded as the arc and can be dragged into graceful curves.

In the figure below, notice that the two Bezier curves on the right are more gradual and less

218

symmetrical than the arc on the bottom left. In the latter, the arc line was "forced" beyond the original line to maintain the symmetry of the arc.

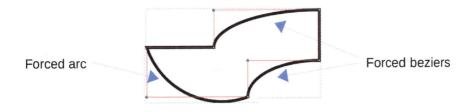

Forced arc   Forced beziers

If you have been operating on more than one corner at once and you want to change fewer knots than you have been changing, check **Change only selected nodes**.

Now, as for **Chamfer** and **Inverse chamfer**, you can use the **Node Arrow** in the same way, but the **Radius** also works. Arcs are obviously irrelevant. What's new is the setting for **Chamfer steps**. To illustrate, I have drawn and duplicated a simple angle, shown at the far left below. The blue line is a guideline that shows how far I dragged the knot. The objects are numbered, the better to identify the process used on each. You can see that **Inverse chamfer** is only relevant when you have two or more **Chamfer steps**. You can't have an inverse chamfer with a single step.

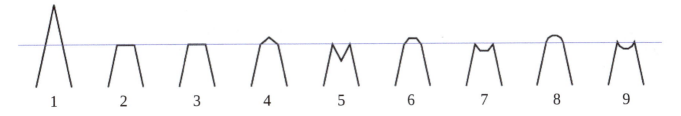

1   2   3   4   5   6   7   8   9

1. The original angle.
2. Chamfer with 1 step.
3. Inverse chamfer with 1 step. Note that at 1 step, inverse chamfer does not differ from chamfer.
4. Chamfer with 2 steps.
5. Inverse chamfer with 2 steps.
6. Chamfer with 3 steps.
7. Inverse chamfer with 3 steps.
8. Chamfer with 4 steps. Hard to see at this size, but there are four short sides in the chamfer.
9. Inverse chamfer with 4 steps. Hard to see at this size, but there are four short sides in the inverse chamfer.

Design possibilities with this LPE abound. For instance, it provides an easy way to make fancy lines or frames. In the example below, a symmetrical jagged line created with node manipulation, as in Chapter 6, can be further manipulated to produce intricate crenelation like this:

Dashed Stroke

Plenty of dots and dashes are available through the standard **Fill and Stroke** menu (**Shift + Ctrl +F**), and will probably provide all you'll ever need. However, this LPE gives you more exact control over the size of the dashes and where they start and stop. The disadvantage is that the dashes produced by this LPE don't count as a stroke that can be filled. If you need a fill, you'll have to put another strokeless but filled object behind the dashed object. Alternatively, you can use the **Fill Between Many** LPE, which is not covered here.

Ellipse by 5 points and Ellipse from points

Probably not very useful to jewelry artists, these two path effects may have been devised to aid with hand-tracing ovals or circles that show up in graphic art: eyes, for instance. **Ellipse by 5 points** is simple. Just draw an object or a zigzag line with five nodes, add the LPE, and bingo, you'll have an ellipse if, and only if, an ellipse running through those five points is possible. **Ellipse from points** offers many more options, including different kinds of ovals and arcs. These are more or less explained by commentary when you point at each option.

You can put the original, probably a raster image, in a separate layer, and then draw on a layer above the original.

Ellipse from points is useful for graphic artists looking for help in drawing ellipses with perspective.

Envelope Deformation

This effect was covered in Chapter 10, the **Text** chapter (see pp. 150 ff.), but you can deform any object or group of objects, not just text, as long as it is a path. Use **Path > Object to Path** if your figure started out as a geometric shape.

The distortion will differ depending on whether you enable only the top & bottom or the left & right paths, even if you only bend the path of one of those pairs.

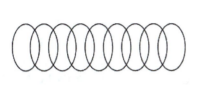

Original group of ovals

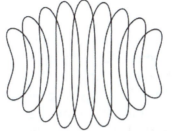

Top and bottom bent with only top and bottom enabled

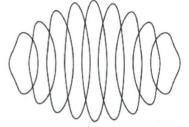

Top and bottom bent with all four paths enabled

Extrude (experimental)

Need a 3-D illusion? This projects an extra face for an object, and then draws sides between those faces.

The **Distance** setting involves the "depth" of the 3-D object; the **Angle** moves the orientation of the object.

Fill between many and Fill between strokes

Not covered here. Useful mostly for colors.

Gears

Inkscape provides two different ways to draw gears. This path effect provides for gears that interlink along a path. In an **Extensions** chapter, we'll look at an extension with more controls for the individual gear. Still, this one is probably quite adequate for our purposes. To run it, you need to draw a path with several nodes and select it. Add the effect. Gears will be drawn immediately, but you can alter their appearance with the drop-down boxes. The distance between the nodes will control where and how large the gears will be. For instance, the path below, left, will produce the gears shown, with the following numbers in the boxes: Teeth, 10; Phi 5; Min Radius: 5.

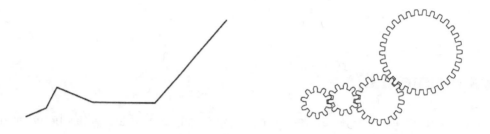

Teeth controls the number of teeth in the smallest gear. **Phi** controls "the ratio of teeth not in contact," which seems to amount here to the shape of the teeth—the higher the number the more pointy the teeth. **Min Radius** controls how small the gears can be. If you make the radius too big for the path, the gears will overlap.

You can, of course, add to this batch of gears in any way you like. If you want the gears as separate objects for your use in further drawing, you can take the set apart. First click **Path** > **Object to Path** and then **Path** > **Break Apart.**

Hatches (Rough)

To use this effect, you need a single path with some volume to hold the hatches. Any shape will do, as will any line with a little curve. The path will disappear when the effect is applied, leaving only the hatches. If you are filling a drawing with hatches, add a "sacrificial" path inside it to hold the hatches so the drawing doesn't disappear.

The effect comes with many options. Try out the settings and see what you like. The lines have both stroke and fill.

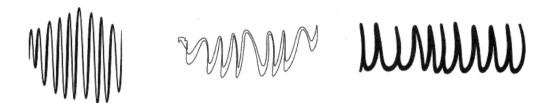

Interpolate Points

This effect changes a path into a different shape based on various mathematical formulas. It's probably of minimal interest, but you may find one or two good uses for it, such as drawing rectangular spirals.

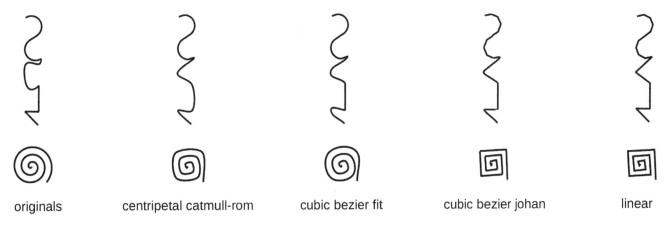

| originals | centripetal catmull-rom | cubic bezier fit | cubic bezier johan | linear |

The fifth option, **Spiro Interpolator**, appears to be quite impractical for us, since it produces an impossibly stretched vertical figure.

Interpolate Sub-Paths

In this effect, one object morphs into another, showing the stages along the way. Let's start with a triangle and a star. I have left some space between the two to contain the resulting stages, or sub-paths. The next step is to **Select** both and **Combine**. Add the **Path Effect**. The default number of steps is 5, but this can be changed as high as thousands, though that would probably turn the result black because the figures would be so close together. Here's the result at 5.

The **Trajectory** arrow adds a handle that can be dragged to allow greater or smaller spaces between the objects. The handle can be rotated and the trajectory line can also be dragged into a curve.

While changing a triangle into a star is really just a novelty effect, there are more practical uses.

You can easily produce numerous copies of an object and neatly line them up. You can also quickly produce hatching if you need it. You can even make stylized hair.

 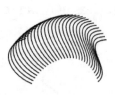 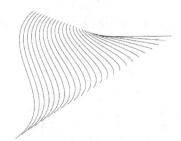 

Still more possibilities are available by starting with concentric objects. Here's the result of two concentric triangles dragged into different configurations with the trajectory arrow.

Join Type

If you need a joint between two path segments that isn't covered by the usual joins in the **Stroke Style** dialogue of **Fill and Stroke**, you may find one here. Most of the options are for tightly angled curves like the ones below. They don't work on straight angles. An ordinary beveled join is shown first. The other four are especially for curves.

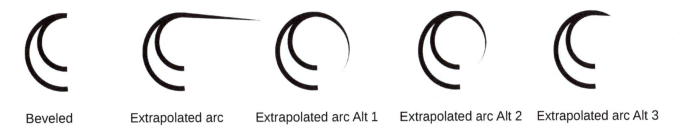

| Beveled | Extrapolated arc | Extrapolated arc Alt 1 | Extrapolated arc Alt 2 | Extrapolated arc Alt 3 |

I find that the miter limit doesn't work well.

Knot

If you're into Celtic designs, you may find a use for this effect. It creates the appearance of a break at each crossover.

The dialogue allows choice about three things: the size of the gap, which line is on top at each crossing, and whether you want gaps in both crossing lines.. The easiest way to set the gap size is by the **Fixed width** drop-down menu, where you can watch your drawing as you raise or lower the number to a gap you like.

The **Switcher size** drop box is relevant when you click on the **Node Arrow**. You will see a round blue circle over one of the line crossings. So that you can see the circle better and see which crossing you are working with, you can make the blue circle larger or smaller with the switcher size. The circle will have a tiny white (or possibly green) diamond in the middle of the crossing. Don't mistake it for a node. Clicking that diamond will cycle you through three choices: one line on top, the other line on top, or no breaks. The blue circle will have an arrowhead that may help you keep track of what's on top.

You can change the shape of the end caps in the **Stroke Style**. Sometimes, especially if you have an acute angle, rounded caps will work better. Unfortunately, there is no option for a cap beveled to just one side, which would often make for a neater design. You could, however, tweak that when everything is done by using the node tool.

After, not before, you have finished getting your drawing exactly how you want it, including stroke width, it is possible to change the drawing to an outlined figure. Click Path > Stroke to Path. Don't panic when you get a black blob. Adjust the fill color (probably none), the stroke color (probably black), and the new stroke width (much smaller).

Lattice Deformation 2

This effect provides a grid of drag points for pulling an object in many different directions. Select the object, add the Path Effect, and click the Node Arrow. The grid will appear, along with the numerous drag points.

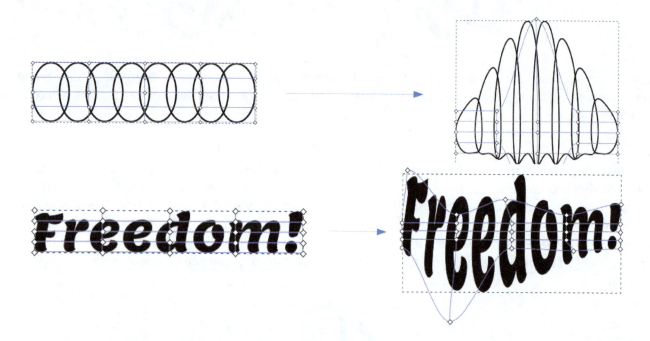

Click outside the object, and the grid disappears.

226

You also have the option of mirroring the drags horizontally or vertically or both, making symmetrical changes to an object very easy. If you have enough computer power, you can check **Update while moving knots**, which will better allow you to see what your drags are doing.

Line Segment (experimental)

Not covered here.

Measure Segments

We've already seen various ways of measuring parts of a drawing. If you want to make measurements visible in your drawing, this is a good way, but it works only for line segments. Here's one example:

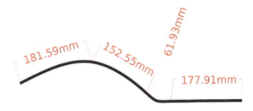

A number of options are available in the settings for this LPE. If the measurements show up very faintly, increase the line width and font size.

Mirror Symmetry

symmetry

To get these reflections, you could make copies, flip them, and position them. You could use tiling. Or, if you don't mind leaving **Text** and converting to a path, you can use this **Path Effect** a couple of times. The effect also gives you sculpting options hard to achieve in other ways.

Mirror symmetry copies and mirrors the original exactly once, but you can, of course, apply it more than once for additional results. This **Path Effect** does basic reflection on geometric shapes as well as paths, but if you want to be able to do the mirrored sculpting covered below, the original must be a path. This effect does not work on unconverted text.

The **Mode** drop-down menu is the key to this effect. The default is **Free from reflection line**, which is the most flexible option. We will return to this in a moment. All the modes provide a reflection line, which can be seen below:

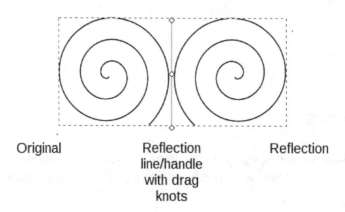

Original   Reflection   Reflection
line/handle
with drag
knots

In the figure above, the original spiral is on the left. The reflection is on the right. The blue reflection line or handle in the middle will appear when the **Node Arrow** is on. The little diamond-shaped knots on the handle will allow you to drag in one direction or another, depending on what the mode allows. It is possible to switch from one mode to another in the middle of an operation to get the advantages of each.

Horizontal and **Vertical Page Center** are both oriented from the center of whatever **Page** you have set up on your canvas. Let's assume an 8 1/2" by 11" page for our examples. The Horizontal mode draws the reflection line across the page through the center. The Vertical mode draws the reflection line down the page through the center. No matter how close or how far the original object is from the center— even out beyond the page boundaries—the reflection will be drawn an equal distance from the center on the other side. These are the least flexible modes. The handle doesn't allow any changes unless you switch to a different mode.

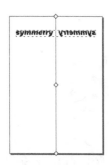   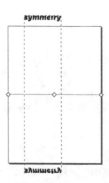   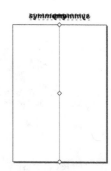

Vertical Page Center with the   Horizontal Page Center with the   Original is so close to the center line
original within the page boundary.   original above the page boundary.   that the reflection overlaps.

The modes **X** and **Y from middle knot** allow you to move the two mirror images back and forth along the X axis or up and down on the Y axis. Again, a reflection line/handle appears between the original and the reflection, but it is not tied to the page. The figures can be anywhere. Here is a spiral on the X axis. Dragging left or right on the middle knot will bring the figures closer together or farther apart. The other knots are inactive.

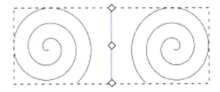

The mode **Free from reflection line** allows other movement. Rather than just moving on the two axes, you can now move freely in any direction from the reflection line. The center knot allows for movement along the two axes, while the end knots allow rotation. When one end knot is dragged, the other serves as an anchor.

If you check **Fuse paths,** the original and mirrored paths will fuse as you drag the original and copy closer together, making for a different, unified figure. Opposite fuse makes the reflection dominant in the fuse. Fuse paths can be applied after you have completed a figure, as well as well as while you are moving things around.

In all the modes, the regular nodes on the original path are also active when you have the **Node Arrow** selected, as long as the object is a path. That makes it possible to sculpt one side of what is now a two-sided path and watch the other side mirror it, an easy way to create symmetrical objects. You can use all the familiar node sculpting tricks.

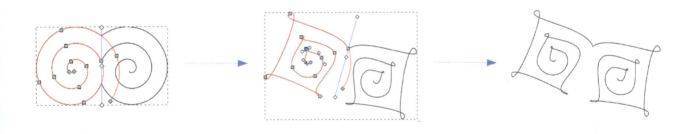

Chapter 14
Path Effects II

This chapter continues the discussion of **Path Effects**.

Offset

We've looked at Inset, Outset and Offset commands before in Chapter 12. Four menu commands under **Path** (**Inset**, **Outset**, **Dynamic Offset**, and **Linked Offset**) provided ways of adding lines inside or outside of an object. This LPE is just another way to accomplish the same thing, and you may find it more convenient because you can experiment with a wide number of different options.
Select the object, add the **Offset** LPE, and consider the options in the dialogue. The most important setting is **Offset**, which is at a default of 0.0. Raising the number produces an outset; lowering the number into the minuses produces an inset. You can hold the plus or minus and watch until you get just what you want.

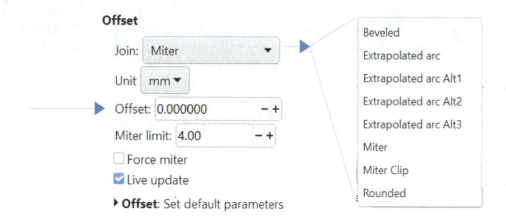

The Join options allow you to choose just how angles will be treated in your offset. Most of the time, you'll want **Miter** or **Rounded**.

If you find the **Live update** feature is eating up too much computer power, turn it off.

If you want to retain the original, **Duplicate** it (**CTRL + D**) before you start. You can leave it in place and work around it, or move it off to the side.

Below is a star shape with outset and inset applied. In both cases, the original has been duplicated.

230

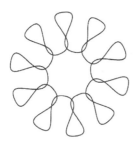  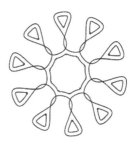

Original star-form Outset with original duplicated Inset with original duplicated

Offset can be used to produce new objects or enhance old ones.. It can also be used, for example, to produce a shadow background for text if you use **Object to Path** first.

Mitered Join at .70 Rounded Join at .70
Original duplicated, raised to top, repositioned, and fill changed to white

Parallel (experimental)

Draws a long, straight parallel line next to where the original was. If you want to keep the original, duplicate it. **Offset** determines how far the new line is from the original; **Length** sets the length, of course.

Pattern Along Path

If this **Path Effect** seems familiar, you're probably remembering **Put on Path** from the Text chapter. This is very similar.

You can put a single or complex objects along a path, forming a pattern or bending a single item. You cannot use a **Group**. Use **Combine** instead.

The first example below duplicates the original path; the others don't.

231

The easiest way to use the effect is the following:

- Copy the object(s) you want as the pattern.

- Draw and select what will be a sacrificial path. It will disappear under the pattern.

- Open the **Path Effect**, choosing **Pattern Along Path**.

- Next to **Pattern copies**, choose **Repeated**, **Repeated stretched**, **Single**, or **Single stretched**.

- Press the **Paste** icon in the **Pattern source** line.

- Make adjustments to the other drop-down menus.

The pattern will take on the stroke and fill colors of the sacrificial path. You can change those afterwards.

Here's an example of putting a **Single stretched** pattern on a wavy sacrificial line.

Pattern (copied to clipboard)   Sacrificial line (pasted)

Once the LPE has worked, the node arrow will bring up handles to manipulate the result further.

After LPE is applied   With node arrow, use handles to make changes

Continue to manipulate as desired

This LPE is often used to make natural looking curves in drawings of lizards, snakes, or caterpillars.

Perpendicular bisector (experimental)

Draws a line perpendicular to the original line. The original vanishes. Seemingly doesn't work on closed lines.

Perspective/Envelope

This effect presents a nice complement to **Envelope Deformation. Perspective/Envelope** changes objects along straight lines, so you end up with a parallelogram or trapezoid deformation, whereas **Envelope Deformation** is friendly to curves. You can use **Perspective/Envelope** on any object, including type, though all must be converted to paths first. You will lose the ability to edit text as text, so be sure you are finished with that editing.

To begin, convert to a path if necessary, select the object, and add the path effect. Then use the **Node Arrow** to do the work. You will see little diamonds in the corners of the bounding box. Drag on any of those to change the shape. You can deform in only one direction, but more likely you will want to check one of the "Mirror" boxes that lets you automatically deform in two directions at once. You won't want to check both, because that would get you the same thing as the regular **Select Arrow**.

   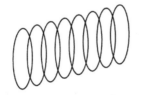

Original   Top right corner dragged   Mirror movements in vertical   Mirror movements in horizontal

If you prefer, you can set the deformation numerically with the drop-down menus.

Next to **Type**, you can choose either **Envelope deformation** or **Perspective.** Try these out and you'll see the difference, especially if you have a significant stroke width. **Perspective** produces more of a 3-D effect and alters the stroke to make "farther" objects seem to recede.

Original   Envelope deformation   

                                    Perspective

Power Clip and Power Mask

Not covered here.

Power Stroke

If you need a line that varies smoothly in width, this may be the path effect for you. Could you achieve the same thing with **Path > Stroke to Path**? Probably, but it would be a lot more trouble to get a gradual variation. Both **Power Stroke** and **Stroke to Path** share the same limitation, namely that the stroke will now have fill, so if it surrounds a space you would like to fill, you will have to do a work-around, such as stacking one figure on top of another. For our black and white purposes, that probably would be an extremely rare problem.

The effect also comes with end caps: three of them are a repeat of the regular ones in the **Stroke style** dialogue, but there are a couple of new ones, **Peak** and **Zero width**. The latter produces a very nice taper.

To use this effect, just select the line you want to adjust and add **Power stroke**.

You will be faced with a number of choices in the dialogue box, but the important thing is what shows up when you click the **Node Arrow**. You will see the usual nodes, along with a red outline. If you look closely at the line, you will also see three tiny pink nodes or knots. These are the nodes that matter for smooth dragging. You can drag these in any direction, including along the red line if they aren't in the right place for where you want to do the widening.

Special pink nodes/knots for dragging smooth lines

Drag the line into the shape you want, and then further experiment with the **Interpolator type**, which will produce slight variations of width. Set the **Start** and **End** caps, and any **Join** you may have.

Various line widths and interpolator types.

You can add extra pink knots by clicking on one as you hold **Ctrl**. The new one will be directly on top of the old. You can move it where you like. More knots provide opportunities for more shaping, including bumps.

If you do add knots, the **Sort points** checkbox becomes relevant. The pink knots remember their original order of creation. Whether the **Sort points** box is checked will influence the behavior of the line. Try it checked and unchecked to get a feel for the difference.

You can delete a pink knot with **Ctrl + Alt + Click**.

Power stroke does not work on closed paths like circles, rectangles, stars, clouds, and so on.

Possible bug: If you happen to end up with a filled line with the fill crossing the curves, try turning off the fill and turning on a black stroke. Then you can select the line again and add black fill. You may have to wait to add the black fill until you have done a little path altering.)

Select line to adjust

Oops! Fill in the wrong place

Turn off fill, turn on stroke, turn fill on again

235

Rotate copies

This effect offers a very useful and powerful alternative to circular tiling or polar coordinates (see pp. 108 ff.). The result can be a 360° kaleidoscopic image , or the effect can put copies only around part of the rotation.

To use this LPE successfully, you must be aware that the pivot point of any figure rotated by this LPE is at the <u>center left edge</u> of the figure as it appears on the canvas when you activate the LPE.

Let's take a simple path meant to look like a petal. The aim will be to produce a stylized flower drawing. The point on the petal is intended to be at the center. Below, the added red dot shows where the pivot point of the LPE will be if the petal is oriented vertically versus two horizontal orientations.

Only the third orientation will put the center where intended. The first petal yields a figure you probably wouldn't expect. The middle petal will put the points on the outside. Here are the results for each orientation above, when the LPE is applied at the default settings:

That odd, crisscrossing kaleidoscope of the figure on the left shows that because of the side pivot, we end up with three pairs of petals, as you can see in the colored version below.

Even if you end up with a mess like this, it is easily fixed with the manipulation tools of the LPE. Here's how.

Activate the on-canvas controls with the **Node Arrow**. Zoom in far enough to be able to see the current pivot handle of the figure—a very tiny white circle and two blue lines protruding from it.

Blue line that shows the 60° angle

Red outline of original figure

Blue rotation line with tiny white handle on the right end

White pivot handle

The line with the white circle on the end is the rotation handle. The tiny white pivot point will turn red when you point at it exactly. Zoom back out a bit so you can get a sense of the whole figure. Holding the left mouse key, you can drag the pivot point where you want. Move it around a bit to get the idea. Now get hold of it and drag it to the petal point of the right side vertical petal. As you drag, you will see the flower taking shape.

When you reach the petal point, let go. You can see that you can correct the shape of the flower, no matter what orientation you started with. As we'll see below, the same dragging action on the rotation point can be used on other figures to create an amazing variety of drawings with little effort.

Now let's take a look at the control dialogue. To the right are the default settings. If the **Method** is **Normal**, the **Number of copies** is 6, the **Rotation angle** is 60.0 (6 x 60° = 360°), and **Distribute evenly** is checked, we get the even kind of rotation in the flower above. The stroke and fill of the original is preserved throughout.

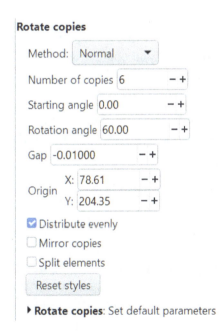

You will note that there is a tiny -.01 gap between copies built into the default to ensure that the copies touch.

If you increase the **Number of copies** by repeatedly clicking the + button, you can watch the number of petals grow. The petals will begin to overlap, producing a sort of pointy mandala overlaying the petals.

If you don't like the internal star produced by that overlap, you'll need to somehow fill the petals with white to make them opaque. At present, simply adding fill won't really have any effect, because white

will just show up between all the black lines. Instead, check **Split elements** and add white fill. This option allows the fill style to apply to one petal at a time. Notice that the pointy mandala has disappeared under the opaque fill.

Now, if the point of that top petal feels wrong, just draw a black center circle to put on top and **Group** everything.

What if you want only part of a rotation? You can <u>uncheck</u> **Distribute evenly** and set a different **Starting angle**. Try 6 copies with a starting angle of 90°, and a rotation angle of 30°.

You'll end up with this figure, which can easily be rotated to sit flat if you wish.

It seems that the only time unchecking **Distribute evenly** does anything is when you want less than a full 360° rotation.

Tip! Remember that at any time you feel you are done manipulating your figure with the LPE, you should click **Path > Object to Path** to stabilize the figure. After that the LPE has no effect. Before stabilizing, you could always duplicate a result you like, stabilize it, and continue to work on the other copy. All copies of a figure will be available for change by the LPE until they are stabilized.

Mirror copies has an effect only if at least two sides of your original object are asymmetrical. Below is a simple squiggle drawn with the **Pencil** tool at a **Smoothing** of 10 and an **Elipse Shape**.

Since the orientation of the squiggle is more or less horizontal and the pivot point is thus at the left point, applying the default rotation with only **Distribute evenly** gets us the figure on the left on the next page. If **Mirror copies** is checked in addition, we get the figure in the middle. The white areas on this middle figure show up because the black fill is overlapping and a fill rule you probably don't need to know about is being followed.

Checking **Split elements** will eliminate fill overlap and result in a wholly black figure like the one on the right.

With **Distribute evenly** only ~ With **Mirror copies** added ~ With **Split elements** added

Now let's take a look at **Method** in the settings, defined as "Rotate methods." All three choices control what happens when the LPE rotates an object, including when you are rotating the object with the rotate handle, as well as the initial rotation that happens when the number of copies is applied. We've been using **Normal**. Change this to **Kaleidoscope**, and now we get what look like pie slices of the squiggle. Exactly what the slices look like can be changed by moving the rotation handle. Here are a few versions that show up as the handle is rotated on the left-hand figure above.

If the **Method** is changed to **Fuse**, the result will be similar to applying **Path > Union** to overlapping objects. This wouldn't be visible with our squiggle figure, first because it's filled and wouldn't show up, and second, because so far we haven't overlapped the copies. The flower figure with which we started, however, clearly shows what happens.

Below left is our flower with 12 petal copies, **Normal Method**. In the middle is the same figure with **Fuse paths**. The figure on the right was formed by moving the pivot point of the middle figure outward and to the side slightly to twist the petals. That's just to show that the Live Path Effect is truly live and fluid until stabilized with **Path > Object to Path** even though those internal lines seemed to have disappeared.

We should touch on one other facet of this LPE. We've scarcely looked at that red line that shows up when you apply the LPE and then choose the **Node Arrow**. Yet that red line contributes greatly to the possibilities for changing these live figures on the fly.

Let's take the 6-copy version of the black squiggle again. You may have noticed that the original squiggle shows up outlined in red and displaying all its nodes when the Node Arrow is selected. Here's a bit of the rotated squiggle greatly enlarged:

Not only can you move the pivot point or the rotating handle, you can also manipulate the nodes themselves and watch what happens to the other five copies of the squiggle arm.

A few examples of messing with the nodes

Finally, it bears repeating that the **Rotate copies** LPE is capable of producing infinite and intricate drawings with little effort. There is no way to show this variety in print, though you can find plenty of videos of the process online. You can begin playing with dragging the pivot point hither and thither and you will soon be astounded at what you are making. Just remember to make copies at various points along the way so you can keep going.

Roughen

As the name implies, the effect roughs up your lines. Here are a triangle, a rectangle, and an oval with minimal roughing. One can question why we would want to do this!

Ruler

The effect adds ruler lines to any object you care to mark.

  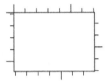

Show handles

This odd little effect is probably for those of us writing directions to Inkscape. The nodes and handles that lie behind every Inkscape drawing can't ordinarily be captured by copying, pasting, saving, or printing so that you can preserve what they look like at a particular stage. You can only take a screen shot. **Show handles** translates the screen view of nodes and handles into a regular Inkscape vector drawing. Unfortunately, it doesn't preserve the colors, but that's the nature of a vector program.

Simplify

This effect is especially useful for the **Pencil tool** and for any path that has an excess of nodes. It's often possible to smooth a jagged line with this LPE. Its use was covered in the **Pencil tool** discussion (see pp. 51-2).

Sketch

Of doubtful use for a metal artist, this effect turns an image sketchy. Perhaps someone might find a creative use for it.

Slice

This path effect does exactly what it says: by default it slices an object or a group of objects in half vertically through the center rotation point. You can choose **Horizontal** from the settings instead if you want. You can split again and again.

Default vertical split   Horizontal split   Further splits possible

You can delete the remaining side if you wish, but if you try to delete the side with the new bounding box around it, the whole object will disappear. Once you are finished slicing, you can use **Path > Object to Path** to stabilize everything, and then you can do with all parts as you wish.

It's also possible to split the object in a different place than the center line. Two different methods are available. If you need to be numerically exact, use the number boxes in the dialogue.

To keep the cut line perfectly horizontal (X) or vertical (Y), the start and end points should be plus and minus the same number (for example, X: +30.66 and X: -30.66); otherwise you get a diagonal.

The other method is to use the node arrow. Select it, and you will see tiny knots at the ends of the initial slice line. These serve as handles. Pull them out from the object so you can see the split line better. Then drag or rotate the line until it's where you want it.

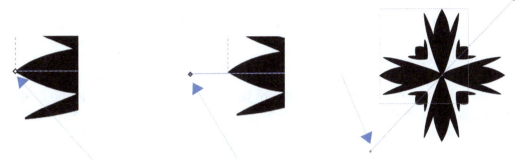

Enlargement shows knot/handle   Handle dragged out for visibility   Handle rotated for diagonal slice

Notice the knot at the center of the object. If you drag that, you can move the entire slice line to a different position on the object.

Object sliced diagonally   Half object altered with a different fill

Once pieces of objects have been split off, they can be altered separately from the other pieces, as in the figure above right.

Spiro spline

This effect was covered on pp. 58-9 in the discussion of the **Bezier pen tool**. It can also be applied to a pencil line after creation.

Stitch Sub-Paths

This effect works much like **Interpolate Sub-Paths**, but instead of adding new lines parallel to the original, the new lines will be perpendicular. The original paths will disappear, so keep a copy if you want to join the new lines with the old.

To use, start with two paths or objects and join them with **Path > Combine**. Add the **Path Effect**. Change the number of paths if you wish. You can also add some variation to where the new paths start and stop. Keeping all the variance options at 0 will result in a tailored set of lines. The node arrow in this menu will allow you adjust the original skeleton lines. Another drop-down menu allows for changes in scale.

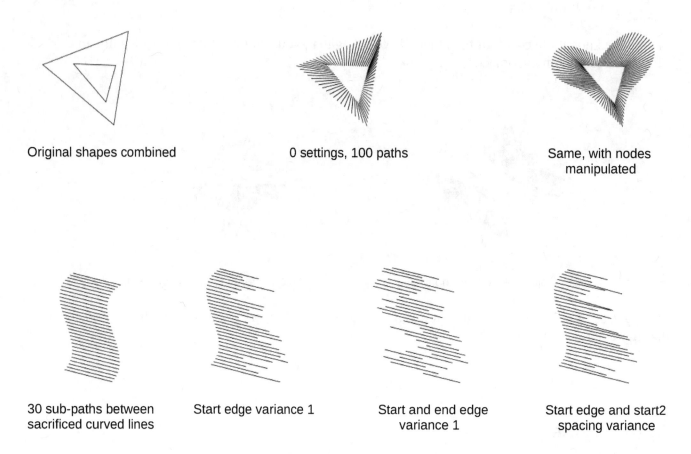

Original shapes combined

0 settings, 100 paths

Same, with nodes manipulated

30 sub-paths between sacrificed curved lines

Start edge variance 1

Start and end edge variance 1

Start edge and start2 spacing variance

If you get what seems to be a crazy reversal half way through the new lines, it may be that the original paths are running in opposite directions. This can produce an interesting result, but if you don't want it you can use **Path** > **Reverse** to change direction on one of the paths. Reversal doesn't matter with concentric paths.

With original paths running in the same direction   With one path reversed

Stitch Sub-Paths is a good way to produce hatching, hair, and other fine lines.

Though the effect was probably intended for use with only two original, sacrificial paths, it is possible to use more than two if you're looking for some odd textures.

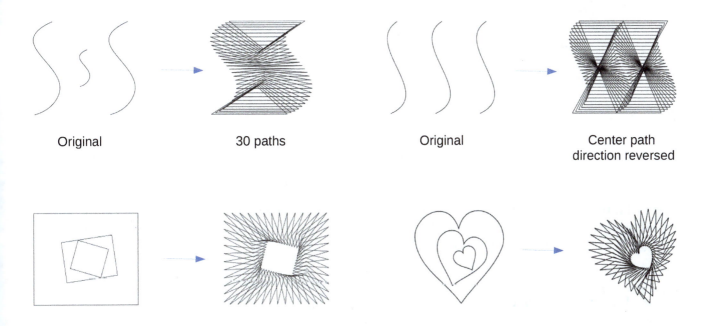

Original   30 paths   Original   Center path direction reversed

Tip! In order to get an interesting line effect on the concentric figures, you must rotate them a little. Otherwise they will only produce straight, continuous lines just as pairs of concentric figures would do.

Stitch Sub-Paths is also capable of producing some lovely symmetrical and non-symmetrical stars and basket-weaves using the **Shape** tools as the originals.

All the objects above use one of two techniques before applying the **Stitch Sub-Paths** effect.

The first four rely on rotation of a symmetrical shape. Here are steps to produce the second one:

- Draw a circle. **Duplicate** it (**Ctrl D**) or copy it and paste in place. Do not move the circles apart!
- Open the **Transform** dialogue (**Object > Transform**). Choose the **Rotate** tab. Put 90 in the **Angle** box for degrees. Click **Apply**. Because you didn't re-select the two circles, this rotation will apply only to the duplicate, leaving the other circle unrotated. You wouldn't think this would make a difference, but it absolutely does.
- Now rubber-band the circles to select both copies. Click **Path > Combine**. The circle shapes will automatically be converted to paths and combined.
- Go to **Path > Path Effects** if it's not already in the dialogue area to the right. Choose **Stitch Sub-Paths** from the little pop-up box.
- In **Number of paths**, put 37. That should do it.

If you have problems, make sure you remembered to **Combine**.

The first and third stars above simply differ in rotation and/or number of paths. Experiment! The fourth was based on a hexagon.

The last three figures above use a different technique. As you can see, the same technique can be used on different shapes. The number of paths determines whether the weave will be open or dense. Here are steps to produce the middle object of the three.

- Use the **Star** tool to draw a ten-sided figure.
- Convert it to a path (**Path > Object to Path**).
- Select the **Node Arrow**. Rubber-band the whole decadron to select all the nodes.
- In the **Node Control** bar, click on the fourth symbol in—**Break path at selected nodes**. Have faith that this happened.
- With the **Select Arrow**, make sure the whole figure is selected and click **Path > Combine**.
- Now open the **Path Effects** menu and select **Stitch Sub-Paths**. You will need very few paths. The figure above has only two. Experiment. Too many paths or a too-wide stroke will turn the figure black.

You can use this technique on a variety of shapes. Some will work better than others. Sometimes you may have to add more nodes, which you can do symmetrically by selecting the whole figure with the **Node Arrow** and then clicking on the **Insert new nodes** button in the **Node Control** bar.

Tangent to curve (experimental)

Draws a line touching a curve at the first node of a curving line. The original curved line disappears. It can work on a group, drawing multiple lines. The line length and angle can be adjusted.

Taper stroke

The **Stroke Style** section of the **Fill and Stroke** dialogue offers only three ends for a stroke: butt, rounded, and square cap. If you want a tapered or pointed cap, this effect will provide it. Drop-down menus offer choices. The longer the line, the more pointed it can be. The first two lines below were both set to a taper smoothing of 0.10. The three right-angle lines were set to 0, 1.2, and 7 for taper smoothing. The join can also be controlled with this **Path Effect**. For the right angles, we have mitered, rounded, and beveled.

For a larger selection of join types, see the **Join Type Path Effect** (pp. 224-5).

Transform by 2 points

This LPE produces what you might think of as an accordion effect: you can stretch or contract a figure along a line.

The effect draws a control line between two points (usually nodes) called "knots" here. The important thing about these knots is that they serve alternately as anchor or as drag point. When you are dragging one, the other is anchored. You can rotate around the anchor or just stretch or contract. You can also use both of them as anchors while you drag on the actual path to deform it in some way.

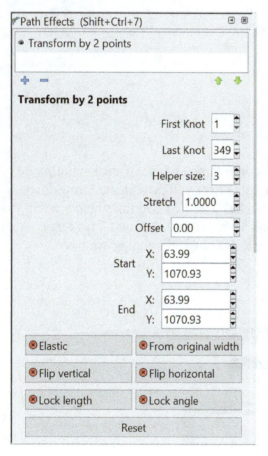

You can choose the positions of the knots by number in the drop-down menu; otherwise the program will choose them for you. You can also set the position of the two knots by the X and Y coordinates in the menu.

> **Tip!** The X and Y coordinates of your cursor can be found at the bottom right of the Inkscape screen. As you move the cursor, the coordinates change. Thus, by pointing, you can tell exactly where you want to set the knots.

One knot is designated as **Start** and one as **End**. The knots can be snapped, *e.g.*, to a grid.

If you want precision, you can <u>stretch</u> or <u>contract</u> between the two knots using the **Stretch** drop-down menu. <u>Contract</u> would be produced by minus numbers.

If you click the **Elastic** button, the expansion and contraction will act like an accordion, changing the aspect ratio (the width versus the length).

Other controls make it possible to lock length or angle so that you can deform the line itself while the knots serve as anchors.

To get started, select the figure you want to transform, open **Path Effects**, and select the effect. Then click on the **Node Arrow** tool. You will now see the figure with a blue line through it from one node to another. Tiny circles at either end are the knots. You can drag one while the other is anchored in place or set them both as anchors. Once you drag, the original figure becomes a red line. The black is the new figure that you are shaping by dragging, while the red remains in place, reminding you of the original dimensions.

Original

Effect activated, node arrow selected,
blue drag-line showing

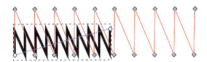

Dragged from top right to bottom left

Dragged with Elastic selected

A curve compacted from lower right
to lower left with **Elastic** on

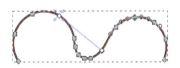

The same curve with the knots
placed at internal nodes

The figure in black after the
previous curve was dragged
along the blue control line

VonKoch

If you are fascinated by fractals, this might be worth a glance, but there's a much easier route to the VonKoch Snowflake and to various other fractal images as well: the **L-System Extension**. Go to **Extensions > Render > L-System** (see pp. 282 ff., especially p. 291) if you want to try a different tack. If it's fractals you're after, time spent on that extension will be much more rewarding than this path effect. That extension will quickly produce the full snowflake if you fill a form with a simple formula.

This **VonKoch** LPE, however, does generate fractals and will have some clever uses in design. You could find it worth playing with.

Here are some basic directions.

Draw an object. A group will work, but to keep things clearer, a simple star-flower shape is used here. Select the shape and add the **VonKoch** LPE. Once the LPE is added, a generation automatically happens; that is, the object suddenly has two mini-objects—babies—positioned just below it in a horizontal line.

In the VonKoch dialogue, you can increase the number of generations, but only two or three are practical before the "babies" are so tiny they're difficult to see. You can add generations at any point in your experiments if you need them.

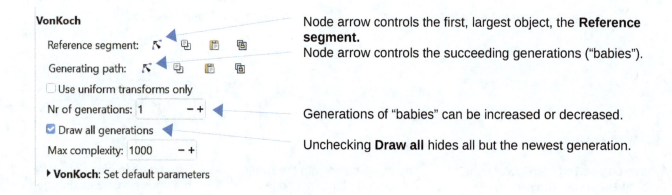

Node arrow controls the first, largest object, the **Reference segment.**
Node arrow controls the succeeding generations ("babies").

Generations of "babies" can be increased or decreased.

Unchecking **Draw all** hides all but the newest generation.

Merely generating pairs of objects is not very interesting. What is more fun is manipulating these objects, which can be done with the node arrows in the dialogue.

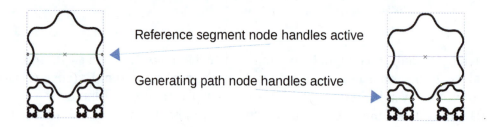

Reference segment node handles active

Generating path node handles active

If you click on the node arrow in the **Reference segment** line, you will see a green horizontal line across the center of the largest object. This line has tiny circular handles at each end. When you point at them, they turn red. You can drag these out to make the "babies" smaller, in to make them larger. You

250

can rotate the handles to rotate the "babies." <u>All</u> of the babies are affected to a similar degree.

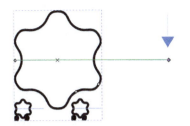

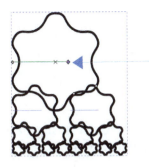

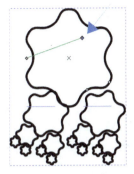

Dragging handle outward
makes "babies" smaller

Dragging handle inward
makes "babies" larger

Rotating handle
rotates "babies"

Similarly, clicking on the node arrow in the **Generating path** line of the dialogue, makes handles appear on the first line of "babies." That means there will be two sets of little green lines with circular handles, since there are only two babies of that generation. The right set will control all the rightmost objects of each generation. The left set will control all the leftmost objects. Other adjacent objects will be changed to a lesser degree.

This time, outward dragging makes "babies" larger, inward dragging makes them smaller, and rotating the handle rotates the "babies." The action just happens to a smaller selection of the generations.

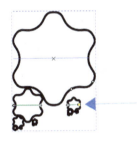

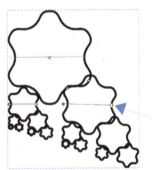

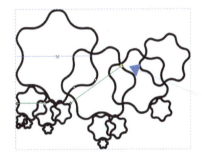

Dragging handle inward makes
makes some "babies" smaller

Dragging handle outward
makes some "babies" larger

Rotating handle rotates some
"babies"

Further control can be gained by drawing separate paths that will be copied to act as remote control lines. Try this out by going back to an unchanged single star-flower.

- Add the Van Koch LPE and increase the generations to three.
- Near the star flower, draw two simple lines, one straight and one curved, for example.

- Select and copy the first simple path with the regular Inkscape copy function, not the one with the copy icon in the Reference line.
- Select the star-flower(s).
- Click the **Link to Path** icon on the **Reference segment** line. This will change the stars' size and position because the first path is now active.
- Select the second path (e.g., the curved path). Copy it with the regular copy function in Inkscape.
- Click the star(s).
- Click the **Link to Path** icon on the **Generating path** line. Again, sizes and positions will change, now that the second path is active.

Using the node arrows within the **Reference segment** and **Generating path lines**, experiment with dragging an end node of each of these two lines in and out, up and down and around.

At this point, you might want to increase the number of generations. Soon you will be producing swirls, cornucopias, and circles of the star-flowers.

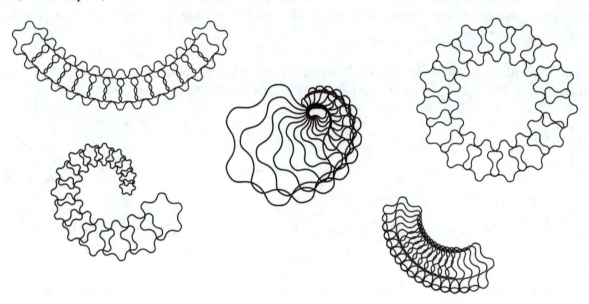

You can also experiment with fill. Using the usual fill option will simply get you an all black or all white object. If, however, you use the even-odd option in the **Fill and Stroke** dialogue ♡ (see pp. 67, 200-2), you can end up with some interesting effects.

Because VonKoch is a **<u>Live</u> Path Effect** you can make changes to the original reference object at any time the effect is active. If you look closely at the reference object in any of the swirly stages you create, you will see that the flower-star has a little cross for the center of rotation and two tiny circular handles somewhere along the perimeter.

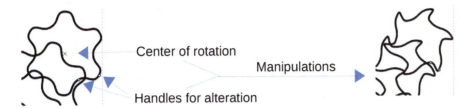

Center of rotation

Manipulations

Handles for alteration

Dragging on the handles will alter the shape of all the star-flowers, as in the right-hand figure above.

You can also drag on the little center of rotation cross for additional adjustments.

Once you are completely finished with all changes to your figure, you will want to stabilize it by using **Path > Object to Path**. That turns your active figure into an ordinary drawing and you will no longer be able to alter it with the VonKoch LPE. It will then be available to change in any of the usual ways.

If the drawings produced above seem familiar to you, you are probably remembering **Chapter 8** on **Cloning and Tiling**. Some of the VonKoch figures are almost identical to figures we achieved with tiling. The difference is in method. You may find the VonKoch LPE a more intuitive way to produce similar results.

Chapter 15
Extensions I

Inkscape comes with a slew of **Extensions**, which are mini-programs somewhat like **Path Effects**. They have been developed by a wide variety of developer-users to meet a wide variety of needs, often quite technical. Some of them may be useful for our metal arts, but most will not be. Some of them come with a help section or at least a short explanation, some don't. A number of them are very similar to **Path Effects** already covered. If there is enough added value for our purposes, the corresponding extension will be covered somewhere in the next three chapters. Here's a list of what will be covered in Chapters 15-17.

An Index to Relevant Extensions as of Inkscape Version 1.11		
Extension	**Brief description**	**Page**
Generate from Path	*Always requires a base path on which to operate.*	
Interpolate	Puts additional objects between two end objects.	256-7
Pattern along Path	Curves a pattern of one or more objects to the shape of a path.	258-9
Scatter	Similar. Gives options for arranging group members along a path.	259
Voronoi Diagram	Produces a random polygon mosaic.	260-2
Voronoi Pattern	Similar, but better for the casual user.	263-4
Modify Path	*Always requires a base path on which to operate.*	
Add Nodes	Another way to add nodes to paths.	264
Envelope	Places one object inside another as a way to achieve perspective.	264
Flatten Beziers	Changes a curved segment to a straight one.	265
Perspective	Places one object inside another as a way to achieve perspective.	265
Rubber Stretch	Compacts or stretches complex paths along a line.	265-6
Straighten Segments	Changes a curved segment to a straight one by percentage.	266
Whirl	Swirls a drawing around the center of the viewing area.	266-7
Render	*Produces something new from specifications you enter.*	
Alphabet Soup	Generates text that looks exotic.	268

Function Plotter	Generates wavy lines and figures from formulae. Can be very useful.	268-79
Gear	Draws one gear at a time to specified measurements.	279-80
Grids	Produces various kinds of grids to specifications.	280-1
Guides Creator	Sets types of guide lines not available in the regular program.	281
L-system	Draws many figures, including fractals, based on branching instructions.	282-308
Parametric Curves	Draws specified curves, including Celtic knot and doughnut, hearts, butterflies, and flowers.	309-14
Polygon Side	Draws equilateral polygons with specific side lengths.	315
~~Seamless Pattern~~	~~Excellent replacement for the regular pattern function of Inkscape.~~ Currently unusable in Windows. (See pp. 320 ff.).	
Spirograph	Draws repeating curves around a center as the children's toy does.	316-7
Triangle	Draws triangles with specific side lengths and/or angles.	317
Wireframe Sphere	Draws a grid texture on a globe for a 3-D illusion.	318

Tip 1! Before you begin to change the parameters in an **Extension** dialogue, copy down the original parameters or take a screenshot. The numbers in most of the extensions will <u>not</u> return to a default once you close the extension—even if you start Inkscape again. You may want a record of the original.

Tip 2! Some extensions may not work until you change your initial object(s) to paths (**Path > Object to Path**).

Tip 3! In Inkscape 1.1 in Windows 10, extension dialogue boxes have the annoying habit of disappearing behind all the other windows on your screen once an operation is complete. Fortunately, the dialogue box should show up on your taskbar as an additional Inkscape window, so you can retrieve it easily. It is greatly to be hoped that the Inkscape developers will fix this glitch in an upcoming version.

Interpolate (Generate from Path > Interpolate)

This extension is very much like the Path Effect, **Interpolate Sub-Paths,** except that it does not give you as many options. It does work for colors, but that is not very useful for our purposes. To use, copy both objects (which must be paths) and fill in how many steps you want between the two. Experiment with the other options if you like. A quirk in this extension is that the order of the nodes in the paths matters. When a path is drawn, even if it starts as a dimensional shape, the nodes in the path get a particular order. When we have two paths that originated as shapes, the first node in one shape may not be in a compass direction matching the first node of the other. Thus the interpolations are skewed, as below.

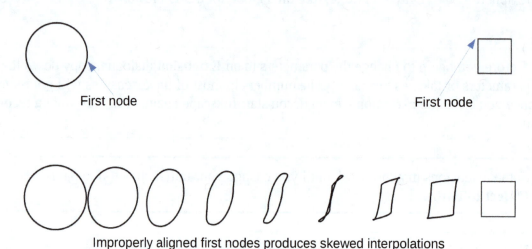

Improperly aligned first nodes produces skewed interpolations

In the figures below, the circle was rotated to put its first node in the upper left to match the square.

Properly aligned first nodes produce even interpolations

If you have done that and you are still getting skewed results, try reversing the path of one of your objects (**Path > Reverse**).

To find the order of nodes, select the path, select the **Node Tool**, and press **Tab**. The first node will be a brighter color.

Exponent controls spacing. An exponent of 0.0 makes all spacing equal if the objects are equal size. Varying the spacing up or down makes spacing vary continuously.

Interpolation steps controls the number of intermediate objects between the end objects.

Interpolation method has to do with how curves are calculated. Try both methods and see what you like.

Like the **LPE**, the **Interpolate** extension can be used for concentric shapes for interesting effects.

It does not work for groups but does work for combined objects, though not particularly well.

Three Similar Ways to Put a Pattern on a Path

Inkscape now has three different ways to put a pattern on a path, in addition to putting text on a path. One of these is a **Path Effect**; the other two are **Extensions**. Information about the path effect will be found in a **Path Effects** chapter (see pp. 231-3). The other two are discussed here.

As you can see in the three control dialogues laid out below, each has slightly different options. The first, the **Path Effect**, allows changes to be made to the path with the **Node Arrow**, which is good for bending. The two **Extensions** don't have that but have other advantages. The best thing about the extension **Pattern along Path** is the addition of a ribbon deformation, which is unique to this alternative. **Scatter** has a couple of nice features: the ability to **Stretch spaces to fit skeleton length** and the choice of how to treat group members.

You may find that a particular task you need to complete will be best served by only one of these alternatives.

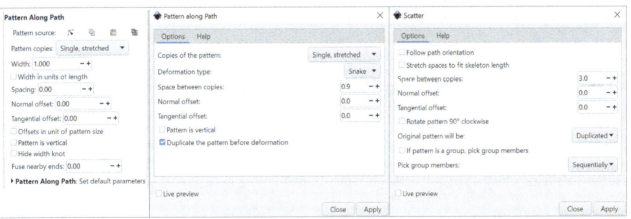

A Path Effect (LPE)   An Extension   An Extension

257

Pattern along Path (Generate from Path > Pattern along Path)

When this extension is working correctly, which is not always, it provides at least one choice that the **Path Effect** does not have: the ribbon deformation.

To use the extension, you need a pattern and a path.
- **Select** the pattern (*e.g.*, a line, a circle, a complex **Group** of objects, etc.). The pattern should be converted to path(s) and should be at the top of the Z order. Click **Shift**.
- **Select** the path (*e.g.*, a line or a shape converted to a path). This is called a skeleton path, but it remains after the process.
- Click **Extension > Generate from Path > Pattern along Path**.
- A dialogue box will pop up. The choices you are offered are fairly self-explanatory. Since there is a **Live preview**, trying out variations is easy. You can use minus numbers in **Space between copies** if you want each pattern object to overlap with the next.
- When you have what you like, click **Apply** and **Close** the dialogue.
- Move the path away from the patterned result and delete the path if you don't want it to be part of the drawing.

Here are a few simple examples.

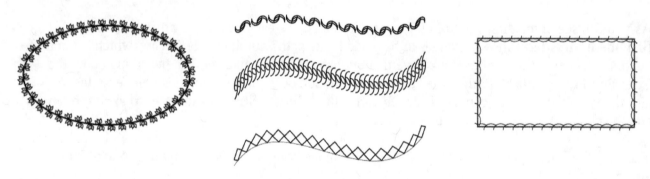

To effectively use the **Single, stretched** option of the **Copies of the pattern**, you need to remember one thing: in order to bend a shape or path, it has to have enough nodes. For instance, consider this rectangular object as the pattern and this curving line as the path:

Pattern   Path

The extension does not add nodes. A rectangle has only four nodes, so the following is the result of applying the **Single, stretched** option with the **Ribbon** deformation type, which slightly skews things as if they are lying along a slightly curled ribbon. Without more nodes, there was nothing to bend.

Here's the result after adding some nodes along the long sides.

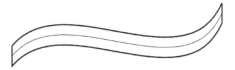

Tip! If you have trouble getting the right item to be the path rather than the pattern, try sending the path to the bottom of the Z-order (**Object > Lower to Bottom**).

Scatter (Generate from Path > Scatter)

This ill-named extension is the third of the pattern-on-a-path type. This one has the helpful option of copying or cloning the pattern before applying it.

In addition, if your pattern is a group of objects, you have three options for how to treat them. If left unchecked, **If pattern is a group, pick group members** just applies the whole group at each spot along the path. If checked, you have two other options next to **Pick group members**. Single group members will be applied to the path either **Randomly** or **Sequentially**. You will see the effect below.

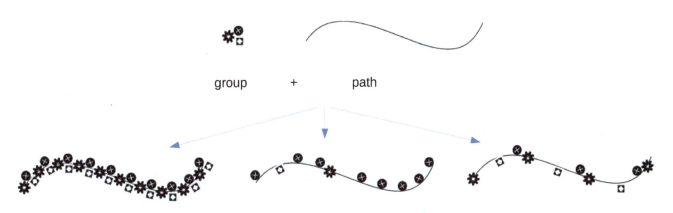

group   +   path

If pattern is a group is unchecked   **Pick group members: Randomly**   **Pick group members:
Sequentially**

The extension is activated the same way as **Pattern Along a Path.** The tip about moving the path to the bottom also pertains to this extension.

At the time of this writing, you <u>must</u> check the box for **Stretch spaces to fit skeleton length** or the extension won't work.

Voronoi Diagram and Pattern

Inkscape has two different extensions for making Voronoi diagrams. The first, **Voronoi Diagram,** makes authentic Voronoi diagrams; the second, **Voronoi Pattern**, produces an Inkscape **Pattern** that fills a space you create but does not allow you to control the points on which a Voronoi diagram is based.

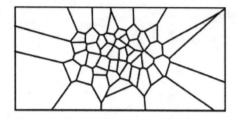

Made with Voronoi Diagram

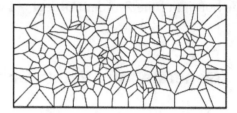

Made with Voronoi Pattern

Polygons like those in a Voronoi diagram can be found in the natural world. Think of the cracks you see in dried mud, the veining in a translucent butterfly wing, or the spots on a giraffe. This may be all you, as a metal artist, may want or need to know about Voronoi diagrams. They can make attractive patterns or textures.

You can skip the following explanation to get to the directions if you wish.

At first glance, a Voronoi diagram looks like a mosaic of random asymmetrical pieces, but it's actually a geometrical construct that creates straight-sided cells around reference points on a plane based on the notion that any point within the cell will be closer to the reference point of the cell than it is to any of the other reference points. Let's take a very simple example. Let's suppose we have five airports in a region represented by the square below. The airports are the black dots in the illustration below.

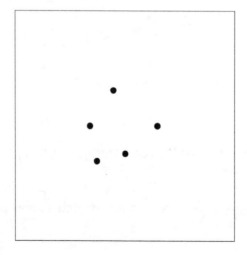

Suppose authorities want to construct a zone map that would tell them the closest airport for a plane in trouble flying over the area (and this is pre-GPS!). Such a map would end up looking like this.

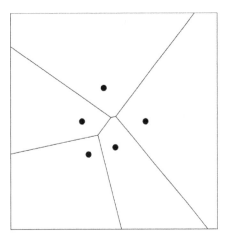

Any point in one of these zones would be closer to the airport in that zone than it would be to any of the other airports.

Here's how the map is constructed. First, the airport dots are connected by triangles where none of the lines of the triangles cross. This is called Delaunay triangulation.

Correct Delaunay triangulation

Incorrect Delaunay triangulation

Next, the center points of each line in the triangles are determined. Then a perpendicular line is drawn through each of the triangle lines at this center point. The closest intersection points of those lines are the points through which the Voronoi diagram lines are drawn. If done by hand, that step can get very confusing with so many lines to track. Fortunately, the Voronoi diagram extension does this for us.

Here's the combination of the Delaunay triangulation with the Voronoi diagram. If you look closely, you can see the lines perpendicular to the triangle lines.

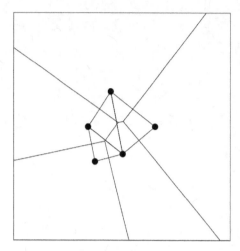

Voronoi Diagram (Generate from Path > Voronoi Diagram)

This extension is the one that can actually be controlled based on objects you provide. In the diagrams above, the "points" are represented by little circles, but the program allows you to use any objects. The centers of the objects are the original points. To achieve anything of much interest for a design, you need many more points to start with. I find it easiest to draw a tiny circle and duplicate it many times, scattering the circles randomly. Be sure to get all of the circles moved away from the original, though, or you will mess up the triangulation. Here are the steps to using the extension.

- Accumulate a bunch of randomly arranged objects.
- Select them all.
- Click **Extension > Generate from Path > Voronoi Diagram**. That brings up the dialogue.
- In the drop-down menus, decide
  - whether you want the Voronoi Diagram, the Delaunay triangulation, or both.
  - whether you want to fill a page or a box
  - what style you want on the Delaunay triangulation, if relevant.

If you have a lot of points, the diagrams may take a while to process.

Admittedly, all this explanation of the Voronoi Diagram may have little to do with jewelry design, but it can yield some usable designs.

Voronoi Pattern (Generate from Path > Voronoi Pattern)

If what you're looking for is an interesting abstract pattern for a texture, skip the **Diagram** extension and start with this one. It's much faster and easier, and you can better control what the outer portions of the diagram look like.

- Draw an empty shape, like a rectangle or circle or irregular blob. Your pattern will be drawn within the shape.
- Select it.
- Click **Extension > Generate from Path > Voronoi Pattern**. That brings up the dialogue.
- In the first option, choose the **Average size of cell**. The sizes will vary. The smaller the size you choose, the more cells will populate the shape you've drawn. Experiment to find what you like.
- The second option allows some control over the appearance of the border. If you want larger cells near the border to create a sort of frame, roughly double the number in the <u>Average size</u> box and make the number <u>negative</u>.

This extension may take time and computer power to produce a result, so if you lack the RAM, you'd be advised to start with a small shape to fill. Then you can enlarge it once the extension is done. Both rectangles below were filled by putting the same sizes in the cell and border options (4 and -10). The difference is that the one on the left started as a very small rectangle that only occupied an inch or so of the page on the canvas, whereas the second one took up half the width of the page. Both rectangles were then resized.

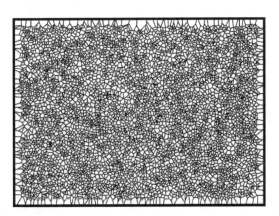

Once you've run the extension, what fills the shape is a **Pattern**, with all the characteristics of a **Pattern**. It takes the place of fill. Like other **Patterns**, it can be scaled, shifted in its frame, and rotated, using the appropriate handles if you can find them (see pp. 38-9). The handles are often hidden within the pattern somewhere.

Because this is a **Pattern**, the width of the stroke can't be changed. To get around that problem, use **Object > Pattern > Pattern to Objects** and then change the stroke width. You may want to make the border transparent and add a different border later. The alternative way to get a different stroke size is to change the size of the whole figure. A bigger figure will get you a wider stroke.

Here is the same pattern with different scaling and rotation.

Note: **Modify Path** extensions all need a path to operate on. Without a path selected, this type of extension will do nothing.

Add Nodes (Modify Path > Add Nodes)

This is a quick way to specify how you want to add nodes to a selection, which must be a path.

Envelope (Modify Path > Envelope)

Requires two selected paths. The first is fitted into the second with a distortion that imitates perspective with the top leaning into the distance.

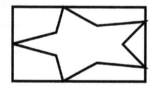

Flatten Beziers (Modify Path > Flatten Beziers)

The extension changes curves to straight segments.

Here's a spiral with varying degrees of flatness.

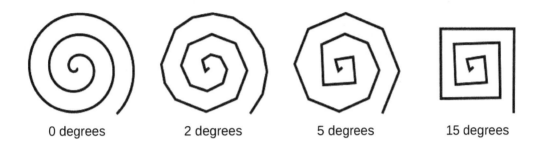

| 0 degrees | 2 degrees | 5 degrees | 15 degrees |

Perspective (Modify Path > Perspective)

Similar to the **Envelope** extension, this places one selected object into a second selected object, skewing it to look as if the top is further from the viewer than the bottom. The result seems to be a horizontal mirror image of **Envelope**'s result.

Rubber Stretch (Modify Path > Rubber Stretch)

This extension distorts a path or paths in a particular way. The vertical sides become concave, while the top and bottom are pulled outwards toward a curved peak. Add some nodes before applying, especially to straight lines. Here are shapes converted to paths with **Rubber Stretch** applied.

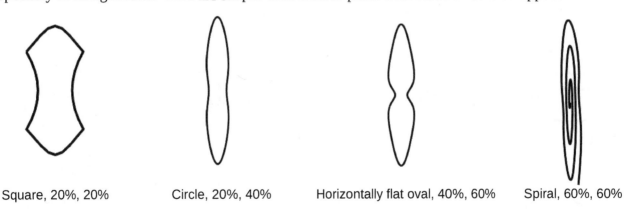

Square, 20%, 20%   Circle, 20%, 40%   Horizontally flat oval, 40%, 60%   Spiral, 60%, 60%

The results may be most pleasing on groups of straight lines. Here all numbers are at 40.

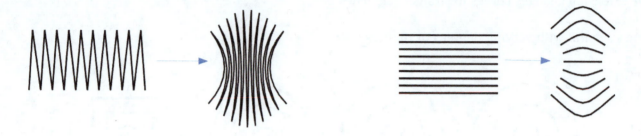

Straighten Segments (Modify Path > Straighten Segments)

Another curve straightening extension, this one allows you to specify the amount of straightening you want by percentage, allowing the retention of some curve. The **Behavior** option allows you to choose between two different ways of moving node handles, which doesn't seem to make much difference.

Whirl (Modify Path > Whirl)

The extension slants paths at nodes in what is supposed to be a whirling effect, with the slanting more pronounced farther from the center. There is really no curving, just the illusion of curving if there are enough nodes on a line. That means you have to add nodes.

Another quirk is that the center around which the whirl takes place is not the center of the figure, but the center of the viewable area of the screen. If you want the action centered, you must take the extra step of selecting the drawing and then clicking **View** > **Zoom** > **Selection**. Then apply the extension.

Group doesn't work. **Combine** does.

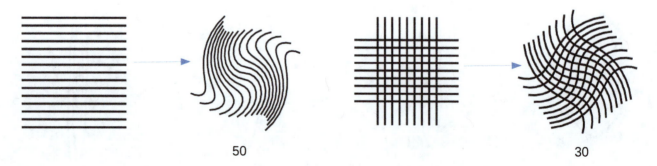

50   30

Here is a simple straight vertical line with six added nodes and with **Whirl** at 50. It's magnified here, so you can clearly see what the extension does and doesn't do.

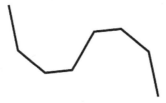

If you want smoother lines, add scads of nodes, and then once you've applied **Whirl**, run **Path > Simplify** to get rid of excess nodes. Here's the same straight line as above with this technique applied —add lots of nodes, apply **Whirl**, and **Simplify** down to a handful of nodes.

Chapter **16**
Extensions II

This chapter continues the discussion of extensions. It is the second of four chapters on the extensions included in Inkscape.

Note: Render extensions may or may not need a path to operate on. Each extension's process may require a different sort of base or nothing but the numbers put into a dialogue box.

Alphabet Soup (Render > Alphabet Soup)

This produces fake exotic lettering readable in English or whatever language you write.

Wɾiξɛ aɲythjɲɡ jɲ ξhɛ ιɛxι бox aɲɖ cιicξ Aββιy

Characters other than letters don't work.

The text will appear at the top of the page on your Inkscape screen.

Function Plotter (Render > Function Plotter)

This extension is for plotting mathematical functions on graphs, which you probably are not going to be doing on jewelry! Some of the lines the plotter can produce, however, might be quite useful in designs. As neither a mathematician nor a Python programmer, about all I can offer here is a few observations about getting started with the dialogue box and a few "recipes" that might be of interest. Each time the plotter is applied, only a single line is produced, but the line can be complicated with many turns so that it may look like many lines.

What we will be drawing will fall into two categories: (1) wavy or zigzag lines; or (2) lines arranged around an axis, like a star or flower.

To operate the extension, you must **start with a dimensional rectangle drawn with the shape tool**. A path won't do. The size and shape of the rectangle will have a direct bearing on the line produced. For the wavy line category, the longer the line you want the wider the rectangle must be in proportion to its height. For the axial figure a square will do nicely.

Because small variations in proportions can make quite a difference to the end result of the wavy line category, it seemed best to give you recipes with the rectangle sizes specified until you are more used to the extension. You can set the rectangle size in the **Rectangle** shape control bar or in the **Select Arrow** control bar after drawing.

For starters, draw a rectangle 1/2" high x 8" wide. We will use the plotter to fill this rectangle with a wavy line, like this one below. We'll get to the circular kind of figure later.

Select your empty rectangle and then click **Extension > Render > Function Plotter**. This brings up a dialogue, which will need some explanation. Notice first that there are three tabs. Click the **Functions** tab. There you'll find a list of most of the functions available in the extension. These functions tell the line what to do, how to behave. Don't panic if they are meaningless to you. They are to me, too. We can use them without understanding the math and programming, although those users who do have the math skills would certainly have an advantage.

One or more of these functions listed gets plugged into the **Function** line of the **Range and sampling tab**. Even with the **Functions tab** selected, you can see that **Function** slot just below the halfway point of the dialogue. Type the function exactly with no extra spaces or upper-case letters. The extension automatically pastes the function into Python computer code, and computer code is picky about format.

In the function slot, write **sin(x)**. This will produce a garden variety wave, assuming the other slots in the **Range and sampling** are filled in properly. We can make a few generalizations about these other items.

Start X value and **End X value** control how close together or far apart the periods of a wave are horizontally. A period is one up and down movement. The greater the difference between the **Start** and **End X** values, the closer together the periods will be and the more periods, or repeats, there will be. In fact, for this particular wave, the number difference between the two values equals the number of periods.

The **Y value of rectangle's bottom** and the **Y value of the rectangle's top** determine how low and high the wave reaches vertically.

If you check **Multiply X range by 2*pi**, you are significantly increasing the effect of the difference between the two X values, which will in this case make the periods closer together. By the way, * is a multiplication sign in computer code.

If you check the **Isotropic scaling**, you may shrink the figure in a particular direction, or checking may have no effect. Here, the figure will shrink vertically.

The **Number of samples** can have a major effect on what is drawn; sometimes it makes little difference. This option controls how many nodes are added to the line. If the line has lots of turns, the more nodes the smoother the line, within reason. How many is enough depends on the figure and on what result you want. Sometimes having fewer samples brings interesting results because it forces more jaggedness or less completion of turns. At other times, you'll want more smoothing. Experiment with holding other factors constant and raising or lowering the number of samples.

Use polar coordinates should be checked when you want to draw a figure around a central point, like some sort of flower or star. For most such figures, you would be better served to just use the **Star/Polygon tool**, because it will easily produce a truly symmetrical figure. However, the plotter can produce some interesting figures that you cannot get with the polygon tool.

Calculate first derivative numerically should be left checked unless you know what you're doing mathematically.

Leave the other boxes unchecked unless you want to automatically **Remove** the **rectangle** from your figure. I like to leave the rectangle so that I can see how the plotting relates to the size of the rectangle I've drawn. Then I can move the rectangle away from the figure afterwards and delete it.

For the first wave drawn above, here are the options used: **Start X value** -1.0; **End X value** 1.0; **Multiply X range** checked; **Y value of rectangle's bottom** -1.0; **Y value of rectangle's top** 1.0; **Number of samples** 6; **Function** sin(x).

If you want more periods, increase the difference between the **Start X value** and the **End X value**, e.g. **Start X value** -2.0; **End X value** 2.0. That will double the periods. You will also have to raise the **Number of samples** because you'll need more nodes. Try it without changing the samples, and you'll see that the line has become irregular. Then try increasing samples to 12.

Now increase the difference between the Y values: **Y value of rectangle's bottom** -2.0; **Y value of rectangle's top** 2.0. Now all the X and Y values are at -2.0 or 2.0. Here's the result:

Note that the figure no longer reaches the top and bottom of the rectangle.

Now let's make a circular figure with the original X and Y values: **Start X value** -1.0; **End X value** 1.0; **Multiply X range** checked; **Y value of rectangle's bottom** -1.0; **Y value of rectangle's top** 1.0. Check **Use polar coordinates**. You'll also need to make a square, rather than a rectangle, unless you want an oval. In addition, we no longer have "enough" samples. Raise the samples to 30. Here's the result. Wow— all that trouble for a circle that begins at the center of the rectangle and proceeds in its curve to the top center of the rectangle before curving back down to meet its beginning.

Here's one instance where changing the **Number of samples** to less than "enough" makes for some interesting results. The reduced number of nodes is forcing differences in where the line goes.

4 samples   6 samples   7 samples   8 samples   10 samples   11 samples

Above 11 samples, the result so closely approaches a circle as to be uninteresting.

Now that you have an inkling of how the extension works, here are some recipes, starting with some more linear waves.

Rectangle 8" x .125"; Start X -2.0; End X 2.0; Multiply X checked; Y bottom -1.0; Y top 1.0; samples 40; isotropic unchecked; polar unchecked; function sin(x)

Rectangle 8" x .125"; Start X -8.0; End X 8.0; Multiply X checked; Y bottom -1.0; Y top 1.0; samples 40; isotropic unchecked; polar unchecked; function sin(x)

Rectangle 8" x .125"; Start X -16.0; End X 16.0; Multiply X checked; Y bottom -1.0; Y top 1.0; samples 80; isotropic unchecked; polar unchecked; function sin(x)

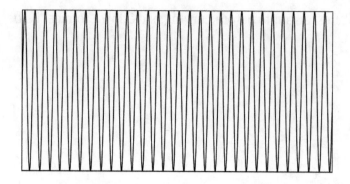

Rectangle 8" x 4"; Start X -15.0; End X 15.0; Multiply X checked; Y bottom -1.0; Y top 1.0; samples 200; isotropic unchecked; polar unchecked; function sin(x)

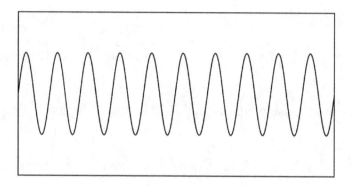

Rectangle 8" x 4"; Start X -5.0; End X 5.0; Multiply X checked; Y bottom -2.0; Y top 2.0; samples 200; isotropic unchecked; polar unchecked; function sin(x)

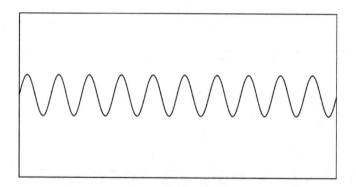

Rectangle 8" x 4"; Start X -5.0; End X 5.0; Multiply X checked; Y bottom -4.0; Y top 4.0; samples 200; isotropic unchecked; polar unchecked; function sin(x)

All three of the last rectangles above have been grouped below to demonstrate that such waves can be combined to good effect one on top of the other. You don't even have to do them on a blank rectangle. Just keep the same rectangle selected and apply the extension repeatedly with the differing values.

You can also give each different wave a different stroke width. I have not changed the stroke widths here.

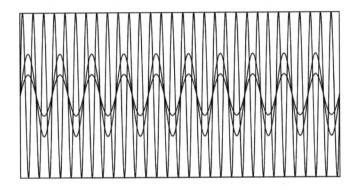

Let's move on to other linear recipes.

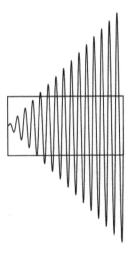

Rectangle 8" x 4"; Start X 0.0; End X 15.0; Multiply X checked; Y bottom -10.0; Y top 10.0; samples 200; isotropic checked; polar unchecked; function sin(x) * x . Source: Kirsanov.

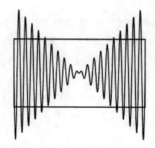

Rectangle 8" x 4"; Start X -10.0; End X 10.0; Multiply X checked; Y bottom -10.0; Y top 10.0; samples 200; isotropic checked; polar unchecked; function sin(x) * x

Rectangle 8" x .5"; Start X -1.0; End X 1.0; Multiply X unchecked; Y bottom 0.0; Y top 1.0; samples 200; isotropic checked; polar unchecked; function x-floor(x)

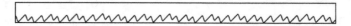

Rectangle 8" x .5"; Start X -1.0; End X 5.0; Multiply X checked; Y bottom 0.0; Y top 2.0; samples 100; isotropic checked; polar unchecked; function x-floor(x)

Rectangle 8" x .5"; Start X -1.0; End X 5.0; Multiply X checked; Y bottom 0.0; Y top 2.0; samples 50; isotropic checked; polar unchecked; function x-floor(x)

Rectangle 8" x .5"; Start X -1.0; End X 8.0; Multiply X checked; Y bottom 0.0; Y top 1.0; samples 70; isotropic unchecked; polar unchecked; function x-floor(x)

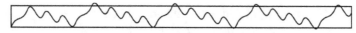

Rectangle 8" x .5"; Start X 0.0; End X 6.0; Multiply X checked; Y bottom 0.0; Y top 1.0; samples 22; isotropic unchecked; polar unchecked; function x-floor(x)

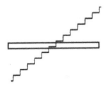

Greatly shrunken

Rectangle 8" x .5"; Start X -1.0; End X 1.0; Multiply X checked; Y bottom 0.0; Y top 1.0; samples 500; isotropic unchecked; polar unchecked; function ceil(x)

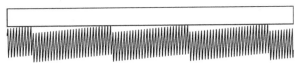

Rectangle 8" x .5"; Start X -8.0; End X 8.0; Multiply X checked; Y bottom 0.0; Y top 0.5; samples 500; isotropic unchecked; polar unchecked; function x-ceil(x)

Rectangle 8" x .5"; Start X -8.0; End X 8.0; Multiply X checked; Y bottom 0.0; Y top 1.0; samples 500; isotropic unchecked; polar unchecked; function x-ceil(x)

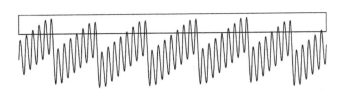

Rectangle 8" x .5"; Start X -20.0; End X 20.0; Multiply X checked; Y bottom 0.0; Y top 0.5; samples 50; isotropic unchecked; polar unchecked; function x-ceil(x)

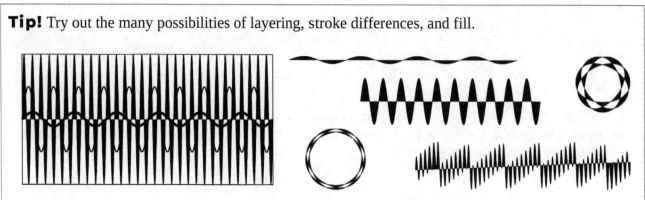

Examples of some of the figures with fill added

The remaining recipes will be for more or less round figures like flowers or stars. All require **Use polar coordinates** to be checked. All use a square as the starting figure.

Start X 0.0; End X 4.0; Multiply X checked; Y bottom -1.0; Y top 1.0; samples 100; isotropic unchecked; polar checked; function sin(6.0*x) End X 6.0 would double petals.

Start X 0.0; End X 8.0; Multiply X checked; Y bottom -1.0; Y top 1.0; samples 50; isotropic unchecked; polar checked; function sin(6.0*x)

Start X 0.0; End X 5.0; Multiply X checked; Y bottom -1.0; Y top 1.0; samples 30; isotropic unchecked; polar checked; function sin(4.0/5.0*x) Source: Bah

Start X 0.0; End X 12.0; Multiply X checked; Y bottom -1.0; Y top 1.0; samples 100; isotropic unchecked; polar checked; function sin(12.0*x) Will draw outside the boundaries of the square by quite a bit.

Start X 0.0; End X 8.0; Multiply X checked; Y bottom -1.0; Y top 1.0; samples 40; isotropic unchecked; polar checked; function sin(2.0*x)

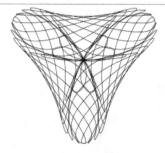

Start X 0.0; End X 8.0; Multiply X checked; Y bottom -1.0; Y top 1.0; samples 40; isotropic unchecked; polar checked; function sin(3.0*x)

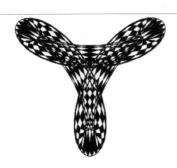

Start X 0.0; End X 8.0; Multiply X
checked; Y bottom -1.0; Y top 1.0;
samples 50; isotropic unchecked;
polar checked; function sin(3.0*x)

Start X 0.0; End X 12.0; Multiply X
checked; Y bottom -1.0; Y top 1.0;
samples 100; isotropic unchecked;
polar checked; function sin(5.0*x)

Start X 0.0; End X 10.0; Multiply X
checked; Y bottom -1.0; Y top 1.0;
samples 500; isotropic unchecked;
polar checked; function
1+0.2*sin(3*x) *sin(100.0/7.0*x)
Source: Bah

Start X 0.0; End X 5.0; Multiply X
checked; Y bottom -1.0; Y top 1.0;
samples 500; isotropic unchecked;
polar checked; function
1+0.2*sin(3*x) *sin(100.0/7.0*x)

Start X 0.0; End X 1.0; Multiply X
checked; Y bottom -1.0; Y top 1.0;
samples 500; isotropic unchecked;
polar checked; function
1+0.2*sin(3*x) *sin(100.0/7.0*x)

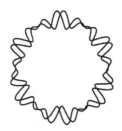

Start X 0.0; End X 2.0; Multiply X
checked; Y bottom -1.0; Y top 1.0;
samples 500; isotropic unchecked;
polar checked; function
1+0.2*sin(3*x) *sin(100.0/7.0*x)

The following figures will be drawn much larger than your square. Use a small one (e.g., 1 mm) with a thick stroke.

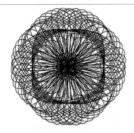

Start X 0.0; End X 500.0; Multiply X
checked; Y bottom -1.0; Y top 1.0;
samples 100; isotropic unchecked;
polar checked; function sin(x) *
cos(x)

Start X 0.0; End X 300.0; Multiply X
checked; Y bottom -1.0; Y top 1.0;
samples 50; isotropic unchecked;
polar checked; function sin(x) *
cos(x)

Start X 0.0; End X 100.0; Multiply X
checked; Y bottom -1.0; Y top 1.0;
samples 50; isotropic unchecked;
polar checked; function sin(x) * x
filled

Start X -1.0; End X 200.0; Multiply X checked; Y bottom -1.0; Y top 1.0; samples 100; isotropic unchecked; polar checked; function sin(x) * cos(x)
filled

Start X -1.0; End X 500.0; Multiply X checked; Y bottom -1.0; Y top 1.0; samples 100; isotropic unchecked; polar checked; function sin(x) * cos(x)
filled

Start X 0.0; End X 100.0; Multiply X checked; Y bottom -1.0; Y top 1.0; samples 25; isotropic unchecked; polar checked; function sin(x) * x
filled

Start X 0.0; End X 10.0; Multiply X checked; Y bottom 0.0; Y top 1.0; samples 150; isotropic unchecked; polar checked; function sin(x) * x
Source: Kirsanov

Start X -10.0; End X 10.0; Multiply X checked; Y bottom -1.0; Y top 1.0; samples 500 isotropic unchecked; polar checked; function sin(x) * x

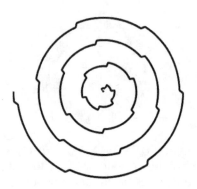

Start X -4.0; End X 0.0; Multiply X checked; Y bottom -1.0; Y top 1.0; samples 500; isotropic unchecked; polar checked; function ceil(x)

The following figures will be drawn about half the size of your square Use a thin stroke.

Start X -1.0; End X1.0; Multiply X checked; Y bottom -1.0; Y top 1.0; samples 100; isotropic unchecked; polar checked; function sin(x) * cos(x)
small

Start X 0.0; End X 500.0; Multiply X checked; Y bottom -1.0; Y top 1.0; samples 500; isotropic unchecked; polar checked; function sin(x) * cos(x)
small

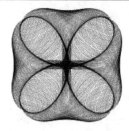

Start X 0.0; End X 1000.0; Multiply X checked; Y bottom -1.0; Y top 1.0; samples 500; isotropic unchecked; polar checked; function sin(x) * cos(x)
small

Note: This discussion of the **Function Plotter** mostly skips recipes for drawing spirals, since we already have the handy **Spiral** shape tool. Technically, the shape tool draws Archimedes spirals, but one other type that nature buffs might want is the logarithmic spiral, found in nautilus and snail shells, galaxies, DNA, hurricanes, whirlpools, sunflowers, and so on. The only way Inkscape can produce a logarithmic spiral is with the **Function Plotter** extension. Here's a recipe: Start X 0.0; End X 5.0; Multiply X checked; Y bottom -1.0; Y top 1.0; samples 100; isotropic unchecked; polar checked; function exp (0.185*x)

Sources

Bah, Tavmjong. *Inkscape: Guide to a Vector Drawing Program*. 4th Edition. New York: Prentice Hall, 2011.

Kirsanov, Dimitry. *The Book of Inkscape: The Definitive Guide to the Free Graphics Editor*. No Starch Press: San Francisco, 2009.

Gear (Render > Gear)

This extension offers two type of gears, a circular gear and a rack gear, which is simply a toothed horizontal track. Each draws only one gear at a time, but allows you to specify the measurements of the teeth. You can put together your own interconnected gears if you are so inclined. Pressure angle, by the way, determines the shape of the tooth: either sharply pointed (higher number) or squared off (lower number).

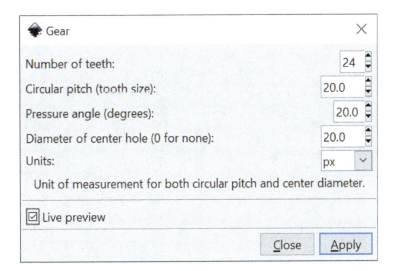

The **Rack Gear** option draws a figure like this:

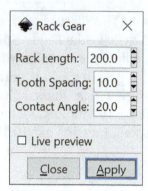

Contact Angle is the shape of the track—the matching option for the
Pressure Angle of the circular gear. A higher number is more pointed; a
lower number is squarer.

Grids (Render > Grids)

These are grids as images rather than as disappearing aids for your drawing. If you need regularly
spaced lines for a design, you'll find just about all you can imagine among the four types offered by this
extension. The settings are fairly self-explanatory. We could wish there were an option to use a white
rather than a transparent background, but a work-around is to draw another rectangle or circle the same
size, add white fill and no stroke, send the new rectangle to the bottom, and group the two.

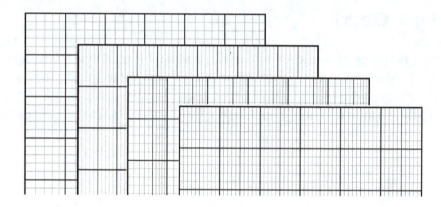

Various Cartesian grids

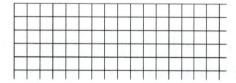

Grid (will cover the whole page)

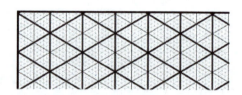

Isometric grid

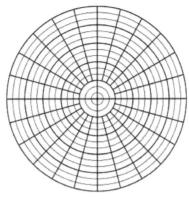

Polar grid

Guides Creator (Render > Guides Creator)

Unlike the previous extension, this one is for setting up guides that will not print with your objects but will help you position objects. The extension gives you more choices than simply setting guides from the usual screen, and maybe best of all, it provides a quick way of getting rid of all the guides simultaneously when you no longer want them.

Chapter 17
Extensions III

This chapter continues the discussion of Inkscape's Extensions. It is the third of these chapters and covers only one intriguing extension among the **Render** extensions.

L-System (Render > L-System)

A twentieth century botanist named Aristid Lindenmayer devised a branching system that would expand strings of symbols into geometric figures. He used these to simulate the way plants grow. Among other things, these formulas can be used to generate fractals, patterns that repeat at an increasingly larger or smaller scale. The Lindenmayer System, or L-System, has been adapted for use in various graphics programs, including this Inkscape extension. You may find some of the resulting images useful for design. Mostly, what will be provided here are "recipes."

Feel free to skip the following explanation and just go to the recipes. If, however, you want to try to make a few interesting lines or figures of your own, it's not hard to pick up enough understanding to do that.

The system adapted for this extension consists of four parts:
- **Axiom**: always includes a starting set of upper case characters on which the rules will build. These will most often represent one of two instructions, either "draw forward" or "move forward without drawing." Sometimes there will also be other letters which just serve as place holders.
- **Rules**: these are applied over and over each time a starting character is encountered. The rules tell how each starting character will develop at each application.
- **Additional characters:** constants that define a particular kind of motion. For instance, + supposedly means "turn left" and | means "turn 180°." Brackets [and] produce branching by telling the program to remember and come back to a certain point and then apply an instruction. Brackets must always come in pairs.
- **Some extra information** about size and angles explained below.

Note: This extension has an unexplained quirk. The **Help** key says + means "turn left" and - means "turn right." In practice, the opposite seems to be true. Maybe there is something going on in the programmer's mind that is totally opaque to me, or maybe this is simply a mistake. If you are attempting to write your own rules, just think of + as "turn right and - as "turn left." The only difference is that the resulting figure will be mirrored horizontally.

If you go looking for other L-system instructions online, you might want to know that the = sign used in our extension often appears as →. It means "becomes" or "leads to" or "expands to." Thus, if you come across online instructions that include → just substitute =.

All of these pieces together provide Inkscape with a road map for automatically drawing a recursive figure. "Recursive" simply means that the same rules are applied over and over.

All the meaningful characters for the **Axiom** and **Rules** slots in the dialogue are listed in the **Help** tab. You will notice that all the letters from A to F mean the same thing: "draw forward." F is very commonly used online. All the letters from G to L mean the same thing: "move forward" (without drawing). Why so many letters for the same thing? Some of the more complicated figures may have two or more rules. The letters make it possible to specify different recursions for different letters. Sometimes, even arbitrary letters beyond L, such as R, Y, and X, may be used just to serve as a place in the equation for another rule to apply.

The remaining slots of the dialogue allow you to specify how <u>much</u> of something will be applied.

Order: how many times should the rules be applied? Keep these in low single digits until you know how many applications will not overtax your computer.

Step length: what distance will "move forward" be in pixels?

Randomize step: how much chance variation do you want to introduce into the step length?

Left angle: when the drawing "turns left," to what degree will it turn?

Right angle: when the drawing "turns right," to what degree will it turn?

Randomize angle: how much chance variation do you want to introduce into the angles?

Let's look at a simple example.

We'll start with an Axiom: A.
We'll add the Rules—in this case, just one rule: A=A+A-A
To begin with, we'll try only one application of the rules, so write 1
in **Order**. We'll draw the lines 10 pixels long, so write 10.0 in the
Step length. Write 60.0 for each of the degree options. We don't
want to randomize anything, so leave those options at 0.0.

What the rule tells the program is this: "Program, every time you see
an A on the left of the = sign, substitute this:
draw forward 10 pixels, turn right 60°, draw forward 10 px, turn right
60°, draw forward 10 px."

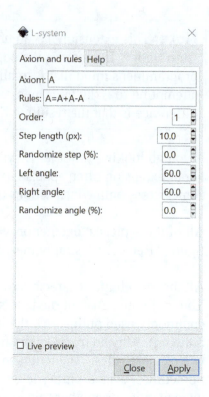

 Drawing starts going up the screen. Here's the result of the
extension with only 1 in the **Order** slot. That means there
are no recursions at this point.

Here's a further elaboration of how these rules work. The figure has been enlarged so it's easier to see.

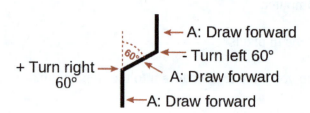

+ Turn right
60°

60°

A: Draw forward
- Turn left 60°
A: Draw forward
A: Draw forward

Now suppose we put 2 in the **Order** slot. This time we are telling the program,
"Start from the result from round one and apply the rule every time you see A.
Leave the extra pluses and minuses in, too." This results in A+A-A + A+A-A -
A+A-A . Now the result is the figure to the right, scaled down a bit to save space.

Remember that each line segment here corresponds to one instance of A, with the
pluses and minuses telling where to turn.

You can see that it wouldn't take many recursions before even this simple figure
would be quite large. When you encounter or devise a more complicated set of rules, keep the order to
4 or so until you see how Inkscape does with it. Otherwise you are liable to hang up the program.
<u>Remember to save often</u>!

> **Tip!** If your experiments do hang up Inkscape, it's not a big deal in Windows. First try the **Close** button to close Inkscape. If that doesn't work, just press **Ctrl-Alt-Delete** and select the **Task Manager**. You might then have to wait a few moments before you see Inkscape in the list of active programs. Select it and click **End Task**. You can restart Inkscape right away.

Below are a number of L-system recipes gathered from various sources on the Internet and often reworked slightly to fit the requirements of this extension. There were also a few happy accidents of my own. Because these formulations may show up in several places, it's sometimes hard to know who to credit, so if an attribution is incorrect, my apologies. Sources are listed at the end of the chapter.

L-System Recipes

Plant-like forms

To get more natural looking plant forms, experiment with the **Randomize step** and **Randomize angle** settings. Some of these recipes will give you a bushier form as you raise the order. Some will just add height. Changing the basic angles may also give variety.

Axiom: F
Rules: F=FF-[-F+F+F]+[+F-F-F]
Order: 4
Step: 5
Left angle: 22.5
Right angle: 22.5
The default formula in Inkscape

Axiom: X
Rules: F=FF; X=F+[-F-XF-X][+FF][--XF[+X]][++F-X]
Order: 4
Step: 4
Left angle: 25
Right angle: 25
Source: Vexlio

Axiom: X
Rules: X=F[+X] [-X]FX;F=FF
Order: 7
Step: 2
Left angle: 25.7
Right angle: 25.7
Source: Prusinkiewicz and Lindenmeyer

Axiom: X
Rules: X=F-[[X] +X]+F[+FX]-X;F=FF
Order: 5
Step: 5
Left angle: 22.5
Right angle: 22.5
Source: Bourke

Axiom: F
Rules: F=F[+F]F[-F]F
Order: 4
Step: 3
Left angle: 25.7
Right angle: 25.7
Source: Prusinkiewicz and Lindenmeyer

Axiom: F
Rules:

F=F[+F]F[-F][F]
Order: 5
Step: 5
Left angle: 20
Right angle: 20
Source: Prusinkiewicz and Lindenmeyer

286

Axiom: X
Rules: F=FF; X=F[+X]F[-X]+X
Order: 6
Step: 2
Left angle: 20
Right angle: 20
Source: Bourke

Filled

Axiom: +F
Rules: F=FF-[-F+F+F]+[F-F-F]
Order: 3
Step: 15
Left angle: 16
Right angle: 16

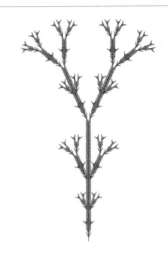

Axiom: Y
Rules: X=X[-FFF]
[+FFF]FX;Y=YFX[+Y][-Y]
Order: 6
Step: 5
Left angle: 25.7
Right angle: 25.7
Will work with angles up to at least 70,
though it starts looking less like a plant.
Source: Bourke

Axiom: VZFFF
Rules: V=[+++W][---W]YV;W=+X[-
W]Z;X=-W [+X]Z;Y=YZ;Z=[-FFF]
[+FFF]F
Order: 8
Step: 10
Left angle: 20
Right angle: 20
Source: Bourke

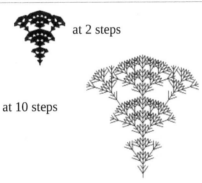

at 2 steps

at 10 steps

Axiom: F
Rules: F=F[+FF][-FF]F[-F][+F]F
Order: 3
Step: 2
Left angle: 36
Right angle: 36

Source: Bourke

Axiom: F
Rules: F=FF-[XY]+[XY];X=+FY;Y=-
FX
Order: 6
Step: 3
Left angle: 22.5
Right angle: 22.5
Source: Bourke

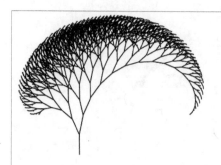

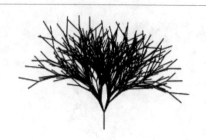

Axiom: --------C
Rules: C=NF[--P]F+C; N=NFF; P=Q;
Q=C
Order: 14-18
Step: 2
Left angle: 12.5
Right angle: 12.5
Source: Zaykov

Axiom: F
Rules: F=F[+F][-F]
Order: 8
Step: 10
Left angle: 25
Right angle: 25
Source: Vexlio

Same fromula, randomized:
Order: 6
Step: 20
randomize Step: 20
Left angle: 20
Right angle: 20
randomize angle 20

Axiom: F[+F+F][-F-F][++F][--F]F
Rules: F=FF[++F][+F][F][-F][--F]
Order: 3-4 more will hang
Step: 5
Left angle: 12   angles to 20 & 30 work
Right angle: 12
Source: Zaykov

rotated
Axiom: --------C
Rules: C=[--C]N[++C]N+C; N=NNF;
P=C
Order: 4-7
Step: 2
Left angle: 12.5
Right angle: 12.5
Source: Zaykov

rotated
Axiom: --------C
Rules: C=N[--C]N[++C]N+C;
N=NNF;; P=C
Order: 7
Step: 5
Left angle: 12
Right angle: 12
Source: Zaykov

288

Axiom: F
Rules: F=F-[-F-F+F+FF]+FF
[+F+F+FF]
Order: 3
Step: 7
Left angle: 8
Right angle: 8

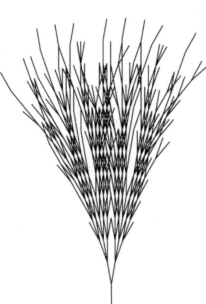

Axiom: A
Rules: A=A[-B][+B]; B=AA[-
B]AA[+A]
Order: 5
Step: 40
Left angle: 10
Right angle: 10

Axiom: A
Rules:A=A[-B][+B]; B=A[-B]A[+A-B]
Order: 6
Step: 30
Left angle: 20
Right angle: 20
Similar to Meyer

Axiom: F
Rules: F=FF[++FF[+FF]][-FF]
Order: 4
Step: 7
Left angle: 20
Right angle: 20

Axiom: X
Rules: F=FX[FX[+XF]]; X=FF[+XZ+
+X-F[+ZX]][-X++F-X]; Z=[+F-X-F][+
+ZX]
Order: 4
Step: 8
Left angle: 20
Right angle: 20
Source: Vexlio

Axiom: F
Rules: F=FF[-F+F][+F-F]
Order: 4
Step: 5
Left angle: 60
Right angle: 60
Source: Trbovich

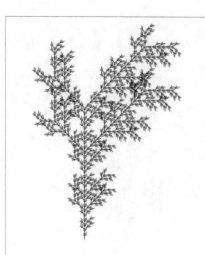

Axiom: F
Rules: F=+-FF[+FF][-F]F[-F][+FF]
Order: 4
Step: 4
Left angle: 45
Right angle: 45
Source: Lawrence

Same formula

Randomize Step: 20
Randomize Angle: 10

Source: Lawrence

Axiom: AF
Rules: A=FFFFFV[+++H][---Q]FB;
B=FFFFFV[+++H][---Q]FC;
C=FFFFFV[+++FA]FD; D=FFFFFV[+
++H][---Q]FE; E=FFFFFV[+++H][---
Q]FG; G=FFFFFV[---FA]FA; H=IFFF;
I=FFFF[--M]J; J=FFFF[--N]K;
K=FFFF[--O]L; L=FFFF[--P];
M=FFN; N=FFO; O=FFP; P=FF;
Q=RFF; R =FFFF[++M]S; S=FFFF[+
+N]T; T=FFFF[++O]U; U=FFFF[++P];
V=FV
Order: 15
Step: 2
Left angle: 12
Right angle: 12
Source: Bourke

Other geometrical figures, including well-known fractals, with variations.

For some, fill works very well.

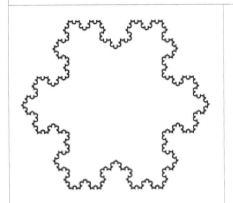

Von Koch Snowflake
Axiom: F++F++F
Rules: F=F-F++F-F
Order:
Step: 2
Left angle: 60
Right angle: 60
Source: Bah

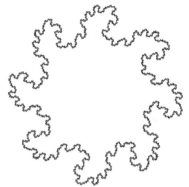

Koch variation by Hasan Hosam.
Axiom: X+X+X+X+X+X+X+X
Rules: X=X+YF++YF-FX--FXFX-
YF+X;Y=-FX+YFYF++YF+FX--FX-
YF
angle = 45
Source: Bourke

Cesàro Fractal
Axiom: F
Rules: F=F+F--F+F
Order: 5   6-7 ok, 8 may hang up
Step: 10
Left angle: 85
Right angle: 85
Source: Corte

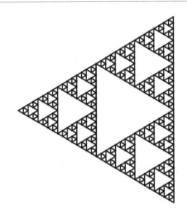

Sierpinski Triangle
Axiom: F-A-A
Rules: F=F-A+F+F-F; A=AA
Order: 6
Step: 5
Left angle: 120
Right angle: 120
Source: Wikipedia

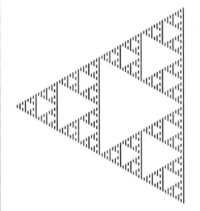

Sierpinski Triangle with dashes
Axiom: A-G-G
Rules: A=A-G+A+G-A; G=GG
Order: 6
Step: 5
Left angle: 120
Right angle: 120

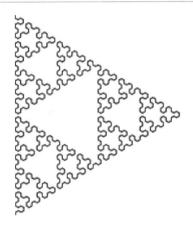

Sierpinski Triangles
Axiom: A
Rules: A=B-A-B;B=A+B+A
Order: 6
Step: 3
Left angle: 60
Right angle: 60
Source: Bah

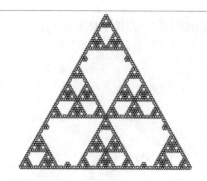

Sierpinski Arrowhead
Axiom: F+F+F+F+F+F
Rules: F=F-F+F+F+F-F
Order: 5 (6 may hang up)
Step: 3
Left angle: 60
Right angle: 60
Source: Kühne

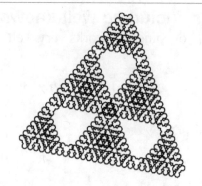

Axiom: F+F+F+F+F+F+F+F+F
Rules: F=F- -F+F+F+F+F+F+F- -F
Order: 4
Step: 2
Left angle: 40
Right angle: 40

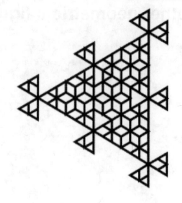

Axiom: F+X
Rules: F=F+F;X=--FXF++FXF+
+FXF--
Order: 6
Step: 5
Left angle: 60
Right angle: 60

With Order 14, Step 1

Heighway Dragon
Axiom: FA
Rules: A=A+BF+;B=-FA-B
Order: 12
Step: 2
Left angle: 90
Right angle: 90
Source: Wikipedia

Vicsek fractal
Axiom: F−F−F−F
Rules: F=F−F+F+F−F
Order: 4
Step: 2
Left angle: 90
Right angle: 90
Source: BoxFractal

Quadratic curve
Axiom: F
Rules: F=F+F-F-F+F
Order: 3
Step: 3
Left angle: 90
Right angle: 90
Source: Bah
same, angles 85
same, angles 80

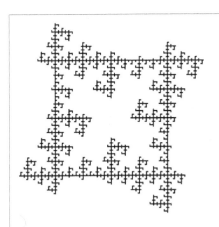

Axiom: F+F+F+F
Rules: F=FF+F++F+
Order: 6: Above 6 may hang up
Step: 2
Left angle: 90
Right angle: 90

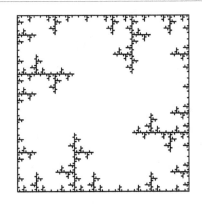

Crystal
Axiom: F+F+F+F
Rules: F=FF+F++F+F
Order: 4
Step: 4
Left angle: 90
Right angle: 90
Source: Bourke

Variation on quadratic snowflake by
Hasan Hosam.
Axiom: FF+FF+FF+FF
Rules: F=F+F-F-F+F
Order: 4
Step: 4
Left angle: 90
Right angle: 90
Source: Bourke

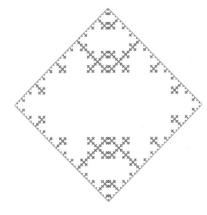

Axiom: F|F|F
Rules: F=F-F+F+F-F
Order: 4
Step: 2
Left angle: 90
Right angle: 90

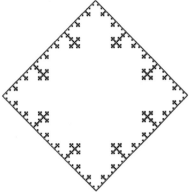

Axiom: F+F+F+F+F+F
Rules: F=F-F+F+F-F
Order: 4
Step: 2
Left angle: 90
Right angle: 90

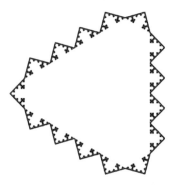

Axiom: F++FFFF++F++FFFF++F+
+FFFF++F
Rules: F=F---F+++F+++F---F
Order: 4
Step: 2
Left angle: 30
Right angle: 30

Axiom: F--F--F--F--F--F
Rules: F=F---F+++F+++F---F
Order: 4
Step: 3
Left angle: 30
Right angle: 30

Axiom:
F+F+F+F+F+F+F+F+F+F+F+F
Rules: F=F---FF+++F+++FF---F
Order: 4
Step: 2
Left angle: 30
Right angle: 30

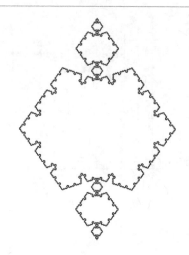

Axiom: F|F|F
Rules: F=F-F+F+F-F
Order: 4
Step: 2
Left angle: 72
Right angle: 72

Triflake or Koch Anti-snowflake
Axiom: F++F++F
Rules: F=F+F- -F+F
Order: 4
Step: 2
Left angle: 60
Right angle: 60
Source: Kühne

Axiom: F-F-F-F
Rules: F=FF-F-F-F-F-F+F
Order: 4
Step: 2
Left angle: 90
Right angle: 90
Source: Prusinkiewicz and
Lindenmeyer

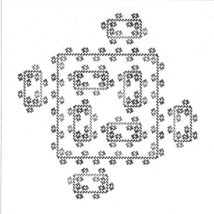

Axiom: F+F+F+F
Rules: F=F+G-FF+F+FF+FG+FF-
G+FF-F-FF-FG-FFF;G=GGGGGG
Order: 2
Step: 5
Left angle: 90
Right angle: 90
Source: Prusinkiewicz and
Lindenmeyer

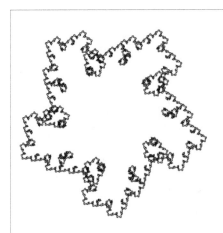

Axiom: F+F+F+F+F
Rules: F=F-F+F+F+F- -F
Order: 4
Step: 2
Left angle: 72
Right angle: 72
Source: Kühne

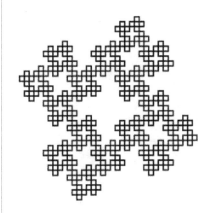

Axiom: F-F-F-F
Rules: F=F-F+F+F-F
Order: 4
Step: 4
Left angle: 90
Right angle: 90
Source: Bourke

Quadratic Flake
Axiom: F+F+F+F
Rules: F=F+F-F-FF+F+F-F
Order: 3 or 4: higher will hang up
Step: 2
Left angle: 90
Right angle: 90
Source: Bourke

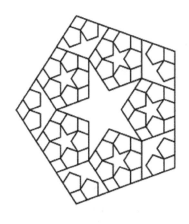

Axiom: F-F-F-F-F
Rules: F=FF-F-F-F-F-FF
Order: 2
Step: 10
Left angle: 72
Right angle: 72
Source: Leszpio

Axiom: F+F+F+F
Rules: F=FF+F-F+F+FF
Order: 3
Step: 2
Left angle: 90
Right angle: 90
Source: Bourke

Axiom: F-F-F-F
Rules: F=FF-F-F+F-F-F-FF
Order: 3
Step: 10
Left angle: 90
Right angle: 90

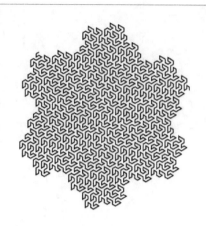

Hexagonal Gosper Curve
Axiom: A
Rules: A=A-B--B+A++AA+B-;B=+A-
BB--B-A++A+B
Order: 4
Step: 4
Left angle: 60
Right angle: 60
Source: Bourke

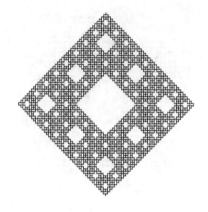

Sierpinski Carpet
Axiom: F
Rules:
F=F+F-F-F-G+F+F+F-F;G=GGG
Order: 4
Step: 4
Left angle: 90
Right angle: 90
Source: Riddle

Axiom: F-F-F-F
Rules: F=FF-F-F-F-FF
Order: 4
Step: 3
Left angle: 90
Right angle: 90
Source: Prusinkiewicz and
Lindenmeyer

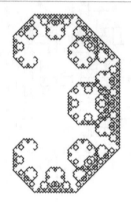

Lévy dragon
Axiom: F
Rules: F=+F--F+
Order: 11
Step: 3
Left angle: 45
Right angle: 45
Source: Riddle

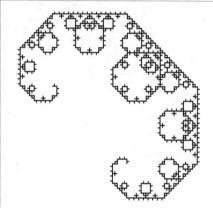

Axiom: F
Rules: F=F+F+
Order: 11
Step: 5
Left angle: 90
Right angle: 90

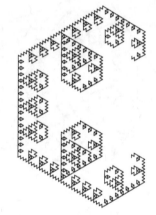

Axiom: F
Rules: F=F+F+
Order: 11
Step: 10
Left angle: 120
Right angle: 120

Durer's Pentagon
Axiom: F++F++F++F++F
Rules: F=F++F++F|F-F++F
Order: 4
Step: 3
Left angle: 36
Right angle: 36
Source: Bourke

McWorter's Pentidendrite
Axiom: F-F-F-F-F
Rules: F=F-F-F++F+F-F
Order: 4
Step: 3
Left angle: 72
Right angle: 72
Source: Browserling

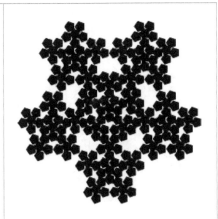

McWorter'sPentigree
Axiom: F-F-F-F-F
Rules: F=F-F+++F+F-F-F
Order: 3
Step: 4
Left angle: 72
Right angle: 72
Source: McWorter

Hexaflake
Axiom: F-F-F-F-F-F++
Rules: F=F-F-F++F++F-F-F
Order: 3
Step: 4
Left angle: 60
Right angle: 60
Source: Leszpio

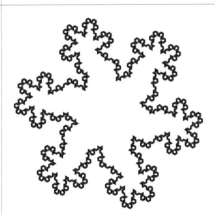

Axiom: F-F-F-F-F-F
Rules: F=F-F++F+F-F-F
Order: 3
Step: 5
Left angle: 60
Right angle: 60

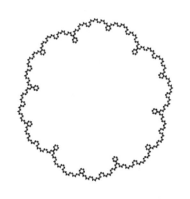

Axiom: Y-Y-Y
Rules: X=F+GF; Y=XY-XY
Order: 7—works to 10
Step: 2
Left angle: 60
Right angle: 60

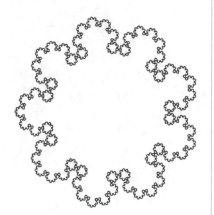

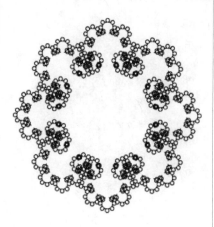

Axiom: F+F+F+F+F+F
Rules: F=F++F-F-F-F-F++F
Order: 4
Step: 2
Left angle: 60
Right angle: 60
Source: Kühne

Axiom: F+F+F+F+F+F+F+F+F
Rules: F=F- --F+F+F+F+F+F- - -F
Order: 4
Step: 2
Left angle: 40
Right angle: 40
Source: Kühne

Axiom: F+F+F+F+F+F+F+F+F
Rules: F=F- --F+F+F+F+F+F- - -F
Order: 3
Step: 2
Left angle: 40
Right angle: 40
Source: Kühne

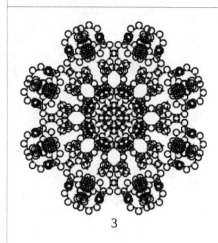

3

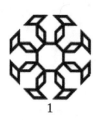

1

3

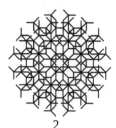

2

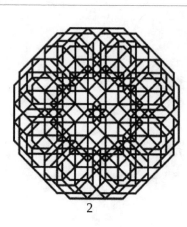

2

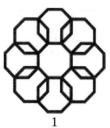

1

Axiom: F-F-F-F-F-F-F-F
Rules: F=F- - -F+F+F+F+F+F- - -F
Order: 3
Step: 4
Left angle: 45
Right angle: 45
Source: Kühne

Axiom: F-F-F-F-F-F-F-F
Rules: F=F- --- -F+F+F+F+F+F- --- -F
Order:3
Step: 4
Left angle: 45
Right angle: 45

Axiom: F+F+F+F+F+F+F+F
Rules: F=F--F+F+F+F+F+F--F
Order: 2
Step: 10
Left angle: 45
Right angle: 45

298

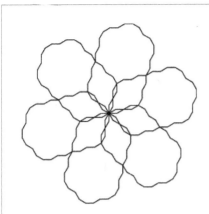

Axiom: F
Rules: F=F+F-F+F
Order: 4
Step: 10
Left angle: 30
Right angle: 30

Axiom: F
Rules: F=F++F
Order: 7
Step: 300
Left angle: 77
Right angle: 77
Source: Browserling

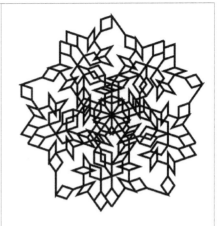

Axiom: [N]++[N]++[N]++[N]++[N]
Rules: M=OA++PA----NA[-OA----
MA]++;N=+OA--PA[---MA--NA]
+;O=-MA++NA[+++OA++PA]-;P=--
OA++++MA[+PA++++NA]--NA
Order: 3
Step: 2
Left angle: 36
Right angle: 36

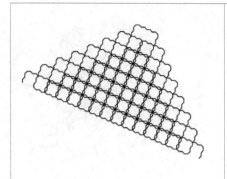

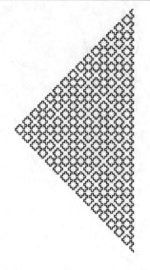

Axiom: F
Rules: F=F+F-F+F
Order: 5
Step: 5
Left angle: 45
Right angle: 45

Axiom: Axiom: W
Rules: W=+++X--F--ZFX+; X=---W+
+F++YFW-; Y=+ZFX--F--Z+++; Z=-
YFW++F++Y---
Order: 7
Step: 4
Left angle: 30
Right angle: 30
Fills nicely
Source: Lawrence

Axiom: X
Rules: X=XF-F+F-XF+F+XF-F+F-X
Order: 5
Step: 5
Left angle: 90
Right angle: 90
Fills nicely
Source: Dickau

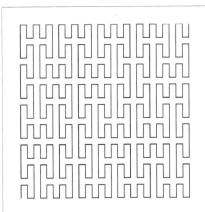

Peano Curve
Axiom: X
Rules: X=XFYFX+F+YFXFY-F-
XFYFX;Y=YFXFY-F-
XFYFX+F+YFXFY
Order: 3-5
Step: 5
Left angle: 90
Right angle: 90
Source: Bourke

Moore Curve or Hilbert Curve
Axiom: X
Rules: X=-YF+XFX+FY-; Y=+XF-
YFY-FX+
Order: 5
Step: 10
Left angle: 90
Right angle: 90
Source: Bourke

Snake Kolam
Axiom: F+XF+F+XF
Rules: X=XF-F+F+XF+F+XF-F-F+X
Order: 4
Step: 10
Left angle: 90
Right angle: 90
Source: Bourke

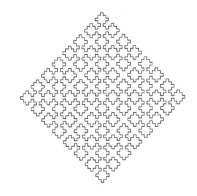

Sierpinski Square Curve
Axiom: F+XF+F+XF
Rules: X=XF-F+F-XF+F+XF-F+F-X
Order: 4
Step: 5
Left angle: 90
Right angle: 90
Source: Bourke

Kolam
Axiom: -D--D
Rules: A=F++FFFF--F--FFFF++F+
+FFFF--F;B=F--FFFF++F++FFFF--F--
FFFF++F;C=BFA--BFA;D=CFC--CFC
Order: 4
Step: 10
Left angle: 45
Right angle: 45
Source: Bourke

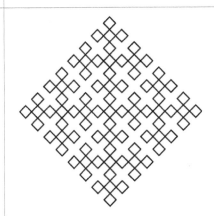

Krishna Anklets
Axiom: -X--X
Rules: X=XFX--XFX
Order: 4
Step: 10
Left angle: 45
Right angle: 45
Source: Bourke

301

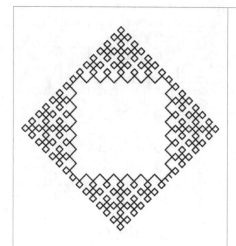

Axiom: -X--F--X--F--X--F--X
Rules: X=XFX--XFX
Order: 4
Step: 5
Left angle: 45
Right angle: 45

Axiom: --D--D-G-D--D-G
Rules: A=F++FFFF--F--FFFF++F+
+FFFF--F;B=F--FFFF++F++FFFF--F--
FFFF++F;C=BFA--BFA;D=CFC--CFC
Order: 3   Does not grow
Step: 12
Left angle: 45
Right angle: 45

Axiom: X
Rules: X=X+F+R-F-X+F+R-F-X-F-
R+F+X-F-R-F-X+F+R-F-X-F-R-F-
X+F+R+F+X+F+R-F-X+F+R+F+X-F-
R+ F+X+F+R-F-X+F+R-F-X; R=R-F-
X+F+R-F-X+F+R+F+X-F-
R+F+X+F+R-F-X+F+R+F+X+F+R-F-
X-F-R-F-X+F+R-F-X-F-R+F+X-F-R-
F-X+F+R-F-X+F+R
Order: 2-3
Step: 10
Left angle: 45
Right angle: 45
Source: Prusinkiewicz and
Lindenmeyer

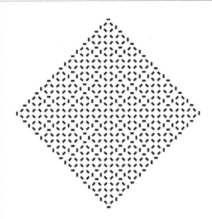

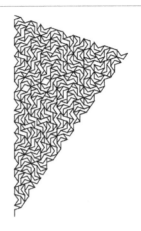

Axiom: L--F--L--F
Rules: L=+R-F-R+; R=-L+F+L-
Order: 9
Step: 3
Left angle: 45
Right angle: 45
Source: McWorter

Same, at Order 8.
Even order produces dashes; odd order produces circle/cross pattern.

Axiom: Q
Rules: F= ; P=--FR++++FS--FU;
Q=FT++FR----FS++; R=++FP----FQ+
+FT; S=FU--FP++++FQ--; T=+FU--
FP+;U=-FQ++FT-
Order: 7
Step: 10
Left angle: 36
Right angle: 36
Source: McWorter

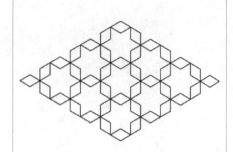

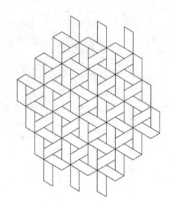

Mango Leaf
Axiom: Y---Y
Rules: X=RF-FRRF-FR--[--X]RF-
FRRF-FR--RF-FRRF-FR--;Y=G-
F+X+F-GY
Order: 4
Step: 20
Left angle: 60
Right angle: 60
Source: Bourke

Axiom: F
Rules: F=FF-F-
Order: 9   10 is iffy
Step: 30
Left angle: 60
Right angle: 60
Source: Trbovich

Penrose
Axiom: [N]++[N]++[N]++[N]++[N]
Rules: M=OA++pA----NA[-OA----
MA]++;N=+OA--PA[---MA--NA]
+;O=-MA++NA[+++OA++PA]-;P=--
OA++++MA[+PA++++NA]--NA;A=
Order: 2-5 Shown: 2, 3, 4
Step: 5
Left angle: 36
Right angle: 36
Source: Lawrence

304

Axiom: X-X-X-X-X-X-X-X-X-X-X-X-
X-X-X-X-X-X-X-X-X-X-X-X
Rules: X=[F-F-F-F[+++X+Y]-----
F--------F+F+F+F];Y=[F-F-F-F[++
+Y]-----F--------F+F+F+F]
Order: 6
Step: 6
Left angle: 15
Right angle: 15
Source: plot::Lsys

Axiom: X-X-X-X-X-X-X-X-X-X-X-X-
X-X-X-X-X-X-X-X-X-X-X-X
Rules: X=[F-F-F-F[+++X+Y]-----
FF+F+F+F];Y=[F-F-F-F[+++Y]-----
FF+F+F+F]
Order: 6
Step: 6
Left angle: 15
Right angle: 15

Axiom: X-X-X-X-X-X-X-X-X-X-X-X-
X-X-X-X-X-X-X-X-X-X-X-X
Rules: X=[F-F-F-F[+++X+]-----
FF+F+F+F]
Order: 6
Step: 10
Left angle: 15
Right angle: 15

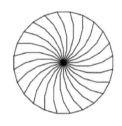

Axiom: X-X-X-X-X-X-X-X-X-X-X-X-
X-X-X-X-X-X-X-X-X-X-X-X
Rules: X=[F-F-F-F[+++Y]-----F--------
F+F+F+F]
Order: 6
Step: 6
Left angle: 15
Right angle: 15

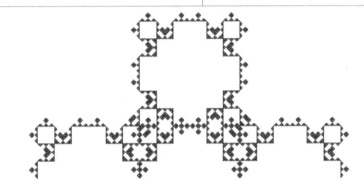

Axiom: F
Rules: F=+F+F-F-F+F+F+F-F-F+F
Order: 4   5 will hang up
Step: 2
Left angle: 90
Right angle: 90
Source: Marilyn

305

Axiom: X
Rules: X=-FF+FF+F+F-F-FFX
Order: 10   okay to go considerably
higher and longer
Step: 5
Left angle: 90   curved: 91
Right angle: 90   curved: 89
Source: Lawrence

Axiom: X
Rules: X=-FF+FF+F+F-F-FFX
Order: 15
Step: 10
Left angle: 93
Right angle: 85

Axiom: F
Rules: F=F+F-F-F+F-F
Order: 4
Step: 5
Left angle: 90
Right angle: 90

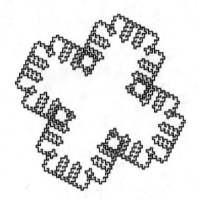
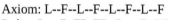

Axiom: L--F--L--F--L--F--L--F
Rules: L=+R-FR-FR; R=--F+FF-FL
Order: 9   4-13 produce other patterns
Step: 5
Left angle: 90
Right angle: 90

Axiom: L--F--L--FL--F--L--FL--F--L--
F
Rules: L=+R-F-R+; R=-L+F+L-
Order: 5
Step: 3
Left angle: 20
Right angle: 20

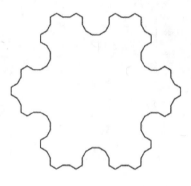

Axiom: L--F--L--F--L--F
Rules: L=+R-F-R+; R=-L+F+L-
Order: 5
Step: 10
Left angle: 30
Right angle: 30

306

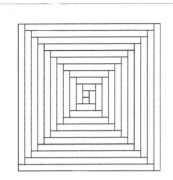

Axiom: -Y
Rules: X=XF;
Y=Y+XF+X+XF+XF+XF+XF
Order: 22
Step: 10
Left angle: 90
Right angle: 90

Axiom: -Y
Rules: X=XF; Y=Y+XF+XF
Order: 22
Step: 10
Left angle: 90
Right angle: 90
Source: Abrate

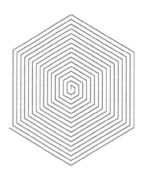

Axiom: -Y
Rules: X=XF;
Y=Y+XF+X+XF+XF+XF+XF
Order: 16
Step: 10
Left angle: 60
Right angle: 60
Source: Abrate

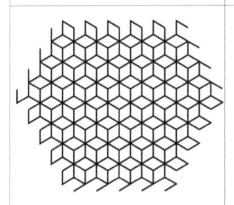

Axiom: Y
Rules: X=F+GF; Y=XY-XY
Order: 10
Step: 20
Left angle: 120
Right angle: 120
Source: Van Evert

Axiom: [F]+[F]+[F]+[F]+[F]+[F]
Rules: F=F[++F][--F][-FF]
[+FF]FF[+F][-F]FF
Order: 3 more will hang
Step: 2
Left angle: 60
Right angle: 60
Source: Zaykov

Axiom: -X--X
Rules: X=XFX--XFX
Order: 4   variations through 7
Step: 5
Left angle: 60
Right angle: 60

Sources

Abrate, Matteo. 2015. *Bl.ocks.org*. http://bl.ocks.org/nitaku/8b9e134ca8bae13bb470
http://bl.ocks.org/nitaku : 2019.

Bah, Tavmjong. *Inkscape: Guide to a Vector Drawing Program*. 4th Edition. New York: Prentice Hall, 2011.

Bourke, Paul. "L-System User Notes." 1991. *Fractals, Chaos, Self-Similarity.* http://paulbourke.net/fractals/lsys/ : 2019.

"Box Fractal." *WolframMathWorld.* http://mathworld.wolfram.com/BoxFractal.html : 2019.

Browserling. "L-system generator: World's simplest math tool." *Onlinemathtools.* https://onlinemathtools.com/l-system-generator : 2019.

Corte, Leo. "L-Systems and Penrose P3 in Inkscape." *The Brick in the Sky.* https://thebrickinthesky.wordpress.com/2013/03/17/l-systems-and-penrose-p3-in-inkscape/ ; 2019.

Dickau, Robert M. "Two-dimensional L-systems." *Math Forum, The National Council of Teachers of Mathematics.* http://mathforum.org/advanced/robertd/lsys2d.html : 2019.

Heijltjes, Wadler. "Turtle Graphics and L-systemsInformatics 1 – Functional Programming: Tutorial 7." *The University of Edinburgh, School of Informatics Website.* http://www.inf.ed.ac.uk/teaching/courses/inf1/fp/2008/tutorials/Tutorial7.pdf : 2019.

Kühne, Andrea. "The Beauty of Fractals: L-system in Houdini." *Motionesque.* http://www.motionesque.com/beautyoffractals/ :2019.

Lawrence, J. C. "Inkscape, L-Systems, SVG, Penrose and other tilings." 2008. *Other Wise.* https://kanga.nu/~claw/blog/posts/2008/11/16/game-design-tools/inkscape-l-systems-svg-penrose-and-other-tilings/ : 2019.

Leszpio. "Hexaflake." *Scratch*, MIT Media Lab. https://scratch.mit.edu/projects/293699541/ : 2019.

"L-system." *Wikipedia.* https://en.wikipedia.org/wiki/L-system :2019.

Marilyn. "Inkscape L-Sytem Turtle." 2011. *Brief Insights.* http://briefinsights.blogspot.com/2011/02/inkscape-l-system-turtle.html : 2019.

McWorter, William. "Fractint L-System True Fractals." 1997. http://spanky.triumf.ca/WWW/FRACTINT/lsys/truefractal.html; webpage archived at *WayBackMachine* (https://web.archive.org/web/20020503212834/http://spanky.triumf.ca/WWW/FRACTINT/lsys/truefractal.html) : 2019.

Meyer, Mark. "L-system." *NodeBox.* https://www.nodebox.net/code/index.php/Mark_Meyer_%7c_L-system : 2019.

"plot::Lsys: Lindenmayer systems." *MathWorks.* https://www.mathworks.com/help/symbolic/mupad_ref/plot-lsys.html : 2019

Prusinkiewicz P., Lindenmayer A. (1990) "Graphical modeling using L-systems." In: *The Algorithmic Beauty of Plants.* The Virtual Laboratory. Springer, New York, NY. Electronic reprint: *Semantic*

Scholar. https://www.semanticscholar.org/paper/Graphical-Modeling-Using-L-systems-1.1-Rewriting : 2019.

Riddle, Larry. "Classic Iterated Function Systems." *Ecademy Agnes Scott College.* http://ecademy.agnesscott.edu/~lriddle/ifs/ifs.htm : 2019.

Trbovich, Pete. "Inkscape Tutorial - L-System Fractals." *Penguin Pete's Blog.* http://penguinpetes.com/b2evo/index.php?p=694 : 2019.

Van Evert, Kelley. "L-systems #2 — using SVG." *Observable.* https://observablehq.com/@kelleyvanevert/l-systems-2 : 2019.

Vexlio, LLC. "Drawing simple generative organics with L-systems" *Vexlio.* https://www.vexlio.com/blog/drawing-simple-organics-with-l-systems/ : 2019.

Zaykov, Dmitriy. "Двухмерные L-фракталы" (L-dimensional fractals). http://dmitriyku.narod.ru/html/gallery_lfr.htm : 2019.

Chapter **18**
Extensions IV

This chapter ends the discussion of extensions included with Inkscape. It is the fourth of the four chapters on these extensions.

Parametric Curves (Render> Parametric Curves)

Most of the curves used in computer graphics are parametric curves. In fact, the Bezier and B-spline curves produced in Inkscape are parametric. This extension, related to the Function Plotter extension, allows people familiar with the mathematics of parametric curves to draw them using Python computer code. Since most of us are neither mathematicians or programmers, the extension may be of minimal use to you. What will be supplied here are a few "recipes."

All the figures produced by this extension must begin with a rectangle drawn by the **Rectangle** shape tool, **not** converted to a path. The dimensions of the rectangle will determine the dimensions of the figure, as long as **Isotropic Scaling** is unchecked.

- -

Celtic Knot

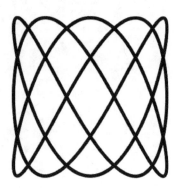

Isotropic scaling checked

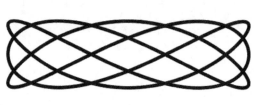

Isotropic scaling unchecked; different sized rectangles.

Parametric Curves: Range and Sampling		
Start t-valu	0.0	
End t-value	7.0	
Multiply t-range by 2*pi		
x-value of rectangle's left	-4.0	-1.0}Makes a longer figure

x-value of rectangle's right	4.0 1.0}
y-value of rectangle's bottom	-4.0
y-value of rectangle's top	4.0
Samples	30
Isotropic scaling (uses smallest of width/xrange or height/yrange)	x for squarer uncheck to allow rectangle shape to influence
X-Function	sin(3*t)
Y-Function	cos(5*t)
Remove rectangle	x
Draw Axes	

Increasing numbers in either the X-Function or Y-Function will increase or decrease the lines in the figure.

- -

Heart

Start with a tiny rectangle. This formula draws a very large heart.

Parametric Curves: Range and Sampling	
Start t-valu	0.0
End t-value	1.0
Multiply t-range by 2*pi	X
x-value of rectangle's left	-1.0
x-value of rectangle's right	1.0
y-value of rectangle's bottom	-1.0
y-value of rectangle's top	1.0
Samples	30

Isotropic scaling (uses smallest of width/xrange or height/yrange)	
X-Function	16*sin(t)**3
Y-Function	13*cos(t)-5*cos(2*t)-2*cos(3*t)-cos(4*t)
Remove rectangle	x
Draw Axes	

Source: Amaro Vita.

- -

Butterfly

End t-value 10   20   100

Parametric Curves: Range and Sampling	
Start t-valu	0.0
End t-value	100.0 A lower number produces fewer lines
Multiply t-range by 2*pi	
x-value of rectangle's left	-4.0
x-value of rectangle's right	4.0
y-value of rectangle's bottom	-4.0
y-value of rectangle's top	4.0
Samples	300
Isotropic scaling (uses smallest of width/xrange or height/yrange)	X
X-Function	sin(t)*(exp(cos(t)) - 2*cos(4*t) - pow(sin(t/12), 5))
Y-Function	cos(t)*(exp(cos(t)) - 2*cos(4*t) - pow(sin(t/12), 5))
Remove rectangle	x
Draw Axes	

Source: Bah

- -

Celtic doughnut

Check Isotropic scaling to make it round.

Parametric Curves: Range and Sampling	
Start t-valu	0.0
End t-value	100.0
Multiply t-range by 2*pi	
x-value of rectangle's left	-4.0
x-value of rectangle's right	4.0
y-value of rectangle's bottom	-4.0
y-value of rectangle's top	4.0
Samples	300
Isotropic scaling (uses smallest of width/xrange or height/yrange)	
x-Function	sin(t)*(1.0 + 0.2*sin(3.2*t))
y-Function	cos(t)*(1.0 + 0.2*sin(3.2*t))
Remove rectangle	x
Draw Axes	

Source: Bah

- -

Flower

Parametric Curves: Range and Sampling

Start t-valu	0.0
End t-value	5.0
Multiply t-range by 2*pi	x
x-value of rectangle's left	-2.0
x-value of rectangle's right	2.0
y-value of rectangle's bottom	-2.0
y-value of rectangle's top	2.0
Samples	100
Isotropic scaling (uses smallest of width/xrange or height/yrange)	
x-Function	(sin(-t)+sin(5*t))*exp(-t*0.01)
y-Function	(cos(t)+cos(5*t))*exp(-t*0.01)
Remove rectangle	x
Draw Axes	

Changing the number after **sin** and **cos** gets more or fewer petals.
Raising the number after **exp** slightly gets other flowers.

- -

Another Heart

Parametric Curves: Range and Sampling	
Start t-valu	0.0
End t-value	50.0
Multiply t-range by 2*pi	
x-value of rectangle's left	-250
x-value of rectangle's right	250
y-value of rectangle's bottom	-210
y-value of rectangle's top	210
Samples	1000 (Distortion sets in below 400)
Isotropic scaling (uses smallest of width/xrange or height/yrange)	
x-Function	(16*(sin(t)*sin(t)*sin(t)))*exp(t*0.01)
y-Function	(13*cos(t)-5*cos(2*t)-2*cos(3*t)-cos(4*t))*exp(t*0.01)
Remove rectangle	x
Draw Axes	

Source: Ragnar.

- -

Sources

Amaro Vita. "How to Plot." *Stack Overflow*. https://stackoverflow.com/questions/49095575/how-to-plot-x2y2-13-x2y3 : 2019.

Bah, Tavmjong. *Inkscape: Guide to a Vector Drawing Program*. 4th Edition. New York: Prentice Hall, 2011.

Ragnar. "Draw a 'perfect' heart shape using Parametric Curves." *InkscapeForum.com*. http://www.inkscapeforum.com/viewtopic.php?t=12951 : 2019.

Polygon Side

Need an equilateral polygon with a specific side length? This extension allows you to specify the number of sides and their length.

Seamless Pattern

Temporarily unavailable. (See pp. 320-22).

Spirograph (Render > Spirograph)

The Spirograph is a toy that first appeared in the 1960s, though its history is actually older than that. It used actual gears to draw lines on paper. This computer version is easy to use and fun to experiment with. Here are a few settings and the figures they yield.

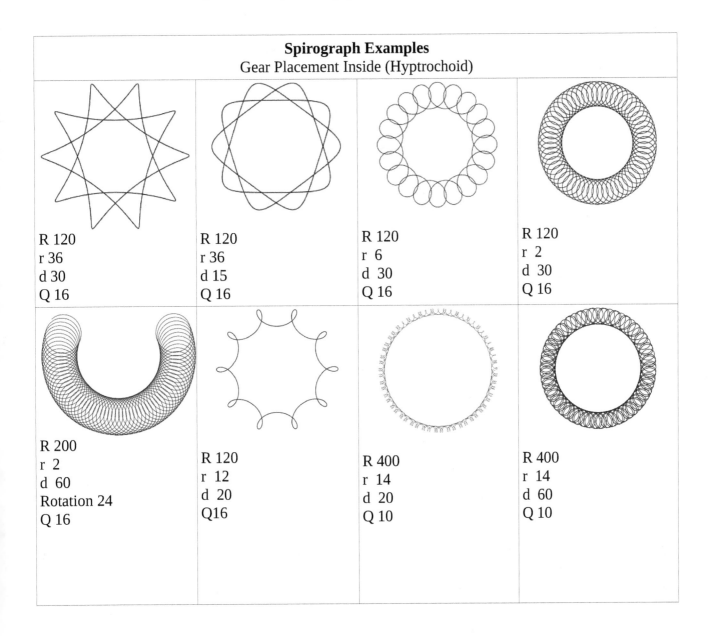

Spirograph Examples
Gear Placement Inside (Hyptrochoid)

R 120 r 36 d 30 Q 16	R 120 r 36 d 15 Q 16	R 120 r 6 d 30 Q 16	R 120 r 2 d 30 Q 16
R 200 r 2 d 60 Rotation 24 Q 16	R 120 r 12 d 20 Q16	R 400 r 14 d 20 Q 10	R 400 r 14 d 60 Q 10

(cont.)

Spirograph Examples
Gear Placement Outside (Epitrochoid)

R 100 r 14 d 60 Q 16	R 48 r 24 d 36 Q 16	R 48 r 32 d 48 Q 16	R 48 r 36 d 48 Q 16
R 42 r 36 d 48 Q 16	R 48 r 44 d 44 Q 16	R 46 r 36 d 48 Q 16	R 100 r 36 d 48 Q 16

Triangle

The extension draws a triangle based on the length of three sides, or a combination of sides and angles. The only measurement is pixels, but that can be altered fairly easily by using a little judicious rotation and the measurements in the object control line. Helpful for making templates for 3-D geometrical hollow-forms.

Wireframe Sphere (Render > Wireframe Sphere)

The extension produces a 3-D sphere that looks like a wire skeleton of a globe. Essentially there are two versions: a see-through globe that shows the wires that would appear on the other side and an opaque globe that shows lines only on the side toward the viewer. The latter is produced by checking "Hide lines behind the sphere."

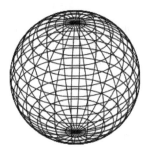

See-through sphere   Opaque sphere

The settings are easily understood. You can opt for more or fewer lines, more or less tilt, more or less rotation, and a different size.

Raising the **Tilt** to 90 results in a pole view:

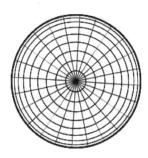

The default settings, in case you lose track of them, are:

Lines of latitude   19
Lines of longitude   24
Tilt (deg)   35
Rotation (deg)   4
Radius   100

Chapter 19
Pattern-making Revisited

We've looked at several ways to create patterns in Inkscape (see especially Chapters 4 and 8), but there are a few additional ways to consider. Of particular interest are seamless patterns. Such a pattern is made up of one rectangle filled with a drawing that can be repeated over and over in a larger space without the viewer being able to see the boundaries of the original rectangle. You can do that with the Pattern maker built into Inkscape, but it's not always easy to figure out how to make these patterns seamless. In seamless patterns, lines or shapes may continue across the boundary of the rectangle without the viewer ever realizing that the boundary exists, and yet elements of the drawing repeat again and again.

We will look at additional ways to create seamless patterns. One is especially designed for the purpose and is named **Seamless Pattern**. The another is based on the **Cloning and Tiling** functions that you have already met in Chapter 8. A third is a hybrid: cloning and tiling done in such a way that the result is similar to **Seamless Pattern**.

In addition, we'll see how to preserve your Pattern swatches in Paint Servers, so that they are available after you've closed and opened Inkscape again, and even after updating Inkscape to a new version.

Warning! Unfortunately, as of the writing of this book, **Seamless Pattern** is not functional. When I first wrote the directions for **Seamless Pattern**, it was an extension that worked very well indeed. Then Inkscape moved from Version .92 to Version 1.1. It was a watershed moment in the history of the program, with numerous improvements and new features. However, the underlying code made some old features tricky to update, and **Seamless Pattern** was one. It currently resides as a template rather than as an extension. You can find it under **File > New from Template > Seamless Pattern**. At the moment, Inkscape crashes when this is opened in Windows.

I have retained this discussion of the former extension in hopes that in an upcoming version, **Seamless Pattern** will be fixed. It may be put back among the extensions or it may remain a template, but in either case, the hope is that the following directions will be helpful.

Seamless Pattern (Extensions > Render > Seamless Pattern or File > New from Template > Seamless Pattern)

Although the regular Inkscape program has a pattern maker built into it (see pp. 38 ff.), some users felt a need for a mechanism to produce patterns that would be more reliably seamless. This extension looks complicated at first, but it is actually rather simple to operate even though the built-in instructions are confusing.

When you open the extension, starting with a new document, the following screen appears.

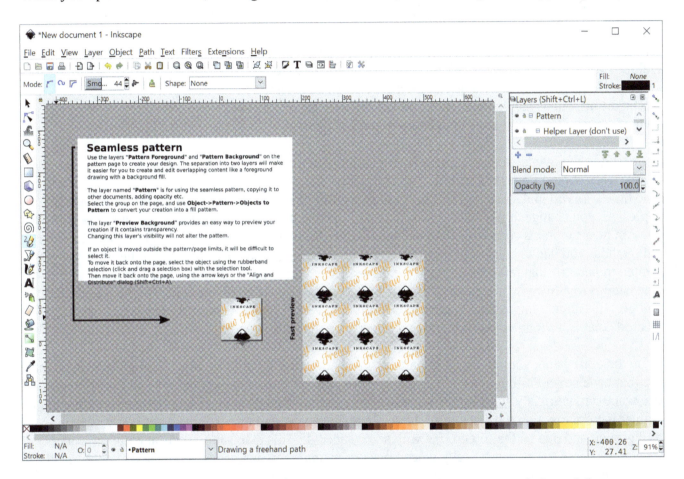

The default size of a pattern is 100 pixels square. You can change this as you wish, but while you are learning, just leave it as is. If you choose a different width and height, click apply.

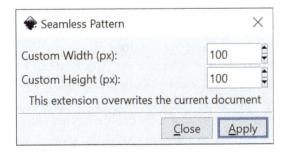

In addition, you will need to call up the **Layers** dialogue (**Shift + Ctrl + L or Layer > Layers**), which will appear in the right-hand panel.

The only active part of the main screen that you will will actually be controlling is the little square that has the arrow pointing at it. To start with, it has the Inkscape logo and motto "Draw Freely." Let's call this the creator square. This is where you will be drawing.

Corresponding to this creator square will be two layers in the **Layers** dialogue: **Pattern Foreground** and **Pattern Background**. Unfortunately, these don't seem to show up at once in the dialogue: you have to scroll down, and perhaps double-click on the edge of the little square. **Pattern Foreground** and **Pattern Background** will appear under **Helper Layer** in this dialogue. Alternatively, you may have to click on **Helper Layer** to see **Pattern Foreground** and **Pattern Background**, but as the dialogue tells you, don't try to <u>use</u> **Helper Layer**. It will mess up any pattern you have drawn.

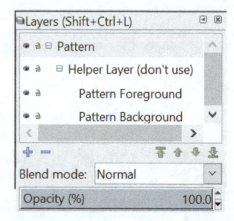

Returning to the overall screen, you will see a larger pattern box to the right, labeled **Pattern Preview**. You will notice that the little creator square is duplicated here nine times. If you look closely, you can actually see faint lines marking the boundaries between the copies. As you change things in the creator square, the results will show up in the **Pattern Preview** so you can position items correctly along the boundaries. To make a seamlessly repeating pattern with the old method, you had to be careful that your items crossed the boundaries correctly; otherwise you were limited to patterns that left space around the edges. Even then, you might see gaps. The point of this extension is to allow you to construct interlocking seamless swatches intuitively, watching the effect as you go. It is almost impossible to create a pattern that doesn't repeat seamlessly using this new method--that is, as long as you are drawing directly on the little square.

If, on the other hand, you are trying to paste elements onto the square in symmetrical patterns, you may run into problems. Pasting one element into the box will produce symmetrical rows of that element. If you want symmetrically <u>staggered</u> rows, however, you may have trouble. Better to use cloning and the regular pattern function for that sort of thing. To achieve staggered rows, I have put one on the background and one on the foreground with some success. This extension excels at patterns where several elements are asymmetrically placed in a group, and then that group is repeated symmetrically as in the example below.

Here's a procedure that seems to work.

1. Start the extension and get the **Layers** dialogue in place, as above. Leave the **Seamless Pattern** size box up, moving it to the side, because you can use it to start the extension again quickly if you want to erase everything you've done.
2. Zoom in so you can see both the creator square and the **Pattern Preview** well.
3. Now, how are you going to see what you're doing on a creator square that is already occupied? You can delete what's there, but <u>don't try to delete everything all at once</u> from the initial logo pattern. If you do, it will make it impossible to use the creator square, and the **Preview** square will also disappear. Then you have to start the extension over.

4. Begin with the background. For our purposes, the background will probably be either plain white or plain black, though we certainly have the option of using a pattern for the background and then overlaying the foreground. We'll use plain white in this example, replacing the gradient fill used by the extension author. If you ultimately want an invisible background, wait until the end to delete it. To start, click along the edge of the creator square to select it. Then click **Pattern Background** in the **Layers** dialogue. Click on the white square on the palette stripe to make the fill white. Lock the background with the little padlock button if you wish.

5. Now you can remove the built-in icons and text that make up the foreground, so you can see what you're doing with a new pattern.

6. You might want to lock the background by clicking on the little padlock next to background in the layers dialogue. That will keep the background from sliding around as you construct the foreground.

7. Click on **Pattern Foreground** and draw your pattern, or copy and paste elements from elsewhere. Here we'll use a simple 13-cornered polygram with a black stroke. As you draw, you can move the items around and observe their effect on the larger pattern in the **Preview**. Notice that if you draw an item that overlaps the edge of the creator square, the rest of the item will show up in the proper place in the **Preview**, so that we have achieved our seamlessly repeating pattern rather effortlessly.

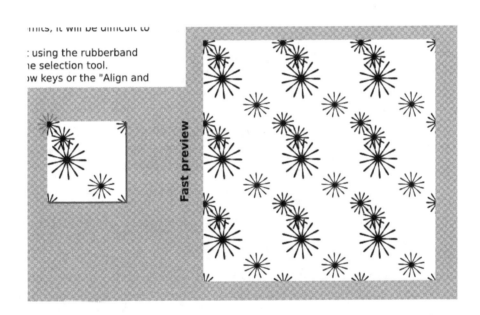

Tip! If you are pasting an element into the creator square, zoom in so the square occupies most of your screen. Chances will be better that all or part of the pasted element will actually show up on the square and not somewhere inaccessible.

The point of having a separate background and foreground designated is that we can lock one or the other or make one or the other invisible in order to work freely on one without messing up the other. Locking is probably less important for our purposes than for those working in complex colors. The little lock and eye symbols can be seen in the **Layers** dialogue to the left of **Pattern Foreground** and **Pattern Background**.

Once you have a pattern, what do you do with it? Continuing with regular work on this extension screen is pretty impossible, so let's get this pattern onto a regular screen. First, click **Pattern** on the **Layer** dialogue. What actually happens behind the scenes is that your pattern is grouped and clipped. At some point you might want to remember that all the scraps hanging over the edge of the creator-square are in fact still there--just hidden. Mostly, you don't have to pay attention to this.

Now click or rubber-band the pattern and **Copy** it. Open a new Inkscape screen (**File > New**). Paste the pattern onto the page. Make sure it is selected and press **Object > Pattern > Objects to Pattern**. The Pattern should now appear in the Pattern list when you go to the **Fill** tab of the **Fill and Stroke** dialogue. To find the Patterns, click the square with the small blue and white checks.

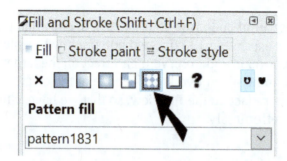

As you can see above, Inkscape has given the pattern a number. You can now use it to fill other objects. Remember you can make the pattern larger or smaller and rotate it using the little control squares and circle outside the object (see pp. 38-9).

Also remember, very importantly, that <u>the pattern will only remain in the **Fill** dialogue as long as this Inkscape screen is active</u>. Once you close the screen, the pattern disappears from the dialogue. Be sure to save a copy of the pattern square itself or save the **Seamless Pattern** screen, giving it a name.

You may wish to start a page of pattern squares that you can activate as patterns when you need them. I keep such a page with dozens of little 100-pixel squares, ready to be copied into new documents and used as patterns.

There is also another slightly more complicated way to save your custom Patterns so that they all show up in the Paint Server dialogue for use in the same way as Pattern fill even after you have closed and reopened Inkscape (see pp. 328 ff.).

Patterns Made by Drawing on Cloned Tiles

In Chapter 8, we explored cloning and the various tiling symmetries available in Inkscape. The method used was to create a drawing and then clone and tile it in various ways. An alternative method used by many artists is to tile first and then draw. You may discover that this is more intuitive, especially if you love line drawing. Those using a pen and tablet may be even more likely to find the method satisfying.

We'll start with a 9-tile setup as an example. You can use more or fewer tiles. Follow these steps!

1. Draw a rectangle. This will land in the upper left corner of our 9-tile setup, so start in the upper left of the page.
2. **Select** and **Group** the rectangle, even though it is a single object.
3. Open the **Create Tiled Clones** dialogue (**Edit** > **Clone** > **Create Tiled Clones**).
4. Choose **P1: simple translation** under **Symmetry**. Next to **Rows, columns** below, enter 3 and 3.
5. Click **Create**. You should now have a 3 x 3 array of rectangles.
6. Keep the original rectangle selected for the moment. It is sitting under one of the cloned tiles. Check the notification area at the bottom of the screen. It should say, "**Group** of **1** object in **Layer 1**...." That is the original rectangle, and that is what you will draw on.
7. Raise this original rectangle to the top of the Z-order (**Object** > **Raise to top**) or use the corresponding icon on line 3.
8. With the base tile selected, **Right Click**. At the bottom of the pop-up menu find **Enter group#_ _ _ _**. The group has been given a number which is relevant only to the inner mysteries of the Inkscape code. Select this command. Now it is possible to draw on the base tile and have that drawing duplicated on all the other tiles.
9. Go ahead and decorate the base tile and watch what happens. What you draw will appear on all the other tiles, creating an instant pattern.

It's fine to draw outside the boundaries of the base tile if you intend to keep the whole array of tiles for making a texture plate with a repeating pattern or for a stencil to be cut with a cutting machine (see pp. 363 ff., 367). If you want, the extraneous bits can be "trimmed" around the outside by clipping (see pp. 113-4).

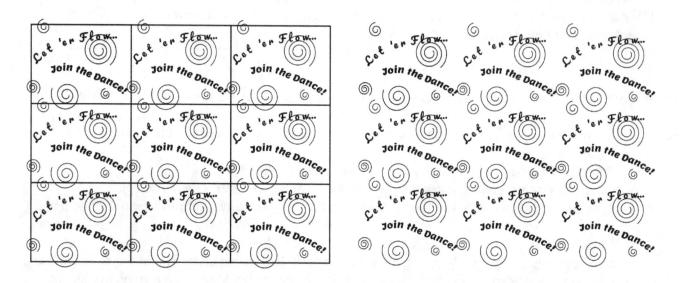

On the left, the base tile has been decorated directly with text and shapes. The rectangle lines have not yet been deleted. On the right is the seamless pattern once the base rectangle's lines have been deleted.

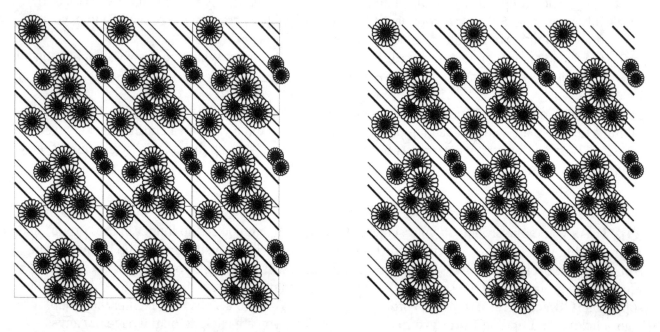

Another seamless pattern with and without the rectangle lines. In this case the base rectangle was a perfect square to make the diagonal lines work. You'll have to look carefully to see the lines of the squares on the left.

Using Cloned Tiles to Make a Seamless Pattern Square for Use with Pattern > Objects to Pattern

This method is essentially the same as using the **Seamless Pattern** Extension/Template. It's just more complicated.

1. Draw a perfect square. As before, put it in the upper left corner of the page.
2. **Select** and **Group** the rectangle.
3. Open the **Create Tiled Clones** dialogue (**Edit** > **Clone** > **Create Tiled Clones**).
4. Choose **P1: simple translation** under **Symmetry**. Next to **Rows, columns** below, enter 3 and 3.
5. Click **Create**. You should now have a 3 x 3 array of rectangles.
6. Keep the original square selected for the moment.
7. Raise this original square to the top of the Z-order (**Object** > **Raise to top**) or use the corresponding icon on line 3.
8. Drag that original base square outside of the array, placing it to the left by itself. Double-check that the bottom notification area says this is "Group of 1 object...." The reason for putting the base square to the left, outside the clone array, is that it's easier to keep track of and manipulate without getting the base square and clone mixed up.
9. With the base tile selected, **Right Click**. At the bottom of the pop-up menu find **Enter group#_ _ _ _** and select it.
10. Decorate the base tile as before, drawing outside the boundaries of the square as needed. Watch carefully what is happening in the array, making sure the whole array looks good, <u>especially the middle tile of the clones</u>.

Warning! When you draw an object outside the boundaries of the square, do not cross two or more boundaries. If you do, the pattern will not be seamless. Crossing one boundary per object works fine.

---

11. When finished, select the whole clone array. Click **Edit** > **Clone**> **Unlink Clone**.
12. **Ungroup** everything. At this point, each object should be surrounded by its own bounding box. Now you want to be able to reach the middle square and all objects inside it and touching it without disturbing those objects. Ultimately, you are going to use the middle square <u>outline</u> as a clipping square.
13. At the very least, you will have to delete the surrounding square outlines, leaving only the square outline in the middle, plus all the objects connected to it. If you delete something you shouldn't, use **Undo**.
14. Once you have clear access to the middle square outline and its touching objects, raise that square outline to the top of the Z-order and click on **Object** > **Clip** > **Set**. Notice immediately that there is now a well-defined square of your custom pattern. Pieces of the border objects have disappeared. They will reappear when you apply the pattern to a new object. This is why you've gone to all the trouble of preserving those extra bits all the way around the outside of the square.
15. While everything is still selected, click **Object** > **Pattern** > **Objects to Pattern**.
16. Test the pattern out in a new object, such as a circle, just to be sure it's working correctly.

Saving Custom Patterns Permanently Using Paint Servers

The **Paint Servers** function, which you met in an earlier chapter (see p. 41), offers some goodies beyond the built-in Inkscape **Patterns** which you can see under the **Fill** tab of the **Fill and Stroke** menu. Not only does it provide another route to those built-in fills, as well as some useful hatch fills; it offers the only reasonably convenient way to keep your custom patterns available every time you open Inkscape, and even after you have installed a new version of Inkscape.

> **Tip!** You were advised earlier to keep at least one page of **Pattern** swatches saved among your Inkscape documents. That advice still stands, even if you follow these directions for adding the swatches more permanently to Paint Servers. It's always good to have a backup.

Single Custom Patterns in Paint Servers

To make a single custom **Pattern** readily available through **Paint Servers**, try following these steps:

1. Draw a pattern. It doesn't have to be square—a square just helps with seamlessness if you have lines leading out of the swatch.

A very simple Pattern drawn with just two spirals, then used to fill an oval.

2. Make your swatch small in relationship to the page. A little under an inch (about 20-25 mm) works well. Otherwise the drawing will show up so large in the Paint Server that it will be hard to identify by sight.
3. Convert the drawing to a **Pattern** with **Object > Pattern > Objects to Pattern**.
4. Make sure it's in a completely clean document. To be sure, you can paste it into a new Inkscape document. You don't want scraps showing up in the **Paint Servers**.
5. Give the document a name. You <u>must</u> do this correctly or **Paint Servers** will crash Inkscape.
   a) Click **Document Properties (File > Document Properties)**.
   b) Select the tab **Metadata**.
   c) Type a name for the **Pattern**. You may <u>not</u> use spaces.
   d) <u>Don't</u> save as default at the bottom of **Metadata**.
6. Save the whole file, maybe with the same name.
7. Copy it.
8. In Inkscape, navigate to where the **Paint Server** files are kept:
   a) Click **Edit > Preferences** (at the very bottom) > **System**.
   b) Find **User paint servers**. At the right is an **Open** button. Click it.

c) You are now in a folder called **Paint**. It will be empty, assuming this is the first time you've used it. Paste the **Pattern** document you copied.

d) Close it and close down Inkscape.

9. Reopen Inkscape. When you go to **Paint Servers**, you should see your **Pattern** file. The name you gave it will be a separate category—a separate **Paint server**—under **Servers**. It will contain only one **Pattern** at this point. The **Pattern** will have a number rather than a name.

Alternatively, you can navigate to the **Paint Servers** files in Windows by this route: **(C:)** > **Users** > [your **name** or the name of your computer] > **AppData** > **Roaming** > **inkscape** > **paint** .

If you need to change or get rid of a custom Pattern, just delete the file or replace it. Remember that a **Pattern** can be edited after you apply **Object** > **Pattern** > **Pattern to Objects**.

Each document you save becomes one **Paint Server**.

Multiple Custom Patterns in One Paint Server

If you have a number of different patterns, a useful way to organize them is to put them all on one document page. If you have more a dozen or so, you may want to set up various documents, each containing several patterns with similar characteristics. For example, I might have a document named *SquaresandTriangles* with several variations of square and triangular shapes like these:

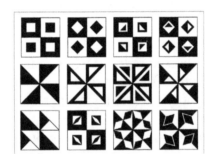

All these Patterns were saved in a single
document named SquaresandTriangles

I could have another document called *Flowers* with various flower patterns, a third document called *Circles* with various configurations of circles, and so on.

The advantage to sorting swatches into documents named according to categories is that the swatches will then show up under that category name as a Paint Server. For instance, all the thumbnails for the *SquaresandTriangles* document above will show up under that name as a single Paint server. Under it will appear the twelve pattern thumbnails, each with a number, ready to fill another object.

In summary, putting more than one Pattern in the same clean document and naming the whole document will result in a number of pattern swatches appearing in the Paint Servers menu under that document name (the name you have given the document in Metadata). The document has become a Paint server, and under it, each pattern will have a separate number. Now as you are working on a drawing, you can choose which Paint server is going to show up in the thumbnails, or you can choose **All paint servers.**

Naming Individual Custom Patterns

As you already know, individual custom Patterns are automatically given a number by Inkscape. It is possible to rename these individual patterns, though not very convenient. I myself find the numbers sufficient since I choose by thumbnails anyway. But if you want to replace the numbers with a name, you can. It just requires going into the .svg code of the document.

Here's how:

1. In the **Paint Servers** dialogue, go through the thumbnails of the patterns in your document. Point at each. The number will appear. On paper, jot down the current number of each pattern and what you want to rename it.
2. Next, find the pattern document in the **Paint server** files on your computer. As before, you can go in by either of two routes:
   a) In Inkscape, click **Edit** > **Preferences** > **System** > **User paint servers** > **Open** button.
   b) Or on your computer, start from **This PC** > **(C:)** > **Users** > [your name or the name of your computer] > **AppData** > **Roaming** > **inkscape** > **paint**
3. Find the document with the patterns you intend to name. Open the document in a basic text processor. (You don't want all the formatting that comes with a major word processor.) Here's how in Windows.
   a) Right-click on the document.
   b) Point at **Open with**. A list of programs will pop up.
   c) Click on **WordPad**. You should now see the .svg code of your document.
4. Find the number of each pattern. It will be in a phrase like `id="pattern6126"` You could try the **Find** function in WordPad if you wish.
5. Change each number to your new name. For example, change `id="pattern6126"` to `id="relic"` or `id="triangle_on_square"` or whatever you want. Just don't leave any spaces if your chosen name has more than one word.
6. Save the document in WordPad.
7. When you close down Inkscape and reopen it, the new name should be visible when you point at each thumbnail.

Chapter **20**
An Add-On Extension

Feeling adventurous? A number of external extensions have been developed for Inkscape by programmers who probably wanted them for purposes of their own and then were generous enough to share them with the world for free. External extensions are not built into Inkscape, so you have to download them separately. The Inkscape organization provides a listing of currently approved external extensions at https://inkscape.org/gallery/=extension/ and additional extensions are found in other places on the Web.

Most of these are highly specialized, having been developed for specific technical purposes. Among the listings, however, is a delightful art-oriented plug-in well worth a look. To use it, you will need to download it, unzip the files, and install them in the right place on your hard drive. Truly, this is not difficult if you follow the directions below.

Here's a little about the extension and why you should bother to seek it out.

Guilloche Extension for Inkscape

This extension is one of the most addictive Internet art aids since programming wizards started making mandala-creating programs available at the touch of a few buttons.

Once this gem is downloaded and installed, the control panel may seem baffling at first unless you are familiar with waveform terminology. Never fear. You'll find some easy explanations here that should get you well on your way to happy experimentation. Do pay attention to advice about what control lines will work well together and what won't.

What is Guilloche or Guilloché?

If you happen to have a very expensive old watch lying around, or if you examine the fancy green margins of a dollar bill, you will see fine-lined engraving in intricate intertwining designs. That is Guilloche. A process first used in the 1500s, Guilloche came to be aided by specialized metal engraving tools like a rose engine lathe. It is still used in many decorative arts, from architectural details to fine jewelry.

The Guilloche Extension in Use

Take a look at the original download page for the extension (https://inkscape.org/~fluent_user/ %E2%98%85guilloche-pattern-extension) and notice the striking color example given by the original programmer, "fluent_user." This figure is <u>not</u> what you will immediately get by applying the extension. Instead, it is a construction made up of several Guilloche figures. The final figure is actually composed of five different concentric outlines. The last is a tiny circle at the center. Between each of these outlines is a network of lines. Note that each of these sets of lines is created separately and the results have been nested by the artist: the program only does one set at a time. The combination is not automatic, but deliberate. This makes for a little additional work but allows for a great deal of flexibility and artistic choice. My own black and white example above is made up of four nested outlines.

In practice, thin lines like those above will not work well for all metal clay and etching techniques. You will have to use your own judgment and experience for the particular techniques you use. Even if you are not using figures as complicated as the one above, the extension still provides a great many choices, including thicker lines that do work well with the techniques reviewed in the next chapter. The outline "contours" will be tremendously useful on their own, even without the internal patterns.

The Guilloche extension is made up of two parts, **Guilloche Contour** and **Guilloche Pattern**. **Contour** draws an outline of waves of varying types. **Pattern** draws waves between two contours. You can use **Contour** on its own to produce many wavy shapes and lines. You can also use **Pattern** with or without **Contour**, though it must have two paths to weave between.

Downloading and Installing the Guilloche Extension

As with anything downloaded from the Internet, be aware that an import can harbor a virus. Take your usual precautions before downloading and installing.

Here's how to download and install in Windows 10. If you are using a different operating system, you may need to seek help on the Internet.

1. Locate the files for **Guilloche Pattern Extension** by fluent_user and revised by DrWiggly.

    The original version, which you will <u>not</u> use, appeared here on the Inkscape Extensions webpage: https://inkscape.org/~fluent_user/%E2%98%85guilloche-pattern-extension

    <u>Don't use this with Inkscape 1.x</u>. However, if you haven't already seen it, <u>do</u> look at the graphic at that location to see what Fluent_user intended. This version was written prior to the big move to Inkscape 1.x and no longer works with the new Inkscape version. However, it has now been rewritten by another coder, DrWiggly (to whom I'm extremely grateful), and is available here: https://inkscape.org/~DrWiggly/%E2%98%85guillocheextensions-for-v1x

Download this one.

2. Press the download arrow. You will it find next to the illustration on the same line as the title. Or you can click the graphic. Save the file where you usually save your downloads and where you can find it again.

3. Find the downloaded folder on your computer. This would be a good time to run your anti-virus scanner on the file. It will take a second or two. If you right click on the file, you may see your anti-virus program in the list.

4. The folder will be zipped. If you are using Windows 10, you can just press the **Extract all** command near the top of the folder and save all the files where you can find them. Keep the folder open.

5. Open Inkscape. Click on **Edit > Preferences**. Find **System** in the left-hand menu. Click on it.

6. Under **System Information** you will see a list of items and their locations. Find **User Extensions**. Press **Open**.

   The folder will be named **C:\Users***Your Name***\AppData\Roaming\inkscape\extensions** .

7. If this is the first time you've added an external extension to Inkscape, the folder will be empty. Copy and paste or drag the following Guilloche files into the Extensions folder:

   guilloche_contour.inx
   guilloche_contour.py
   guilloche pattern.inx
   guilloche_pattern.py

8. You can now close the folder.

9. The final step is to close and restart Inkscape.

Getting Started with Guilloche

Oddly enough, the two-part extension will be listed under
                    Extension > Examples > Guilloche Contour
                                       and
                    Extension > Examples > Guilloche Pattern

Contour always requires one <u>control path</u> to build on. Usually you will want this line to disappear after you run the extension. This line can be closed or open: a simple straight line, a curved line, a circle, an oval, a rectangle, a wandering blob, and so on, as long as it is a single line. <u>All control objects should be converted to paths</u> (**Path > Object to Path**) if they've started as **Shapes**.

Pattern always requires <u>two control paths</u> between which to weave its lines. These can be produced by **Contours** or can be simple lines or shapes. Again, <u>all control objects should be converted to paths</u> (**Path > Object to Path**) if they've started as **Shapes**.

You are meant to use the **Contours** first to create two decorative outlines, one inside the other. Then **Patterns** will be used to draw a network of lines between the two outlines, as in the example above. You can, however, use the **Contours** alone to produce decorative shapes and lines for other purposes, or you can use your own two nested shapes or lines as the base for the **Guilloche Patterns**.

Both the **Contours** and the **Patterns** are based on waveforms like these:

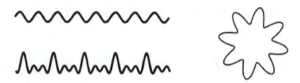

The Settings

The settings, which are almost the same for both parts of the extension, look rather complicated at first, but a bit of explanation should help. The color settings will be ignored here because they are not relevant to us as metal artists drawing in black and white.

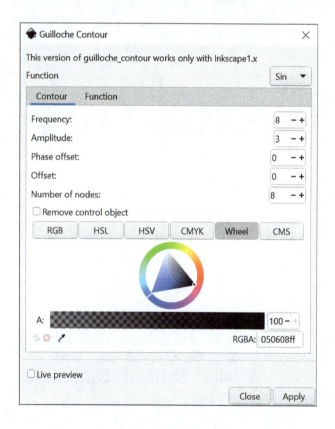

334

Starting with the first tab on the gray bar in the settings boxes, here are the settings and what they control. As already noted, both parts of the extension operate on control lines that you provide. In the examples below, I have left the starting control lines in place so you can see where the wave forms are drawn. Remember, **Contours** is used to draw a wavy line on a <u>single</u> control path. **Patterns** draws a wavy line or lines between <u>two</u> control paths.

Frequency: Determines the number of repetitions of a wave in a given space

Here a frequency of 8 produces 8 sine waves along a line or around the circumference of the space between two circles.

Amplitude: Determines the height and depth of the wave pattern.

Amplitude of 2   Amplitude of 4

For the **Pattern** setting, amplitudes are in percentages. An amplitude of 100 will cover the entire distance from one contour to the other; 50 will cover half the distance between one contour and the other. In the second case, the waveform(s) will be hanging in the middle.

Amplitude of 100   Amplitude of 50

Phase offset: Starts the wave at a different point. With the **Pattern** setting, the pattern appears to rotate from where it would have started without **Phase offset**. Compare these figures with the previous ones.

Phase offset of 50   Phase offset of 25
Compared to the earlier figures, the waves start (and end) at a different place in the curve.

Offset: Expands the figure upward or outward, as if blown up like a balloon. Minus numbers do the opposite.

Offset of 10

Note: I have reversed the order of the **Series** and **Phase Coverage** explanations below because more than one series is needed before phase coverage is meaningful.

Series (**Pattern** part of the extension only): Determines how many overlapping wave forms are produced. You can't have fewer than 1.

Series of 1   Series of 2   Series of 3   Series of 4

Phase Coverage (**Pattern** part of the extension only): Determines what percentage of the space around the circumference will be covered by the waveforms. This only works if the **Series** is more than 1. Each instance of a single wave blip is one phase. Since the number is a percentage, in order to cover the entire space with the waves, insert 100. 50 will cover half the space. Both figures below have a Series of 4. The difference is in the **Phase Coverage**.

Phase Coverage of 100

Phase Coverage of 50

Number of nodes: Determines the nodes per wave blip. Too few will produce jagged lines. Too many will increase the byte size of the figure considerably and will take a great deal of time to process, possibly hanging your computer. It's best to keep the nodes as low as possible for the waveform you want. You only need as many nodes as are required for each individual waveform, so often 8-12 nodes are plenty.

Exploring the Guilloche Contour Half of the Extension

We will continue looking at the settings as they pertain to the **Contour** portion, though much of what is said here will apply to the **Pattern** portion as well.

Preset function settings

Function appears twice in the settings panels, once at the top and once as a tab in the gray line.

Let's take the **Function** settings at the top first. These are **presets**, as opposed to the custom function settings you can work out for yourself in the **Function** tab. We'll look at the custom functions later. Meanwhile, there are 15 presets offered in the drop-down menu, and these may be all you'll ever want. It's instructive to see their effect on a simple line, and indeed these function settings can be useful for producing wavy lines that could be used in many contexts, not just Guilloche drawings.

 In order to make the **Function presets** work, we will need to make sure the settings in the two **Function** areas don't conflict. Just go into the **Function tab** in the gray line and make sure everything is set to 0.0. For the **Contour** tab, we'll use the following settings:

Frequency:	4
Amplitude:	6
Phase offset:	0
Offset:	0
Number of nodes:	12
Remove control object:	checked

We begin by drawing a line, which will be our **control object**.

———————————

control line

We have set it to disappear after applying the extension. On the next page are the results if we apply each of the preset **Function** options to this line.

Line		Env 6	
Sin		Env 7	
Cos		Env 8	
Env 1		Env 9	
Env 2		Env 10	
Env 3		Env 11	
Env 4		Env 12	
Env 5			

What happens if our control object is something besides a line? We'll try a circle (converted to a path) with the same settings and a few of the various function options.

Sin

Env1

Env4

Env10

Env11

If all of these objects seem to be based on a square, rather than a circle, it's because the **Frequency** we have set is 4. That means that the pattern of waves is going to repeat four times, giving us this squarish appearance.

Let's run the same circle with a **Frequency** of 8 and see what happens.

Sin

Env1

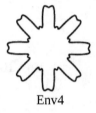
Env4

Env10

Env11

These look a little more circle-based.

Here's an **Env1** at a Frequency of 21:

Tip! Depending on the size of the control figures you draw and the width of the stroke, your figures based on these settings make look a little different from the ones here. The basic shape should be the same, however.

The color example by author fluent_ user has contours that are not nearly this complicated or jagged, so let's reduce the amplitude to make the waves shorter. Here's the same Env1 circle redone twice:

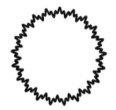 

Frequency 21, Amplitude 2   Frequency 8, Amplitude 2

If you want to imitate the outer two contours in the color example figure for fluent_user's extension, try these settings: **Sin** for the **Function, Frequency** 8 for both, **Amplitude** 4 for the outermost contour, and **Amplitude** 3 for the next contour in.

If you want the figure to be rotated so that that the contour is straight up and down, you can either **Group** the two and rotate them in the usual Inkscape way (guidelines help), or you can figure out what **Phase Offset** will work.

Other **Shapes** and lines can certainly be the opening figure for producing a contour. Just be sure to do **Object > Path** and raise the **Frequency** enough to make it all the way around the figure.

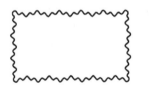    

Custom function settings on the Function tab

If you want to go beyond the preset functions you can set your own. You can choose up to five amplitudes with different phase offsets. Set the **Amplitude** on the **Contour tab** to 1.

Here are some examples on a line and on a circle, all based on a **Frequency** of 8, an **Amplitude** of 1, and **Offset**s of 0 on the **Contour** tab. On the **Function** tab, an additional amplitude has been added to each new figure. The phase offsets are all 0.

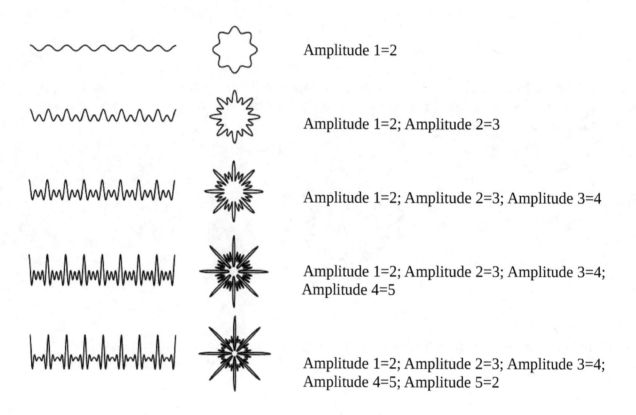

Amplitude 1=2

Amplitude 1=2; Amplitude 2=3

Amplitude 1=2; Amplitude 2=3; Amplitude 3=4

Amplitude 1=2; Amplitude 2=3; Amplitude 3=4; Amplitude 4=5

Amplitude 1=2; Amplitude 2=3; Amplitude 3=4; Amplitude 4=5; Amplitude 5=2

Obviously, you can mix up these amplitudes in many different ways, resulting in countless figures. And that's before adding **Offset**s, which will skew the periods in sometimes unpredictable ways (at least to a non-mathematician).

Using the Guilloche Pattern Portion of the Extension

To use contours as the basis for the **Guilloche Pattern** part of the extension, you will need two and only two contours. The two contours must not overlap, but the inner one can be off-center. Squared or pointed contours do not work well, if at all, as the inner contour, but they work for the outer contour. You can use contours that you have made with the **Guilloche Contour** part of the extension, or you can use a circle, a blob, or any old shapes, as long as you convert them to paths.

You can also use two lines. However, these two lines <u>must start and end at exactly the same places on the X axis</u>. We'll explore this more below.

The settings box will look familiar, since it is almost the same as the box for the **Contours** settings. The two additional settings on the **Pattern** tab are **Phase Coverage** and **Series**, which were discussed briefly in the overview.

Let's walk through the process, using examples of settings for a couple of different nested pairs of contours. We'll start with circles.

1. Make sure you have used **Path > Object to Path** on your circles. Use **Align and Distribute** if you want the circles perfectly concentric.
2. Select both circles.
3. We'll use a preset function, so leave all the **Function** tab settings at 0 and choose **Env11** from the drop-down menu next to **Function** at the top.
4. Keep the **Frequency** and **Series** settings low; otherwise the lines will be too crowded. We'll use these settings:

   Frequency: 4
   Amplitude: 100
   Phase offset: 0
   Offset: 0
   Phase Coverage: 100
   Series: 3
   Number of nodes: 60
   Remove control objects: unchecked

   Here's the result:

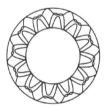

We could, of course do another pair and then stack the two results. The first below leaves the control circles in place; the second removes the circles; the third uses the even-odd fill rule with black fill on the outer and white fill on the inner.

Because you must have two and only two contours to use for a pattern, if you are going to stack patterns as in the example above or in the example that begins this entire description, it is a very good idea to make several copies of each contour you plan to use. That way, you will be able to deal with each pattern and then put them all together at the end, or build them level by level as you go along. It's never a bad idea to have backups.

Difficult Contours for Guilloche Pattern to Handle: A Fancy Example

First, nearly any contour will work as the <u>outside</u> figure as long as the inside is relatively smooth. Squares, rectangles, and anything with acute angles will not work on the <u>inside</u>.

In addition, some of the contours produced by Guilloche Contour do not work well, if at all, with some of the other contours. You can probably predict which contours are likely to spell trouble. We'll explore these quirks and some work-arounds by using a few contours produced by the **Contour** half of the extension. We'll make three different ones using the preset **Functions**.

1. Control figure: circle; Function: Env9; Frequency: 8; Amplitude: 3; Number of nodes: 10.

2. Control figure: octagon; Function: Env10; Frequency: 8; Amplitude: 4; Number of nodes: 10.

3. Control figure: circle; Function: Env1; Frequency: 8; Amplitude: 1; Number of nodes: 10.

Resize these as you wish, and duplicate them so that you have more than one copy to work with.

344

Start with the first two: put #2 inside #1, align by centering horizontal and vertical axes, and select both. On the **Guilloche Pattern** settings box, try these settings: Env 3; Frequency: 8; Amplitude: 100; Phase Coverage: 100; Series: 6; Nodes: 30.

Press **Apply**. <u>This combination is unlikely to work</u>! You have run into one of the extension's quirks. You'll notice that both of the contours are rather pointy—incompatibly so. Sometimes the settings make a difference. You may get a better result if the frequency in the pattern and the frequency in the contour are the same or multiples. Here we have 8 and 8, so that is not the problem. For these contours, the only solutions I've found are either to use the same contour for the interior and exterior of the pattern or substitute a circle for the inner contour.

Here are the results with these two substitutions:

With the same contours inside and outside   With a circle on the inside, then removed

Now, after the fact, we can add the second contour. The pattern will not cover to its edges, but this may be an acceptable work-around. However, you may wish to do the second set first, before you try putting things together.

The second set, contours 2 and 3, are going to have the same problem, though not as severe because the inner circle is more regular. However, even though the pattern may fill, it might be uneven:

The fill is sparser on top than on the bottom

We can do the same trick of using a circle for the inner contour, removing the circle, and then adding the third contour line after the fact. If we use a wide enough stroke, the difference will not be noticeable here.

Stacking Patterns

Now we need to put the figures together. There are still decisions to be made about whether to emphasize or eliminate the contour lines and how wide any of the lines should be. Fill, too, should be considered. The effects will differ, and if you are using the figure for photopolymer plates and most etching, you will certainly need to think about the feasibility of tiny lines. Such figures as these will not work well for that purpose.

Contour lines retained; lines a little wider

Contour lines deleted; lines thinner

Reversing Lines on the Contours

When you create a **Guilloche Contour**, the direction of the nodes on your control line will have an effect on how the waves appear. To reverse the direction, use **Path > Reverse**. The peaks will now be upside down in respect to the control circle. This can be useful, depending on the look you want.

The same settings were used on both control circles. The path on the second circle was reversed.

Guilloche Pattern Between Unclosed Paths

Guilloche Pattern actually works surprisingly well between two separate lines as long as the lines begin and end at the exact same places on the X-axis. They can be slanted or straight; the X-axes just have to match.

The easiest way to make the X-axes points match is just to duplicate the line, position the two, and align.

Duplication won't work if one or both lines are slanted at different angles. If you want one to run along the X-axis and the other to be slanted, the easiest way to assure they both end at the same X-axis point is the following:

1. Use **Align and Distribute** to align, say, only the left end of the lines.
2. **Combine** the two lines.
3. Draw a perfectly vertical line longer than the space between your two target lines.
4. Position the vertical line so that just a bit of both target lines sticks out to the right.
5. Select the vertical line and then the others. (The vertical line must be at the top of the Z order.)
6. Apply **Path > Cut Path**.
7. Click outside the figure and then **Select** and **Delete** each tiny end.
8. If you need to reposition the remaining lines, you can now use **Align and Distribute** to make sure they are at the same X-axis points.

Sometimes the **Pattern** half just seems to decide that it doesn't like the open lines you throw at it, even if you've done the same combination before. You'll start getting "Selected paths are not compatible" messages. You may be trying combinations that really _aren't_ compatible. For instance, I haven't been able to get lines with two different **Contours** to work. If, however, you find that a combo that has worked before is not working now, try shutting down Inkscape and starting again with the most reliable combo, a circle in a circle. Then try your two open lines.

As with concentric control lines, open lines are less likely to work if they are too pointy or if the settings are not compatible. Hand drawn curvy lines work well as long as they are fairly smooth.

Here are a few examples with control lines left in place. All use Amplitude 100, Phase offset 0, Offset 0, Phase Coverage 100.

Env 10, Frequency 10, Series 1, Nodes 12

Env 1, Frequency 6, Series 1, Nodes 30

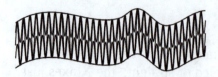 Env 2, Frequency 10, Series 3, Nodes 30

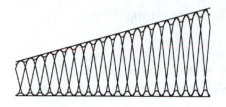 Env 4, Frequency 4, Series 5, Nodes 30

 Sin, Frequency 12, Series 3, Nodes 30

 Env 1, Frequency 8, Series 6, Nodes 60
(Contour is Env 12)

Tip! Don't forget to try your figures with **Even-odd fill**. Some results will be more pleasing than others.

If the thin lines of your figure are unusable for your favorite metal technique, you may find that fill will change the prospect for success.

A Final Technical Note

Both parts of the Guilloche extension were written so that each cycle—each trough and peak—of a wavy line is an individual piece joined to the other pieces of the complete line with **Combine**. You can see this if you apply **Path > Break Apart** to a Guilloche contour:

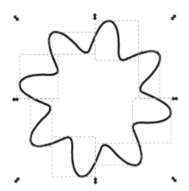

Each cycle now has its
own bounding box

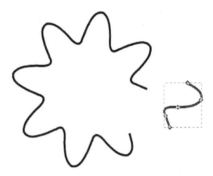

Pieces can now be moved away

If for some reason you need to have a line more permanently unified than is the case with **Combine**, you could use the **Bucket Tool** to produce an unbroken line. That, however, would be very complicated if you tried to use it with the **Pattern** part of the extension and wouldn't work with unclosed lines.

Most likely this little oddity will be of no importance to you whatsoever. If you ever need a portion of a closed contour, however, this might be a way to make one.

Chapter **21**
From Drawing to Jewelry

You've produced a few gorgeous original drawings on Inkscape. Now what? The end goal is a sharply etched or cleanly impressed piece of jewelry, but the processes for metal clay and etching begin to differ even with the printing of the graphics you plan to use. While it is impossible here to cover all the steps of etching or metal clay jewelry making, this chapter will at least get you well on your way to turning your drawings into surface decoration on metal.

Thinking in Black and White: the High Points

Take a look at one of your drawings and imagine it in metal. Whether you are etching or doing metal clay, a drawing from Inkscape will produce two levels, high points and low points. What in your drawing do you want to be the high points in the <u>final</u> <u>product</u>?

In etching, black <u>always</u> produces the high points. In metal clay, black produces the high points in the <u>finished</u> piece if you are using your design to make a photopolymer plate (PPP). If you are etching metal clay with a cutting machine or turning your design into a custom rubber stamp to impress the clay, black will usually produce the low points in the final piece.

Black → high points
in
- Etching
- Metal clay
  impressed with
  PPP
- Custom rubber
  stamps themselves

White → high points
in
- PPPs themselves
- Cutting machine
  etching
- Metal clay
  impressed with
  rubber stamps

If you intend certain parts of your design to be the high points, it's not too late to go back and rework your drawing <u>before</u> you print it. To end up with the white—raised—flower on the metal clay version of the piece on the right above, it was necessary to make a black oval background, move the flower on top, use the **Object > Raise to top** command, and change the fill and stroke color to white. In Inkscape all this can be accomplished quickly and easily. Maybe you'll even want to print two versions of your design, one the negative of the other.

Another thing to consider is what to do about fine lines. If your lines are too fine, they may not make a clean etching or metal clay piece. They may not show up at all, or they may become muddled with other lines. In general, fine lines work better as low points than as high. For one thing, they are less likely to wear off. For another, they will at least have a better chance of taking a patina.

Pay particular attention to typeface. You want any words you have included in your design to be clear. If you are impressing metal clay with a photopolymer plate or rubber stamp, anything smaller than about 12 point could get lost. That may depend, of course, on the particular font. On the other hand, etching metal clay on a cutting machine may allow you to go as low as 11 point. If you decide to push the limits of small size type, at least make sure the words are the low points.

Facing the mirror

Think about whether your drawing will be reversed on the final jewelry piece. When you etch or use a rubber stamp or the photopolymer process with metal clay, the drawing will be mirrored.   That means any typeface you are using must be reversed before you print or the words will be backwards.

To keep the final result looking just as you planned it in your drawing, the last step before printing must be to mirror the image horizontally. Just select the entire image in Inkscape, and click **Object > Flip horizontal (H)**. For totally symmetrical images, of course, this does not matter.

In etching with a cutting machine, the image will not reverse. Keep it as is.

351

Preparing Inkscape Drawings for Etching

Etching on metal requires an **etchant** (such as acid) to eat away background areas of the metal and a **resist** to keep the design portion of the metal from being eaten away. When you print an image for use with etching, the black portion of your design will, of course, be ink, which will be the resist.

The process is the same one used for etching circuit boards, so you'll find lots of information about the process from computer geeks on the Internet.

The directions laid out here will get you sheets of metal covered with your design and ready to put into the etching solution. You may already have your favorite methods and etchants. If not, information about both the etchants and the process is readily available on the Internet.

Printing your drawings for etching

Arrange your drawings on an Inkscape **Page**, as outlined on p. 9.

Print or copy on the correct material with the correct "ink"—actually toner. <u>Inkjet will not do</u>! You will be melting the toner onto the metal, so the right choice of toner is essential. Use a laser printer or copier. Even some brands of laser printer toner do not work as well as others. Brother printer toner, for example, is not satisfactory. Your best bet may be a copy store with good printers or copiers.

Paper
- Option 1: Glossy "magazine" paper. This is the easiest and least expensive option. It produces excellent results. An example would be Hammermill 32 lb. premium laser gloss. Some artists even reuse glossy paper from old magazines. The print allegedly does not come off upon transfer, but your image will. Not a bad way to recycle! You might not be able to use a copy-store for printing on this used paper, however.
- Option 2: Press-n-Peel Blue Image Transfer Film (PnP).
- Print or copy onto the dull side—the emulsion side—of the film. If you are using a copier, set it to dark. PnP will get you a good image, but it is definitely fussier, more expensive, and harder to remove from the metal once the etching is done. The paper deteriorates over time.
- Option 3: Pulsar Toner Transfer Paper (PCB Fab-in-a-Box)
  Similar to PnP, but may be more satisfactory. The paper will come off in water after the heat transfer process. The paper also lasts longer than PnP in storage.
- Option 4: Yellow thermal transfer paper
  A cheaper alternative to the previous two options, this comes in rolls or sheets and will vie with the magazine paper for price and effectiveness. For convenience, try to find the sheets rather than the roll. Print or copy to the glossy side.

Metals to Etch

Copper, brass, and bronze sheet work well. You can also etch silver sheet, but the chemical used to do that is more toxic than those commonly used for base metals.

Your metal sheet should be very flat and at least 24 gauge. That will be thick enough for a light etch. For a deeper etch, 22 gauge is better. To etch both sides you would need 18 gauge.

You can cut your metal sheet into pieces before you etch. A shear works best. File off any burrs, and if necessary, flatten your sheet further with a leather mallet.

Clean the metal well. Use medium wet/dry sandpaper or a Scotchbrite, along with some Bar Keepers Friend. Paper towels can leave fibers behind; try rags instead. Denatured alcohol also works for cleaning. Handle the metal by the edges after you've cleaned it.

Transferring the printed image to metal

The best results come from applying heat to the top and bottom of your image on metal.

Prepare your heat source and tools.

Setup option 1:
Two irons and a vise. One iron goes in the vise upside down to form a flat surface.

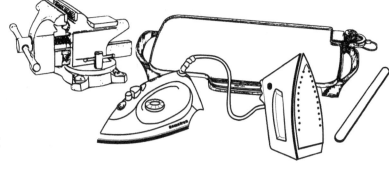

Setup option 2:
One iron plus an electric griddle or frying pan capable of keeping heat about 350°.

Setup option 3:
One iron, a clamp, and a Popsicle stick for burnishing.

The irons or electric griddle/fry pan should be dedicated to this purpose. You don't want toner on your favorite shirt or strip steak.

Check garage sales.

Using the heat to transfer

The iron(s) should be on cotton or linen heat. No steam, of course. A griddle or frying pan, if you're using one, should be on about 350°.

Let's assume you're using magazine paper and two irons, one upside down in the vise. Dip your cut-out image into denatured alcohol, holding it with tweezers, and quickly position it face down on the metal. Using tweezers, place the metal and paper combination paper-side up on the bottom iron. Immediately apply your other iron, tacking the paper with the tip and then working across the entire paper, pressing firmly but gently. You need to work quickly to get the paper burnished before the alcohol dries up.

Continue to burnish for about a minute until you see the toner coming through the paper. At that point you should have a decent transfer.

Using tweezers or old pliers, dump the metal and paper into cold water. Most of the paper will float off as it soaks. Rub off the remainder with your fingers, not fingernails, but be careful not to scrape the toner.

If you are using only one iron in a clamp, use a Popsicle stick to tack down the wet paper and burnish it thoroughly.

If you're using one of the other paper options, follow the package directions.

Tip! Some people use a thin sheet of silicon (*e.g.*, 1/16") on top of the paper. It transfers heat but compensates for unevenness between paper and metal.

Examining the transfer for gaps

Look carefully at the transfer image to make sure the lines are clear and black. If the transfer did not work well, the toner can be cleaned off with denatured alcohol and some scrubbing and the transfer can be tried again.

If there are only a few empty or faint spots in the transfer, you may be able to fill in the area with Stazon ink and a fine brush, or you can try one of the following, which work fairly well:
- a Sharpie marker, especially the oil paint type
- a red Staedler Lumocolor marker

Additional preparation of the metal piece

The back and edges of the metal must be covered so that they do not etch. The easiest way to do this is to cover them with duct tape or electrical tape. A thin line of tape along the edge lapping over to the back will create a nice raised border around the piece.

If, by chance, you are etching a cylinder, such as a piece of copper pipe, cover each end with tape so that no etchant will seep into the interior of the pipe.

You will also need to consider how to suspend your piece face down in the etchant for the best etch. A piece of duct tape attached to the back of the piece can be used to suspend the piece from chopsticks crisscrossing your pan. Another great solution to the problem is to tape your metal pieces to the underside of pieces of Styrofoam and float them in the etchant with the transfer side toward the liquid.

Completing the etching process

Your metal sheet covered with your design should now be ready to etch in your choice of solution. As previously mentioned, a discussion of factors such as cost, toxicity, and efficiency of etchants are beyond the scope of this book, but such information is readily available. If you have not already made a choice, you might want to look into the following etchants for base metals: electrical etching with salt or copper sulfate; or acid etching with ferric chloride; or acid etching with hydrochloric acid (muriatic acid or "pool acid") plus hydrogen peroxide. Silver will require more toxic chemicals, even for electrical etching. These include silver nitrate or copper nitrate for electrical etching; or ferric nitrate or nitric acid for acid etching.

Turning Inkscape Drawings into Photopolymer Plates for Use with Metal Clay

A photopolymer plate starts as a light-sensitive sheet of material that can be washed out with water. Exposure to ultraviolet light hardens it and keeps it from being washed away. Putting a film like a negative over the sheet blocks the ultraviolet light to selected areas while allowing clear, unblocked areas to be hardened. The blocked areas can then be washed out. The hardened areas are left as raised portions of the sheet.

For use with metal clay, we print the design on a transparency, put the printed transparency over a photopolymer sheet, expose the sandwich to ultraviolet light, wash out the dark, blocked areas, and use the remaining raised design to press into the metal clay.

1. The design is printed on a sheet of transparency film.

2. The transparency is placed over the photopolymer plate. The sandwich is exposed to ultraviolet light for a specified amount of time.

3. The exposed areas harden and the unexposed areas can then be washed away by water, leaving the backing and the raised design. The design can then be pressed into metal clay.

What you'll need to make photopolymer plates

- A page of designs. You can print this on paper at home if you have a good printer. If you're printing directly on transparency film, you must have the right transparency film with the right printer.
- Transparency film. This can be purchased by the individual sheet when you print at a copy shop or by the package if you are printing at home. Best is film for laser printers with toner, but not all home laser printers work well for this. Transparencies are also available for inkjets, though the black print may not be as dark as the laser transparencies. I prefer copy shop printing. That way I know the transparencies are fresh and I will get a dark copy.
- Photopolymer sheets. These can be purchased from metal clay vendors. A more cost effective way is to purchase directly from a letterpress company like Boxcar Press. This company offers a variety of photopolymer sheets and is friendly to metal clay artists. You will have a choice of depth and backing (plastic or steel). Some artists prefer steel backing, feeling that it is better for fine detail like type. They also believe that it keeps the plates flatter longer. While that is true, over time the photopolymer may separate from the steel back and curl anyway. In addition, steel-backed plates are much harder to cut. You may want to try different types to learn your own preferences for various uses.
- A ruler and Sharpie for marking the sheet for cutting into smaller plates.
- Stout shears for cutting metal-backed plates or stout scissors or box cutter for plastic backed plates.
  - An exposure "sandwich" made up of the following:
  - A piece of glass a little larger than the largest photopolymer plate you will be making: 4" x 6" is a good size for most setups. The edges should be smooth so you don't cut yourself. Sometimes you can find a good piece of glass as part of an inexpensive frame, or a frame shop might be willing to cut you a piece.
  - A thin, but stiff, piece of wood, hardboard, or plexiglass the same size as the glass. This will be the backing.
  - A piece of thin foam or bubble wrap to act as cushioning and compensate for unevenness. Again, this should be the same size as the glass.
  - Four strong clips to hold the edges together. Bulldog clips are excellent. Alternatively, four heavy rubber bands, one on each side close to the edges, may hold your sandwich securely enough.

- An ultraviolet light source.

An ultraviolet nail polish curing lamp will do, although the size of the opening will limit what size exposure sandwich you can use.

357

Or...

An ordinary, inexpensive florescent light fixture with an 18" UV or black-light bulb works well. This can be raised above a counter surface with a couple of bricks or small pieces of scrap 2" x 4" lumber nailed together. Soup cans also work nicely. The bulb needs to be about 3-4" above the exposure frame.

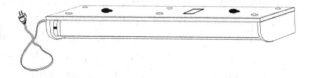

- A timer
- A soft brush to brush and wash out the softened part of the exposed plate. A soft toothbrush will do.
- A hairdryer on a cool setting to dry the plate.

Printing your drawings for photopolymer plates (PPPs)

Arrange your drawings on a **Page** in Inkscape, as outlined on p. 8. The first time you get ready to make a design sheet for PPPs, include a test design for the exposure time. See below for an example of such a design.

Print or copy the page onto a transparency using a printer or copier compatible with the transparencies. As mentioned above, your best bet may be a copy store with good printers or copiers. You can usually purchase transparencies as part of the printing deal. Since unused transparencies degenerate over time, you may not want to purchase a whole box anyway.

You can take the page to a copy store on a plain piece of paper or take the .PNG file on a thumb drive.

Until you have experience with the process, consider printing <u>two</u> transparency copies of each page of designs. Even with the best printer, a single transparency may not be dark enough to block sufficient light for a really sharp result. You can cut out a design from both sheets, place one on top of the other <u>exactly</u>, and tape the edges with transparent tape to hold the two copies together. This step is tedious, but the result may be better. Until you have experience with the printer and transparencies, you may not know if you can forgo this step. Thankfully, I've finally found a copy shop that produces dark enough single transparencies. Perhaps you will, too!

Preparing the photopolymer plate (PPP)

Important! Anytime you are not using them, store unexposed PPPs in a light-safe envelope or box, perhaps the bag the PPPs came in when you bought them. Black garbage bags can work.

When you take the photopolymer sheet out of its envelope, it should be in a room with no ultraviolet light. Regular florescent lights are okay. Try to minimize light from outdoors.

Cut the plate a little larger than your design. Keep a good margin: you probably will not want the corners of the PPP to press into the clay inside your cut line. Steel backed plates will require bench shears. Plastic backed can be cut with with shears or possibly even tough scissors.

As you cut, you will notice a sheet of clear plastic over the top of the plate. <u>Remove it</u> before you put the plate in the exposure sandwich. Your plate will be ruined if you forget to do this.

Preparing the exposure sandwich

Arrange your sandwich in the following order, with the PPP under the glass, emulsion side up.

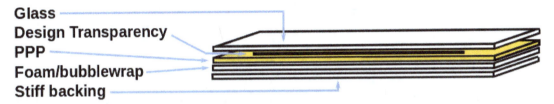

Glass
Design Transparency
PPP
Foam/bubblewrap
Stiff backing

Arrange your clips around the edges. Place the stack under the light.

 Setups, lights, and distances vary: the first time you expose a plate, you should do a test run, as outlined in the next section.

Testing the exposure time

Before exposing a real design, run a test PPP to check the proper exposure time. Once you have the height of your light set and the exposure time figured out, you will seldom have to retest the exposure time. Here is an example of a chart you can put on your first transparency so that you can test a range of times at once. The test plate can be small, so you don't waste a lot.

11111111	22222222	3333333	4444444	5555555	666666666
111111111	22222222	3333333	44444444	5555555	666666666
11111111	2222222	3333333	4444444	5555555	66666666
1111111	2222222	333333	444444	555555	6666666
11111111	2222222	333333	4444444	555555	6666666
1111111	222222	333333	444444	555555	666666

Here's how the testing works.
- Put this transparency into your exposure sandwich, as shown in the section above. Check to make sure the clear plastic is discarded.

- Lay a piece of heavy card over all but the 6's. You can put this over the top of the glass so you don't have to keep opening the sandwich. Turn the light on for 20 seconds, using a timer.

- Leave the sandwich under the light and move the card so the 5's and 6's are uncovered. Turn the light on for 20 seconds.

- Next you'll uncover the 4's 5's and 6's. Proceed in this way, uncovering another number and exposing for 20 seconds each time until all are uncovered and exposed for the last 20 seconds.
- Remove the plate from the sandwich and wash it out. Use a soft brush, such as a soft toothbrush or nail brush. Gently scrub the plate using a circular motion.
- Blot the plate with a lint-free cloth or sponge.
- Dry the plate thoroughly with a cool hairdryer. Once dry, the plate should not feel sticky.
- Now you have a sample plate that will show you the result of exposure from 20 seconds to 2 minutes in 20 second intervals. The 1's are exposed at 20 seconds, the 2's at 40 seconds, and so on. Probably the 1's will wash out too much and the 6's will wash out too little. If there is no happy result, you may have to run the test again and adjust the exposure times.
- Examine the lines of the plate carefully to determine which is the best exposure time. Write down the results of your test so you will remember in the future.
- Re-expose the plate for whatever time you have settled on as ideal. You don't need to put the plate back into the sandwich.
- Once you have figured out the timing, you should be able to use it unless you change your lighting setup or the bulb or PPPs degrade.

Following the procedure for design plates

For an actual design, you will follow the same process just outlined, except that you now know the correct exposure time. Here's a summary:

- Put the transparency into the exposure sandwich.
- Position it under the light.

- Expose it for your ideal time.
- Remove the plate and wash it under cool to warm water using a soft brush in a circular motion.
- Blot and dry the plate with a cool to warm hairdryer.
- Re-expose the plate for the same length of time or longer.

Using and storing the PPP

When you roll a design into metal clay using a PPP, you will, of course, need to use liberal lubrication so the plate doesn't stick to the clay. You can use olive oil, Badger Balm, or whatever you usually use with other texture plates. Consider brushing your oil onto the clay rather than the plate.

Clean your plate before storing, making sure that no clay is left in the crevices.

Store in an airtight container. A zip-lock bag will do.

If the plates curl over time, you should be able be able to flatten them by running them under warm water and drying them with a warm hairdryer.

Turning Inkscape Drawings into Rubber Stamps for Use with Metal Clay or Etching

A number of companies now produce custom rubber stamps for Internet customers. These can be used either to texture metal clay or to apply an etching resist ink such as StazOn® to sheet metal. Rubber stamps should last longer than PPPs and should remain flexible indefinitely. If you are only doing a handful of designs, it may be as cost effective to order rubber stamps as to invest in the plates and equipment to make PPPs. Of course, there is the time lag to contend with. You can't convert a brilliant design idea to jewelry in a day as you can with PPPs you make in your own workshop.

For metal clay, especially, you will want these rubber stamps to be <u>unmounted</u>: that is, not glued to a wooden block. Etching doesn't require a rubber stamp to be mounted either, although a handle is nice for placement on the sheet when you're dealing with wet ink. On the other hand, an unmounted stamp is certainly better if you want to stamp a cylinder. For that, you can simply place the inked stamp face up on your bench and roll the cylinder along it.

To find companies to make you a stamp, search the Internet for something like "unmounted rubber stamps." The price will range from $3 to $50, depending on the size of your stamp. You will be able to upload your design directly to the site. You will need to export your Inkscape design as a .PNG file, save it to your computer, and then follow the upload instructions on the rubber stamp site. For instructions on exporting a .PNG file see pp. 12-13.

When you order, pay close attention to the instructions. Usually the company will reverse your image on the rubber stamp itself, so that when it is stamped, the image will be going the right direction. This applies especially to text. In other words, don't try to reverse your image to get the correct orientation; the company will do it for you.

This is not true for high points and low points. What is black in the image you send to the company will be raised on the stamp itself. That will translate to low points in metal clay and high points in etching.

Making Templates and Stencils

Templates and stencils are best produced by cutting machines (see below), but some templates can be hand cut if you wish. Stencils are usually too complex to cut by hand.

Templates and Layout

A template is simply a pattern shape used for cutting something out. Templates can be used as guides for sawing metal sheet or for cutting shapes in metal clay. They are commonly used for bails or for layered constructions, as well as base shapes. Metal clay supply outlets sell dozens of such templates, but you can easily make your own from cardboard or plastic.

A template can be a shape cut out around the outside edge, meant to be glued on the metal sheet or laid on metal clay. The edge is then cut or sawed. Conversely, the template's shape may be cut from the inside, with the blade or needle tool cutting along the inside edge. Templates can also be used with a stylus to impress a line on metal clay or metal.

In all the illustrations of templates and stencils that follow, gray shows the solid sheet of card or plastic and red shows the cutting line. Red has come to be the customary color used with cutting machines like Silhouette to signal the blade what lines to cut.

Cutting lines in red

Outside-cut template   Inside-cut template

If you are constructing a multi-layer piece, you may want to take advantage of another strength of Inkscape, the potential for exactly laying out different elements of a piece using the various measuring tools of Inkscape and possibly even separate Inkscape layers which can be locked and unlocked at will. A template of cardstock or plastic can be made for each layer or element, pieces stacked and shuffled in cheap paper before getting to the expensive metals or metal clay. Plain paper sandwiched between two pieces of packing tape makes an easy, waterproof template for metal clay.

Stencils

Stencils are very like templates, though they are often considerably more complicated in design. They have at least three different uses for metal artists:

1. A stencil can be laid on top of a piece of sheet metal and inked over, so that when the ink dries and the stencil is peeled off, an inked design is left on the metal sheet. The sheet is then acid-etched, leaving behind a raised design where the ink is.
2. A stencil can be pressed into a sheet of metal clay with a roller just as one would use a texture sheet. The holes in the stencil produce the raised areas of the clay.
3. A stencil can be used in enameling. Enamel is sifted onto metal through the stencil holes and blocked from other parts of the metal by the solid areas of the stencil.

When you make your own stencils, the tricky part is making sure the solid, non-hole parts of the stencil are interconnected sufficiently to hold the whole stencil together. Using a stiff material such as plastic from a polypropylene folder helps to stabilize any long, thin parts of the design. In the example below, the material along the holes could warp to the side or fail to release well if the stencil isn't made from stiff enough plastic or card. Long and continuous holes like these are not always a great idea, especially for metal clay.

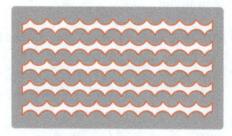

These long thin supports between holes may not be stable enough.

Visualize the holes of the stencil as discreet objects on an empty background. You should have no crossing strokes. If you have groups of objects, each member should be separated by background space unless an overlapping pair will clearly be read as the objects you intend.

Some Inkscape functions you've learned will be especially useful when you construct stencils. Tiled clones will be indispensable for stencils with a repeating pattern. Tiling can produce rather formal arrangements, much more casual arrangements, or arrangements with groups of objects rather than single repeating objects, as can be seen below.

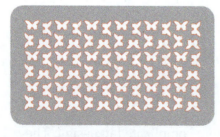

Rather formal tiling

Casual arrangement

Tiling of a group

Can you do the same thing with **Pattern**? Sure. But then you have basically only one choice about how your pattern is arranged, namely in straight rows and columns. Here's the butterfly group sent to a **Pattern**. As you can see, it's very similar to the third stencil above, differing only in spacing, which can't be adjusted in **Pattern**.

Stencil made with **Pattern**

The **Bucket Tool** is tremendously helpful in producing silhouettes that can become the discreet objects of your design. For example, the **Bucket Tool** can turn the figure on the left below, which is unusable as a stencil figure, into a group of objects that will work very well as a stencil. Granted, using the **Bucket tool** can become tedious if there are lots of cells to fill, but the figure below took little time. I used blue simply as a bright distinguishing color. The original black and white figure was simply dragged away from the blue pieces. Another advantage of the Bucket Tool is that you can "grow" or "shrink" what is filled. It's a quick way of adjusting the spacing between cells and would even allow you to round corners if so desired.

Unusable as a stencil because each white cell needs a separate stroke line.

Bucket tool produces individual cells which can have their own strokes.

Cells are now sufficiently separated and have their own strokes.

Occasionally, you may want to turn the <u>strokes</u> of objects into the holes of a stencil. You'll want to make the stroke thick and then use either the **Bucket Tool** or **Path > Stroke to Path** to put new strokes around the holes. Consider, for instance, spirals. The spiral below has been given a thick stroke and converted from shape to path. Then **Stroke to Path** was run and the new object was given a red cutting stroke. The spiral holes could, of course, be multiplied in patterns.

Stroke to Path can produce usable stencil holes from lines that don't cross

Another terrific tool for stencils is the inset option of the **Offset Path Effect**. Below is a complicated **Guilloche Pattern**-generated figure. **Offset** with negative numbers was applied, resulting in the figure on the right. The outer circle was deleted. The center circle remained too large, and so a smaller circle was substituted. If you use **Offset** in this way, don't forget to stabilize the new figure with **Object > Object to Path**.

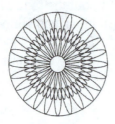 

Offset with negative numbers can produce usable stencil holes from complex figures

If you're thinking of using **Text** in your stencils, keep in mind that in most fonts quite a few letters and numbers have internal spaces that won't work for stencils. That's why there are special stenciling fonts that insert a small connecting tab in strategic places. You can either use such a font or alter the characters you draw after converting the text to paths.

Finally, don't forget the special use of **Bitmap Tracing** with Multiple Scans considered earlier (see pp. 172 ff.).

Tip! If you need to move objects in a design farther apart to make the network of connecting plastic wider and stronger, **Ungroup** everything, select all, and use **Object > Transform > Scale**. Check **Scale proportionally** and **Apply to each object separately**. Try shrinking 75-80% and see how you like the result. Once satisfied, **Group** the whole thing and enlarge the pattern as you like.

366

Using Inkscape Drawings with Cutting Machines Like Silhouette and Cricut

Inkscape designs can be imported into the software used with cutting machines. A metal artist can then use a cutting machine to do several tasks:

- Cut a stencil to press into metal clay or use as an outline for cutting it.
- Cut metal clay directly.
- Etch metal clay directly.
- Etch thin metal sheet.

This section does not discuss how to use a cutting machine, only how to import Inkscape files.

Inkscape's native file type is .SVG, a vector file. Some cutting machines can import these files directly into their own software; others cannot. For the latter, there is usually an easy work-around.

Converting to Paths

No matter what machine you're using, it's probably a good idea to convert everything in your design to paths before going further. Some cutting machine softwares don't like Inkscape's shapes or text. If you think you might someday want to alter your design's text as text or change your shapes as shapes, then make an Inkscape copy of your file before you convert elements to paths. Otherwise you will lose the ability to, say, change the font or change the number of points in a star.

To convert the design to paths, select the whole thing using **Edit > Select All** or **Ctrl A**. Or you can just rubber-band everything. Then click **Path > Object to Path**.

Cricut

You can directly import Inkscape's .SVG files into the Cricut software.

Silhouette

Silhouette offers several models. Any of them are capable of making cardboard or vinyl templates and stencils for use with metal clay. If, however, you wish to use a machine directly on metal clay, the best model is the Curio and the best metal clay is a flex clay. Unfortunately, Silhouette has discontinued the Curio and they are hard to find. Another option is the Cameo 4, which now has enough clearance to be usable. Either machine will work best with steel engraving tips made by Chomas Creations. Instructions about how to prepare your clay and set up the machine itself can be found on several sites on the Internet.

Tip! Etching directly on metal clay with a cutting machine allows you to use finer lines than are possible with Photopolymer Plates or most other stamps.

Inkscape designs can be used with all the Silhouette software versions, but it's best with one of the paid upgrades (Silhouette Studio Designer Edition, Designer Edition +, or Business Edition). In any of these upgrades, your Inkscape .SVG file can be imported directly. What you import is the entire Inkscape document, so be aware that any scraps you have in the document will show up in Silhouette Studio.

Inkscape's .SVG files <u>cannot</u> be imported directly into the basic Silhouette Studio software that comes with all the machines and is free to download even without a machine. Instead, you can save your design file as a .DXF file and open that in Studio. It is possible that some information will be lost in this conversion.

Another option that will work with all the software upgrades is to export your Inkscape design file as a .PNG and import that into the Silhouette software. Then trace it in the Silhouette program. You can also simply do a screen capture and paste the result into Silhouette Studio for tracing.

You will probably find that the lines of your design need to be assigned a color for cutting or etching. For instance, the system Cindy Pope uses for the Silhouette assigns red for cutting and blue for etching. Line colors can be easily changed either in Inkscape or in the cutting machine software.

Silhouette's proprietary software is really quite a good vector program, and you will find some functions easier and more intuitive in Studio than in Inkscape. There are, however, many things that Inkscape can do that Silhouette Studio's versions cannot. Using Inkscape and Silhouette Studio in tandem, especially the Designer Edition or above, would give you the best of both worlds.

Where to Find (and Give) More Help

The Internet has many, many Inkscape tutorials, both video and written, some more useful than others. Keep in mind that Inkscape's Version 1.x is relatively new as of this writing. Consequently, some information you find on the Internet will be outdated. When you do a web search for a particular Inkscape problem, you may wish to include the term "Inkscape 1.1" (or whatever your version is) in your search phrase, at least for starters. Much of the function of earlier versions remains in 1.x, but some functions, such as **Path Effects**, have changed a great deal.

The most important sources of information are accessible from Inkscape itself, namely the **Help** tab.

- *Inkscape: Guide to a Vector Drawing Program*, a manual written by Tavmjong Bah, is somewhat outdated but still the bible. When in doubt, it's a good place to start.
- **Keys and Mouse Reference**: if you're a keyboard aficionado, you'll want to peruse the time-saving possibilities exhaustively listed here.
- **Ask Us a Question**: this points users to some live human help in the form of a chat line and a user forum. Helpfulness varies, but this can be a source of fairly quick recourse for tricky problems.
- Do try the Forums, especially if something doesn't seem to be working correctly: https://inkscape.org/forums/
- **Tutorials**: these certainly don't cover a fraction of what you might want to know about Inkscape but can be a wonderful addition to some of the explanations in this book and have the advantage of excellent graphics. You'll find plenty of extra hints and shortcuts here.
- **FAQ**: these should be the first place you look when you have a question not covered in this book and its index.

When a new version of Inkscape appears, it's a good idea to check out the **Release Notes**, which will sometimes give you some helpful hints about new features, though often the information will be more technical than most of us can use. These notes can be found by going to the page https://inkscape.org/, pointing at **Download**, and clicking on **Current Version**. (Remember, if you install a new version, you must first uninstall the old).

You can also keep an eye on the external **Extensions** page (https://inkscape.org/ > Download > Extensions). Occasionally someone will come up with a truly useful extension that you might want to download and try out in the same way you tried out the Guilloche extensions. Be sure that the extension you choose has been updated for Inkscape 1.x, or it may not work.

Finally, if you like Inkscape, consider a donation to keep the project going. Remember that the program is free and open source, meaning that it is entirely user supported and user developed. You'll find a **Support Us** tab on Inkscape's main page.

Index